Post-Backlash Feminism

Post-Backlash Feminism

Women and the Media Since Reagan-Bush

KELLIE BEAN

McFarland & Company, Inc., Publishers
Jefferson, North Carolina, and London

LIBRARY OF CONGRESS CATALOGUING-IN-PUBLICATION DATA

Bean, Kellie.
    Post-backlash feminism : women and the media since Reagan-Bush / Kellie Bean.
        p.   cm.
    Includes bibliographical references and index.

    ISBN-13: 978-0-7864-3118-2
    softcover : 50# alkaline paper ∞

    1. Feminism — United States.   2. Feminism and mass media — United States.   3. Feminism — Political aspects — United States.   4. Feminist theory — United States.   I. Title.
    HQ1426.B37   2007
    305.420973 — dc22   2007027053

British Library cataloguing data are available

©2007 Kellie Bean. All rights reserved

No part of this book may be reproduced or transmitted in any form or by any means, electronic or mechanical, including photocopying or recording, or by any information storage and retrieval system, without permission in writing from the publisher.

Cover photograph ©2007 Corbis Images

Manufactured in the United States of America

McFarland & Company, Inc., Publishers
    Box 611, Jefferson, North Carolina 28640
        www.mcfarlandpub.com

Contents

Preface — 1

Introduction — 3

1. Fellating Patriarchy: Men's Magazine Feminism — 15
2. The Vexed Body Politic: Ms. Lewinsky, Mr. Clinton and the Feminist Establishment — 40
3. "A Gaggle of Dutiful Daughters": Feminism Does the Waves — 65
4. Booby Traps and Botox: Putting the Fun Back into Politics — 93
5. What a Wonderful World It Would Be — 122
6. "MacKinnon Was Wrong": A Little Rape Never Hurt Anyone — 149
7. Conclusion: A Signifier of One's Own — 176

Bibliography — 187
Index — 191

Leslie, Stephanie, Mom, Janet, Sherri, Judith
and, of course, Jordan and Christopher....
This is for you.

Preface

The year I graduated with a Ph.D. and entered the academic workforce (1994) Tad Friend authored perhaps the most famous article of the post-backlash era. A cover story for *Esquire Magazine* entitled "Yes!" the piece inaugurated the age of pre-fix feminisms. Friend coined the phrase "Do-Me feminism" to describe the politics of the women featured in the piece, writers like Naomi Wolf, Susie Bright, Camille Paglia and Katie Roiphe. Heralding the end of "feminism as usual" and urging women to embrace their inner slut,* "Do-Me feminism" takes its cue from pornography and regressive notions of female sexuality. The Do-Me feminist presents herself as a provocative political player, a vixen with a whip and a graduate degree; indeed, her politics entirely replace issues of social justice with a focus on men's erotic needs, fantasies, and fears. The Do-Me attempts to achieve social parity through a sexualized submission not only to male fantasy, but also to male aggression.

This sexed-up feminism offers not a whit of female empowerment; and didn't strike me as particularly new. Ph.D. at the ready, I was anxious to move into academe and do some good, perhaps open some minds, start a few fruitful arguments on sexuality, gender, social identity formation. Confronted by classrooms of students schooled in revisionist, watered down, do-nothing feminism I found myself surrounded by qualifications and disclaimers: "I'm not a feminist but..." and a litany of TV news misinformation. So began my work on media treatments of feminist politics.

I also confronted my students' reluctance to make direct statements of liberal politics or unalloyed feminist ideology; they preferred the strategy commonly found in the mainstream media — an uncritical endorsement, of all "choices" made by all women. The strategy eases political

---

*Naomi Wolf famously informed Friend that what feminism really needs is more "sluts for the revolution."

anxieties and obviates the (equally anxiety-provoking) possibility of political disagreements among women. But to drain the meaning from terms crucial to women's political progress, like "choice" or "feminism," and fail to bring conflicting ideological positions into conversation is neither an intellectual nor a productive gesture. It is, rather, a kind of making nice and quieting down, things women are encouraged to do throughout their lives and which do not serve them well.

With a woman third in line to the presidency for the first time in history, another poised to make a serious run for that office, and more women in Congress than ever before, now might appear to be women's moment. Certainly women have achieved unprecedented media visibility; it is, then, crucial to take stock of how women are represented there and with what seriousness their political concerns are addressed. Therefore, it is not my intent here to make nice; it is my intent to begin a conversation that may not be easy to have but whose timing is urgent.

Introduction

It is in the nature of power and position that those who have it do not relinquish it graciously...
  Susan Brownmiller, "The Enemy Within"

It's a confusing time to call oneself a feminist. For the past 20 years women have been fairly knocked unconscious by an American media machine pounding out the good news that we can stop worrying, feminism was a success. At the same time, we are told that American feminism is experiencing an identity crisis. And that if we hold liberal, feminist views, we really shouldn't talk too much about them. What we can say for sure is that as feminism moves into the twenty-first century a deeply entrenched ambivalence has characterized nearly all feminist discourse over the past two decades — ambivalence regarding the success, relevance and function of the movement as well as a more personal, immediate uncertainty regarding women's presence in public political discussions. That is, often those women upon whom feminists have so long relied, so long considered our strongest public voices, seem not quite sure what we are doing anymore.

Take, for example, the conflicting responses to two major scandals of our era, the Clarence Thomas hearings and the Lewinsky-Clinton affair, and the questions they raise for feminism. Are we agitating against workplace harassment — à la the general feminist response to Anita Hill? Or, can we now assume that women in the workplace are fully empowered to say no — as in the feminist response to Monica Lewinsky? It is commonplace to hear that women have "arrived," that feminism's work is done, playing fields have been leveled, and 21-year-old interns may safely rebuff a superior's advances.

But, *have* we arrived? If we still identify as feminist, did we miss something? If we continue to see oppression, are we overly sensitive? Are feminists desperate for continued relevance and therefore imagine slights where none exist? How one answers such questions depends in large part upon how one defines "feminism," of course, since the very meaning of the term has become contingent upon who uses it and where. This study investigates notions of feminism popularly produced and marketed, images readily available to the reading and TV-viewing public, seen in places like Border's and Barnes and Noble, at airport newsstands, on network and cable programming.

The discussion of feminism that concerns me here, then, takes place in the U.S. mainstream media, whose influence must not be underestimated. The media's capacity for enormous cultural influence grows directly out of the myth that the free market media works to democratize the distribution of information and ideas within American culture. On the contrary, American media limits and manipulates the distribution of ideas and information in an emphatically ideological, and often misogynist, manner. And as the media have ossified around a conservative point of view over the past twenty-five years, we've seen a corresponding decline in liberal, feminist voices welcome there. The movement toward the Right has opened a market niche for anti-feminist punditry and rhetoric; anti-feminism, indeed, misogyny, sells in America. Significantly, anti-feminism is largely practiced by conservative women with established voices within the mainstream press. The dominant conservative take on women's issues makes a liberal feminist argument not only unwelcome, but also virtually non-existent in the most widely viewed and read media venues.

Any far-reaching social movement will reflect the variety of its adherents and their various approaches to politics; this has always been true of feminism. The most common and recognizable divisions within feminism have reflected generational identities as well as ideological ones. For example, First, Second and Third Wave feminisms tether politics to a particular historical moment and its dominant concerns for women. Academic categorization of feminism further refine these concerns. Radical, Marxist, and eco-feminisms, for instance, advocate specific individual philosophies toward the proper treatment of others and the world; lesbian feminism, addresses lifestyle concerns and liberties; and postmodern feminism takes a philosophical approach to the category of "women" and encourages skepticism toward the production of knowledge. Finally, multicultural feminism embraces the concerns of women in a variety of global circumstances defined by location, race, class, and sexual preference.

The past two decades have produced an explosion of prefix feminisms, which, while seeming to reflect the proliferation of political issues for women, in fact, work to weaken the movement by parsing its concerns into narrow, personal rationales for, basically, behavioral choices. To modify the meaning of "feminism" in order to better reflect a more up-to-date or forward-thinking notion of women and society would be one thing; to co-opt feminist terms to promote emphatically anti-feminist politics is entirely another. While academic inquiry has produced more nuanced approaches to women's politics, reflected in the terminology mentioned above, popular arguments over women's politics have produced an increasingly shallow approach as reflected in shorthand, brand name prefixes. Welcome to the age of equity-, sex-positive, pro-life, anti-, post-, cyber-, neo-, power-, lipstick-, girlie-, Do-Me, The Happy-, dissident-, rogue-, and independent feminisms, all of which call for women to embrace domesticity, sexual display, the production of children, marriage, fashion and/or sex work as empowering and definitive of feminist politics.

A liberal feminist might argue that the crisis for women has not passed; in fact, only from the point of view of the most privileged among us might the women's movement be called a "spectacular success," as Christina Hoff Sommers famously claims. The thing is not done, and women (including those who do not embrace the term "feminist") ought to be worried. Consider, for example, that: just under 16 percent of congressional seats are occupied by women (even after the 2006 mid-term elections); notoriously conservative FBI crime statistics still report that one in four girls (one in seven boys) is sexually assaulted before the age of eighteen; a Hispanic female college graduate can expect to make less than a white male high school graduate; in the summer of 2000, police fail to respond to reports of group sexual violence in New York's Central Park; the Violence Against Women Act civil rights protections for victims of gender-based crimes are removed by the Supreme Court in May of the same year; during his first day in office, George W. Bush reinstates the Global Gag Rule; adequate abortion facilities exist in only about 16 percent of U.S. counties; the U.S. remains the only industrialized nation not to ratify CEDAW (Convention on the Elimination of All Forms of Discrimination Against Women); half of families living under the poverty line are headed by single mothers; between 1995 and 2000 seven out of ten industries experienced deepening wage gaps. In some cases, women lost as much as 21 cents for every dollar earned.* White women make around 76 cents

---

According to a study conducted by the General Accounting Office (GAO), the independent congressional research office. As reported in The New York Times, *January 24, 2002, the GAO "looked at salaries in the 10 industries that employed the most women from 1995 through 2000."*

for every dollar a man makes; the number falls to 68 cents when women's earnings are compared only to the earnings of white men; African American women make 65 cents for every dollar a white man makes; Hispanic women make only about 53 cents; the U.S. ranks 68th for percentage of women serving in the national government; and on average three American women are killed per week by their intimate male partners.

Nonetheless, in a foundational work of the anti-feminist canon, *Who Stole Feminism?*, Christina Hoff Sommers make the following claim:

> American women owe an incalculable debt to the classically liberal feminists who came before us and fought long and hard, and ultimately with spectacular success, *to gain for women the rights that the men of this country had taken for granted for over two hundred years* [17; my emphasis].

Such an assertion surprises many feminists, and would certainly surprise women and children living under the poverty line, the families of women killed by their partners, or Hispanic women working for virtually half of what white men make. Under what circumstances, then, might the above claim accurately be made? In which segments of American culture have women in fact gained the same "rights the men of this country" enjoy? Obviously, embedded in such a claim reside assumptions regarding class and race. Above, "men" refers not simply to members of a particular gender category, but also indicates a cultural situation: the privileged, largely white identity position occupied predominantly by men who do enjoy access to the "rights" they guaranteed themselves "over two hundred years" ago. Which women share this access with them? Those who have achieved similar cultural positions, similar privileges of relative safety, wealth and status. Women like Hoff Sommers. Women now making a career out of the anti-feminist position resemble, then, privileged men. Their claims about women generally are true for them specifically.* The work of what Hoff Sommers calls "classically liberal feminists" *did* pay off for a certain population of American women, the anti-feminist woman who, likely, does not fret over pay scales and enjoys virtual carte blanche in the popular media, for example. Even *Esquire* (*The Magazine for Men*) can see that members of this movement preach "to a receptive socioeducational elite."

As Katha Pollitt pointedly notes, however, "Denial is not an explanation of a social fact but an adaptation to it." Yet, as I am not the first

---

I should add here that Hoff Sommers does not refer to herself as an "anti-feminist." She considers herself an "equity feminist." Hoff Sommers distinguishes herself from the kinds of women who concern themselves with things like rape statistics, congressional representation, and wage gaps. These women she calls "gender feminists." More on this later.

to suggest, the anti-feminist trend is not motivated by denial alone; it is a class-driven, opportunistic, media phenomenon made possible by the conditions of late patriarchal capitalism and the monopolization of media. To make her outrageous claim, Hoff Sommers, a resident scholar at the American Enterprise Institute (AEI), would have to ignore giant swaths of evidence, be a poor researcher, or workman arena where such assertions could reasonably be made — and, more significantly, received. Perhaps understanding the class culture out of which her work evolves, and with which it primarily concerns itself, explains her insistence that we no longer need a woman's movement. Before moving to the AEI, Hoff Sommers was a tenured associate professor at Clark University, whose tuition ranks with the most expensive first-tier universities. Perhaps in this world she feels safer than many other women; clearly she does, and some of her neighbors apparently include Camille Paglia, Katie Roiphe, Naomi Wolf, Cathy Young, and Rene Denfeld, among others, all of whom have a similar pedigree and thriving anti-feminist careers. Indeed, the author who introduces her work with casual references to her education as follows, "At Harvard, and later at graduate school in English literature at Princeton," also announces her class privilege.* The anti-feminist position ignores the fact that those women for whom feminism has *not* produced such results (like access to the upper echelon of American education) constitute the vast majority of American women. Susan Faludi identifies a similar class trend in *Backlash: The Undeclared War against American Women* (1991) — the conservative woman calling herself a feminist, who rejects the most basic tenets of feminist thought, sitting in her well-appointed office, arguing that American women belong at home. In both cases, the rhetorical stance exploits a conservative backlash that has been in full swing for decades.

But why an anti-feminist career for female intellectuals? If feminism has indeed successfully empowered a particular category of American women, why are they not writing books celebrating its success, praising its proponents and keeping it moving? Because the anti-feminist argument offered by Hoff Sommers, Roiphe, et al., is as much about class as it is about gender; if we tease out a bit of the class investment in the rhetoric, then perhaps the gender politics will become clearer. First, an ideological alignment with the upper tier of American society is necessarily an

---

*Katie Roiphe's sentence continues, "At Harvard, and later at graduate school in English literature at Princeton I was surprised at how many things there were not to say, at the arguments and assertions that could not be made, lines that could not be crossed, taboos that could not be broken. The feminists around me had created their own rigid orthodoxy" (The Morning After, 5).

alignment with patriarchal hegemony; second, in the cover of that class privilege, a professional woman might feel herself empowered — and, perhaps, inclined — to ignore the lives of women outside her immediate experience. Third, despite the successes of the women's movement, the remaining truth is that there are still limited opportunities for women at every class level. Finally, the surest way to secure one's position as a successful member of an embattled group (like women in patriarchy) is to limit others' access to that position. Class ambition, then, might be said to motivate the gender argument.

Indeed, the divide-and-conquer mentality of the anti-feminist campaign enacts my point that there still exist limited spaces for female discourse, feminist or otherwise, in American mainstream culture. The anti-feminist goal seems to be to occupy as much of this space as possible, without expanding that space to include more opportunities for more women. In anti-feminist arguments offered by women, we hear the same disingenuousness that colors, say, graduation speeches delivered by the very rich lecturing the newest Ivy-League graduates on the equality of opportunity in America. Of course, this is absolutely false. Competitive self-interest constitutes the very basis of patriarchal capitalism. Without the kinds of selection facilitated by competition, the hierarchical class structure upon which American hegemony (and celebrity) relies would not exist. Membership within an oppressed group renders competition even more acute, and often motivates successful members into the untenable position of defining the larger oppressive culture as genuinely inclusive in order to rationalize their own positions. That is, by denying the possibility of their own exceptionality, they solidify a position (and career) within the status quo, using their own exceptional status as evidence of the myth of inclusion. The feminist movement recognizes this myth as a lie in its fight against repressive social forces, so any movement claiming the label "feminism" yet working in favor of the status quo must be exposed as not only contravening the work of pro-women politics but also misrepresenting feminist ideology. There can be no such thing as a status quo feminist, then, or an anti-feminist feminist.

Reclaiming a pro-woman politic begins in reclaiming pro-woman language. This is the primary goal of my study. The anti-feminist pundits and authors have, since their first appearance during the Reagan era, systematically misrepresented feminist politics and deliberately sought to dismantle the liberal feminist voice in the mainstream; this book seeks to expose the more egregious and important moments of post-backlash anti-feminism.* Only after such misrepresentations have been exposed and analyzed can the necessary work begin of recovering ground lost since Reagan-Bush and through the second Clinton administration.

Further, my hope is to begin the work of reclaiming the language of liberal feminism for practitioners of pro-women politics and to anatomize the pernicious effects of the anti-feminist rhetorical backlash. Within the mainstream media, where analysis is necessarily truncated and history often collapses into the present, the rhetorical appropriation of feminist terms has proven to be the smart move for anti-feminism. As a result, it is my belief that liberal feminists must aggressively, publicly, re-appropriate those terms and reorient the discussion in our own favor. The first steps must be the reclamation and redefinition of the language that has traditionally represented our goals but has recently been used against us.

The trajectory of the anti-feminist backlash requires that feminism exist as the antagonist to its ideology; for the works I am investigating take feminism as their subject while simultaneously insisting on the movement's waning relevance. The fact of the movement's end — or success or redundancy — inaugurates nearly all anti-feminist discourse. It is perhaps redundant on my part, then, to note that in labeling herself an "anti-feminist feminist" Camille Paglia activates the feminist argument her titular ideology requires. She also sets in motion the transformative process of replacing the actual feminism of which she speaks with an idea that best serves her ideological goals; the "feminism" she critiques is, in the main, pure invention, one tailored to the needs of her political agenda. That agenda depends upon misreading (or failing to read at all) the cultural circumstances that motivate a woman-centered political movement. It requires, further, that the anti-feminists portray women's circumstances as their opposite and insist that a privileged, safe few represent the majority. Why such careers concern me is that they exist at the expense of a movement that has experienced many setbacks in the past twenty years, setbacks that have caused tremendous harm to real women.†

---

*I cannot hope to cover each media event exploited to anti-feminist ends in the post-backlash era. For example, however, consider that coverage of the sufferings of the victims of Hurricane Katrina included attacks on feminism, the injuries suffered Jessica Lynch in Iraq provided misogynist fodder, as did the attacks of 09/11/01, and the recent resurrection of the Mommy Wars.

†Consider for example the following small sampling of regressive policies issuing from the White House in the past twenty years: Mexico City Policy ("Global Gag Rule"); the dismantling of the Women's Education Equity Act; invention of the "welfare mother"; chastity training for women receiving public assistance; dramatic increase in pro-life federal nominations and appointees; the closing of the White House Office on Women's Issues; and the recent decision to tie prenatal aid to poor women to identifying the fetus as an "unborn child."

Moreover, in politics labels matter; they produce beliefs and therefore material consequences. Remember Ronald Reagan's "Welfare Queen"? Reagan claimed to know of a Chicago woman who had stolen $150,000 from the government, using 80 aliases, 30 addresses, a dozen social security cards and four fictional dead husbands. Many swallowed this fiction whole, and Reagan exploited the resulting public outrage to cut welfare benefits. The welfare system could not possibly produce those kinds of results.* One still hears the occasional racist rants against "Welfare Queens" driving their "Welfare Cadillacs." Significantly, it is during this period that anti-feminist ideology finds its way into the mainstream; indeed, as I've said, a market opens in the media for conservative women offering anti-feminist commentary.

So, at this time we begin to encounter women in the public domain making the confusing claim that women no longer require the services of the women's movement, and no longer need concern themselves with those issues about which feminism has always cared deeply, like equal pay, daycare, abortion rights, sexual harassment, and domestic violence. Thrust into the mainstream — critics now breezily refer to a feminist "establishment" — this move into the American nomenclature renders feminism vulnerable to the media instruments of American patriarchy. The mainstream media, as an emphatically patriarchal, seriously conservative, willfully biased capitalist institution can be nothing but pernicious to liberal political thinking. That it also represents the best access to the largest audience is the double bind of any liberal political movement.

While the feminist movement relies upon the participation of many men as well as women, the regressive media trend under discussion here targets women, not only the feminists whose work it attacks but also the women for whom those feminists hope to speak. In the main, anti-feminism begins and ends in academe; that is, the anti-feminist often foregrounds her status as an academic, generally has or has had a university appointment, and takes academe as a favored target. Academic women who speak or behave in a manner that threatens the patriarchal status quo are singled out for especially vituperative treatment. For example, Camille Paglia labels academic feminists as "beaming Betty Crockers, hangdog dowdies, and parochial prudes" (*Sex, Art*, 5); Katie Roiphe asserts, stunningly, that Alice Walker is "just a bad writer" (*Morning*, 5); and, in a

---

According to various reports Reagan based his grotesque exaggeration on a woman convicted of using two aliases and defrauding the government of $8,000. Even after his misrepresentation of the actual facts was made public by the press Reagan never modified his story.

touchy defense of pornography, Patty Califia observes, "Do I think Catharine MacKinnon is a great fuck?" "No." (in *Esquire*, 55). Following the logic of this movement, the political sin committed by feminists lies not in that they continue a defunct struggle, or have truly overrun American universities; the problem, of course — as with poor black women during the Reagan era — is that they exist at all.

Anti-feminism isn't merely about discrediting a woman-centered politic, then, but about maintaining a man-centered ideology that enables and rewards anti-feminist careers. In its paradoxical preoccupation with feminism and demonstrated lack of interest in all but a very few real women's lives, the anti-feminist movement boils down simply to misogyny and its attendant anxieties regarding the female body, power, and threats to patriarchal hegemony. Tapping into patriarchy's appetite for women cut to the measure of patriarchal desire, proponents of this movement market themselves as recovered from the excesses of the older, liberal version of feminism. Inoculated by the soothing rewards of patriarchy, anti-feminists renounce feminist politics and offer themselves as ambassadors of conservative politics. Positioning themselves as having regained their senses, as disenfranchised from their intellectual sisters in the academy, these recovered feminists claim an authority within popular discourse that derives from experience in the university. The anti-feminist performs her repudiation of the academy like this: first demonstrating her own erudition by using the language of academic feminism, then undercutting such highfalutin language with a kind of homespun jargon designed to render academic-speak ridiculous. Her message? She's encountered uppity academic feminists firsthand, and, like a dutiful daughter delivering the desired intelligence, she serves up report after report exposing the dangers posed by the other side.

One of these good daughters, Wendy Shalit, suggests that what women really need is to reconnect with their softer, more emotional selves — to be "ladies." In *A Return to Modesty* (1999) Shalit argues that, thanks to the failures of feminism, women now face the following dilemma: "A young woman today has basically two options open to her: to pretend she's a man, or to be feminine in a desperate, victim-like way" (74). Shalit offers her own theory of feminine identity as a panacea for what ails not just women but American culture, which is, she says, our failure to couple for a lifetime and our lack of modesty. The solution to the problem is for women to embrace "sexual modesty," and save themselves for marriage. Actually, she encourages her female readers to reserve "a part of you for someone else," that is, a husband, as a means of securing safety from masculine violence and abandonment in marriage. For "if it lasts, maybe then you can finally be safe," she assures her reader (212). Shalit may not recognize her debt to conservative anti–Equal Rights Amendment rhetoric of Phyllis Schlafly; nonetheless, the notion of protecting women by requiring them to be more lady-like and traditional served this anti–ERA anti-feminist well more than thirty years ago. Mobilized by the threat of the passage of an Equal Rights Amendment, Schlafly launched an anti–ERA, anti-feminist campaign, with claims very much like Shalit's.*

Shalit's ahistorical approach to feminism exposes the mutually contradictory foundational assumptions behind anti-feminism, for privileged benefactors of feminism's earlier work claim as evidence of that movement's success the luxury of returning to a fictional golden age, a pre-feminist period when men were gentlemen and women were ladies (and everyone was straight). The implicit narrative of this mythical time goes something like this: women and men existed happily; there was no rape, for example, because men respected and protected women. Then feminism happened (the violent struggles which brought the movement about are invisible in this fairy tale), and women lost track of their proper place, the culture grew dangerous, and men got confused about how to behave. Still, feminism prevailed; women won more independence and freedom and are now more fortunate than ever. This family-values tale insists we embrace patriarchy (which is itself unproblematic), then thank and dismiss feminists. In fact, Shalit recommends taking Peter's advice to Christian wives to heart; women ought to "live in a way that makes womanliness more a transcendent, implicit quality than a crude, explicit quality" (97). As in most fairy tales, this version of social history blames women for negative masculine behavior. For instance, Shalit scolds her reader, "If women want ... men to be good, they have to want to be good too." This rhetorical trajectory leads Shalit to the following astonishing assertion:

> It is a respect for this transcendence that once *made it impossible* for men to view women merely as sexual objects. Rather, women become something deeper, more elemental: possessors of a deep and wondrous secret that is revealed only to the one who proves himself deserving of her [97; my emphasis].

The efficacy of such a strategy is evidenced by the fact that the ERA remains the only constitutional amendment to be passed in Congress and not fully ratified by the states.

Here Shalit's argument underscores the generational point I am making in my comparison between herself and Schlafly; schooled in the rhetoric of the past 20 years of feminist thinking, Shalit speaks the oxymoronic language of an educated, empowered woman defining herself as a feminist apologist for patriarchy. The above statement also demonstrates the denial required by anti-academic, anti-feminist argumentation. Shalit, who in many ways is a sophisticated and engaging thinker, here finds herself believing, à la the most saccharine Disney film, in a fairy tale. Claiming that there was a time when it was "impossible" for men to objectify women is not unlike claiming that there was a time when violence didn't exist, and birds tied bows in Cinderella's hair.

This rhetorical move into the fantastic is crucial, however, to the anti-feminist position. For example, Camille Paglia's assertions about rape make no sense outside of this fairy-tale paradigm. "Society is not the enemy," Paglia argues. "Society is woman's protection against rape" (*Sex, Art*, 51). In perhaps crasser terms than those used by Shalit, Paglia similarly maintains a faith in a golden age of masculine defenders of feminine honor: "I come from a fierce Italian tradition, where, not so long ago in the motherland, a rapist would end up knifed, castrated, and hung out to dry" (50). Paglia's family drama places power exclusively with men — either the rapists or the avengers — and reifies patriarchal gender roles. The victim is neither saved nor is the crime prevented in this story; rather, the rape of a woman provides an opportunity for additional masculine violence designed to announce family rights over the body of a woman. Focusing exclusively upon masculine authority, Paglia reproduces here the kind of utterly canonical narrative feminists have been interrogating for decades, when, for example, we press for sexual harassment protections or study feminist theory in the university.

Despite years of conservative protestations to the contrary, it remains my conviction that the university acts as an important institutional force for encouraging and producing social action, and that scholarly, theoretical inquiry enhances one's political awareness. In her Foreword to Chela Sandoval's *Methodology of the Oppressed*, Angela Y. Davis suggests that the time has come to subvert "the idea of the social passivity of theory" (Sandoval, xiii). I agree. As a politically engaged academic, my work is always grounded in my experiences with theory, whether my texts explicitly describe this engagement or not. The experiences of actual women, the concrete conditions under which all women live, the difficult work of volunteers and activists who struggle day-to-day to protect women, these material concerns amplify and motivate my discussion. We live in a time when information seems endlessly available, through the internet, the television, talk radio, and we tend to turn to the major media outlets to make sense of it all, seeking common sense, clarifying distillations of complex events from such places as Fox News, MSNBC, the *New York Times*, CBS Evening News, *Time*, *Newsweek*, and even the Walt Disney Company. As a politically engaged academic, I offer my work here and elsewhere as a defense against totalizing pronouncements of cultural values and ex cathedra enforcement of those values produced by such media institutions. My cultural inquiry, then, is always academic, politically inflected and theorized. The tools of the academic world are emphatically political and always potentially liberating. That is, learning to read closely, interrogate assumptions, question received ideas and examine our own belief systems will necessarily makes us more enlightened (and therefore better) citizens. These skills enhance our ability to understand the implications of political rhetoric, like Op-Ed pieces, stump speeches, television and print media, and enable us to read with equal skepticism and confidence, for example, the *American Spectator*, the *National Review*, or watch FoxNews or *The Daily Show*. Approaching the analysis of the mainstream media's output as a political task, then, potentially empowers us to identify and resist — perhaps, even reverse — regressive developments that have always threatened women's political progress. It is my hope that my work will help to correct misrepresentations of women-centered politics not by prescribing a rigid definition of feminism, but rather by calling attention to those notions that cannot reasonably be called feminist. The chapters that follow endeavor to reorient public discussions of feminism back toward issues of women's safety and political empowerment. By exposing the mainstream co-optation of the "feminist" label to the detriment of women's political progress, I hope, further, to demonstrate the need for an unapologetic response to this co-optation and to model the reclamation of the terms of feminist discourse.

1
Fellating Patriarchy: Men's Magazine Feminism

> *Women hate both themselves and other women. They try to escape by identifying with the oppressor, living through him, gaining status and identity from his ego, his power, his accomplishments. And by not identifying with other "empty vessels" like themselves. Women resist relating on all levels to other women who will reflect their own oppression, their own secondary status, their self-hate.*
>
> Radicalesbians, "Woman-Identified-Woman"

> *To many Americans, the word feminism conjures up the image of angry women picketing strip clubs.*
>
> "Outlaw Feminists," *Penthouse* magazine

As the Clinton administration failed to take up the hypermasculine political rhetoric and agenda of the Reagan-Bush days, conservative discourse began blaming feminism for the actual and perceived failures of American (masculine) culture. Since the Reagan Revolution, anti-feminist sentiment has become a kind of editorial growth industry, and within this industry the prevailing voice is female. This trend takes off in the early days of the Clinton administration, but the roots are plainly in the events of the Reagan-Bush era.* The anti-feminist argument of this period both alleviates and articulates the fear that as patriarchy is forced to accommodate more feminist demands, men themselves — those who occupy the privileged class, race and gender positions within patriarchal culture — risk irrelevance, or, the undifferentiated status of equality.†

For example, Naomi Wolf sees the demands of patriarchy as simply

---

*As Susan Faludi so meticulously demonstrates in Backlash: The Undeclared War Against American Women.

†*In this context, I am using "men" as a marker of cultural privilege, a position that speaks to race and class as well as gender. As American politics have become increasingly identity (continued)

unfair to men. Feeding, sheltering and sexually satisfying women have taken a toll, she explains, and were she a man, she'd cling to any "masculine prerogative" she could get her hands on (*Esquire*, 48). Indeed, masculine prerogative will emerge as precisely the point within anti-feminism.

Ask Camille Paglia, who, in a May 1995 *Playboy* interview, famously, rationalizes the wage gap as follows: naturally men earn more because "women don't want the dirty jobs." She observes that women don't collect garbage or work as janitors, and that's why "they are still secretaries" (53). Further, women are too precious about where they work, insisting that offices "be nice, happy places" (53). This attitude to work and the workplace, she adds, is "bullshit." Paglia has made a career of slinging this kind of misogynous rhetoric, and of waging fallacious arguments propelled by the sheer momentum of her writing style and the outrageousness of her convictions. Famous for rhetorical assaults like the above, Paglia bulldozes not only women laborers and blue collar men, but also feminism and logical thinking. In suggesting that garbage men and janitors are making all the money and that most women are secretaries, Paglia embraces the sepia-toned fairy tale told by the privileged about the laboring class*: men happily take out the trash and cash checks; women, well supported by these men, opt for the less demanding jobs and keep things clean.†

If the mid-90s was the right time for anti-feminism, men's magazines provided the right place. Grounded in the belief that feminism has always been equivalent to man hating, men's magazine anti-feminism declares the old feminism dead and offers itself as a progressive alterna-

---

politics, any attempt to depict an identity position has become problematical. That is, how to generalize — an unavoidable requirement in any discussion of cultural trends — without excluding, misrepresenting or otherwise offending specific identity positions? Take, for example, the difficulty in describing what we mean when we talk about female oppression at the hands of men. "Men" in this case refers both to literal, biological individuals and an abstract notion of cultural identity. For the purposes of feminist discussions, one must acknowledge the presumption that a measure of privilege inheres to all members of the cultural identity position we call "men"; this privilege varies widely in accordance with class, race and sexual preference. Still, I am uncomfortable that my own assertion is too categorical. It ignores, for example, the analogous oppression suffered by men who occupy subjugated identity positions, like men of color or gay men. Still, I want to argue that feminism is a social movement committed to transforming structures within patriarchy that plainly undermine women's access to power and favor an identifiable, privileged category often described as "men."

*For like-minded examples of this class mythology see Peggy Noonan's treatment of the "grunts" of New York City in OpEds posted just after 09/11. I will discuss Noonan's work in a later chapter.

†For an informed discussion of labor, class and gender, see Barbara Ehrenreich's Nickel and Dimed.

tive. Arguments contained in these publications move well beyond softening relations between feminism and patriarchy, their nominal goal; they showcase political accommodation on the glossy pages of magazines that routinely devalue women. Further, while claiming to promote a new woman-centered ideology, anti-feminism simply carves out a new publishing niche, and offers another product for men's magazines to sell: the reprogrammed feminist. An ideological symbiosis begins to emerge at this time; in featuring ostensibly feminist pieces, magazines for men appeared to take a progressive step forward, while, in fact, the feminists whose work they chose to feature merely validate (and promote) the misogynous ethos of men's glossies. This "rogue feminist" (*Penthouse*'s term) promises to resuscitate women's politics by embracing and promoting regressive images of women — images characterized in large part by female surrender to masculine erotic and political desire.

Consider the work of Naomi Wolf. Just three years after the publication of *The Beauty Myth* (1991), Wolf categorically backs away from not only identifiably feminist assertions, but also too pointed a tone. In *The Beauty Myth*, Wolf made hard-line claims concerning the "violent backlash against feminism" which undermines women's political advancement in numerous ways, including standards of feminine beauty deployed as political weapons and men raping women "as a normal course of events" (10). But by 1994, she and other women were sharing their "feminist secret[s]" with Tad Friend on the pages of *Esquire*. Chief among these confidences was a desire to be found conventionally attractive and a need to seek erotic validation from the opposite sex. Erotic fantasies, then, constituted Wolf's "feminist secrets"; for instance, a ring of underage ("nubile") soccer players encircling her and aching to fulfill her every need. The "male body," she confided, "is home to me" (49). Such ideological backpedaling at this time underlines the masculine anxiety exposed so clearly by the overdetermined Reagan-Bush domestic and foreign policies: bellicose militarism, Family Values intolerance, and White House public relations. Susan Jeffords describes Reagan's constructed persona:

> It cannot be an accident that one of Ronald Reagan's most powerful and effective activities in the White House was to convey certain distinctive images of himself as a president and as a man — chopping wood, breaking horses, toughing out an assassination attempt, bullying Congress, and staging showdowns with the Soviet Union [12].

Such activities imply an invisible, passive female presence acting as a foil for a terrifically active male persona, a female presence that waits quietly for the hero-cowboy's return, takes strength from his efforts, and nurtures his identity at the expense of her own. The cowboy president, Ronald Reagan, portrayed himself and his administration as "distinctively masculine," that is, "not merely as men but as decisive, tough, aggressive, strong, and domineering men" (Jeffords, 11). Add to this manly mix a healthy dollop of "spiritual strength" and you have the recipe for the Reagan Revolution. The Reagan White House promoted a set of conservative Christian values that authorized and fueled the administration's embrace of the New Right and Family Values. The harmful effects of this ideological strategy, which was specifically responsible for the birth of the politics of personal responsibility (who can forget the invention of the "welfare queen" or Reagan's racist coding of the "truly needy?"),* have already been widely documented and interpreted. What is important for my purposes is that the transition from the Reagan-Bush days to the Clinton administration produced what Susan Cheever calls "gender-based road rage" among women†— a full-scale media assault, featuring women attacking women and feminism (Jong). In flavor and tenor, these attacks reflected the Reagan-Bush Family Values machine, employing, as they did, the rhetoric of personal responsibility, identity politics and ad hominem attacks.

For example, Camille Paglia channeled Pat Robertson on the pages of *Playboy*, saying that "the price of women's liberation is being paid by the children," and "AIDS is a price paid for sins committed in the Sixties, and by gay men who took free love to extremes" (53, 58). An obvious paradox exists in how welcome a Family Values agenda found itself at this time inside the covers of publications like *Playboy* and *Hustler*. This Family Values "feminist" championed male sexual authority, patriarchal marriage and family, and she strutted this ideological stuff next to air-brushed, surgically enhanced, soft-core fantasies of femininity. This editorial coupling is rendered less surprising when we consider that celebrations of highly eroticized, impossibly constructed female bodies constitute no more of a fiction than the Family Values notion of gender roles. With this in mind, the timing of a Clinton-era (or post–Reagan) anti-feminism makes sense, for no two presidents in recent memory have so thoroughly saturated politics and policy with issues of gender identity. More than

---

*See Reagan's 1982 State of the Union Address.

†*In a 1992 piece in the* Canadian Review of Sociology and Anthropology, *Erin Steuter observes, "While supported by religious and political organizations of the New Right, the rank and file membership as well as the leadership of the contemporary anti-feminist movement in the U.S. remains overwhelmingly female" (29 [3]: 288–306).*

commanders-in-chief or makers of policy, these men — Ronald Reagan and Bill Clinton — were masculine personalities, what we might call embodiments of identity politics. Halfway through his first term, Clinton represented a softening of the great American tumescence erected by the Reagan White House.* Clinton's comfort with women in general and feminist politics in particular demanded a response from the firmly entrenched New Right and others whose ideological desires and policy demands were previously satisfied by "the quintessential macho president" and his successor, George H. W. Bush (Orman in Jeffords, 12). This response largely took the form of editorial invective aimed at both the president himself and the category of women with whom he was perceived to sympathize, feminists. In the case of the president, his personal behavior was relentlessly scrutinized, from his marriage to his life as governor of Arkansas, from what he ate to whether he jogged regularly. In the case of the women, feminists were blamed for everything from divorce rates to Monica Lewinsky's dress size, from female infertility to the decline of liberal education.

For example, citing feminism's pernicious influence upon American culture, Christina Hoff Sommers, author of the 1994 blockbuster antifeminist work, *Who Stole Feminism?: How Women Have Betrayed Women*, claimed that liberal feminists were "quietly engaged" in literally "hundreds of well-funded projects" designed to radically transform college curricula and "[drive] out the scholars on many campuses" (33). There may have been hundreds of projects, but as any director of women's studies will attest, there were very few "well funded" ones aimed at women on campuses at this time. This kind of muscular overstatement typifies the particular strand of anti-feminist rhetoric that concerns me here. Such hyperbole frequently led to flatly misleading statements. For example, Hoff Sommers' book was published at a time when women did not dominate the American university system; according to the American Association of University Professors (AAUP), only about 10 percent of tenured university positions were occupied by women, and there were *no more than a dozen* full-blown Women's Studies Programs in place nationwide. Further, a few years later, the AAUP's "Faculty Salary and Faculty Distribution Fact Sheet" (for 2000–2001) puts the percentage of female full professors at just 7 percent.

Post-Reagan anti-feminism claimed to be rethinking feminist poli-

---

Clinton's own predilections notwithstanding, I am here discussing metaphorical, rhetorical representations of these administrations.

tics, realigning the movement to meet the demands of a changing society. This description of the project was accurate; however, the changes in society to which it claimed to respond hadn't actually taken place. Rather than urging a reorganization of feminist political goals to accommodate the actual gains women had made and to suit realities of the changing political landscape (which they claimed now favors women), the female anti-feminist, in fact, recommended that women abandon women-centered political thought and behavior altogether. What better way to align the movement with the demands of patriarchal society? Claiming the untenable position that feminism has become simultaneously irrelevant and corrosive to American culture, these authors avow an oxymoronic political point of view, calling an emphatically anti-woman ideology "feminist." Indeed, I find myself disinclined to refer to these authors as "feminists" at all. However, they have in the main successfully appropriated the term and are generally referred to in this way, often with a qualifying prefix like "anti-" or "post," "equity-" "sex-positive" or "post-backlash." While no modifier entirely satisfies, I will use "anti-feminism" to describe the trends and their adherents which claim the feminist label while endorsing a regressive politic designed to undermine the women's movement; "post-backlash" will serve as an indicator of the timing of these trends.

Hoff Sommers' *Who Stole Feminism?* appeared within months of Katie Roiphe's *The Morning After: Sex, Fear and Feminism on Campus* (1993) and the same year as Naomi Wolf's *Fire with Fire: The New Female Power and How It Will Change the Twenty-first Century* (1994), works which quite specifically and emphatically altered mainstream connotations of the terms "feminism" and "feminist." Indeed, the years 1991–2000 produced a wave of anti-feminism in the form of editorials, books, news stories, films, and magazine articles; of particular interest to me here are the pieces that appeared in mainstream men's magazines. Widely construed, and often expressly positioned, as a response to Susan Faludi's *Backlash: The Undeclared War Against American Women*, the reaction begins in earnest in 1991 around that book's publication. The appearance of this book — and its almost immediate movement into American nomenclature — coming one year before the first presidential election visibly affected by women voters constitutes a genuinely noteworthy historical moment. So, just as anti-feminism was proliferating (and being documented), women made one of the strongest political statements of the women's movement. Terminology becomes almost immediately problematic in the media, as the term "feminism" itself undergoes a redefinition, and, in the context I am identifying, begins to function very much as an entirely new signifier. For example, in anti-feminist hands, "feminist" became shorthand for, as Cathy Young would argue, "politically correct college professors" or unhappy women committed to "policing sex jokes at work."

As discussions of women and politics migrated from academic, book-length studies into more colloquial venues, from library shelves and university classrooms to newsstands and late-night television, definitions of "feminism" influenced public perceptions and therefore mainstream conversations and so must be carefully considered — and interrogated. The migration of previously academic subject matter into the mainstream pleases one's activist inclinations, of course, as academic feminism is a discipline grounded emphatically in political activism. The move from academic to mainstream venues, then, reminds us that feminism functions not only as an ideological lens, but also a social project with material consequences for the lives of women; these facts have always demanded that we follow and engage in conversations regarding women's politics in these newer venues. Academic, liberal feminists do just that, and with mixed success at this time; conservative women appropriating the term fare much better.

> *Sexual Power is a pistol loaded with only one bullet.*
> — Elizabeth Austin

Men's magazines — like *Esquire, Penthouse, Playboy, Hustler, Maxim, Details*— began featuring pieces on women's issues whose covert goal was to discredit feminism. I am arguing here that publications like *Esquire* and *Details* exist on the same ideological continuum with works like *Playboy* and *Hustler*, in that these magazines promote fantasies of masculine sexual domination and employ images of women strictly in service to that fantasy. The former folds sexist and misogynist images of women in with fashion layouts, relationship advice and movie reviews; while the latter forgoes such niceties in favor of unabashed misogyny. In this context, feminists are the spoilers of men's fun, and the term becomes synonymous with "hate-intoxicated little zealots," or, say, the familiar and generic "ball-busting bitches" (Sommers, in *Penthouse*, 67). For example, the cover of the December 1992 *Hustler* promised the following piece, "Sticking it to the Victims: How Feminists Exploit Rape." Inside, the author, Rene Denfeld, fails to address women and rape or to suggest any relation between feminism and rape victims; rather, she portrays the women's movement as overrun with "the emotional sensationalism of male-bashing and separatism" (39). The placement of this article, which is renamed inside, "Cry Rape: The Feminist Crime against Women," is telling. On the page previous to the article, ads for "phone domination" include one inviting readers to "Fuck my sister Mary up her ass! And then do me!" (The attendant visuals are predictable.) Turn the page and learn how feminists have dramatically misled all of us regarding rape statistics, dear reader, in order to satisfy a small "separatist faction" which does not properly appreciate sex with men. In fact, Denfeld warns, this faction would like women to "cease all intercourse with men whether sexual or social" (39).

Such a move would be a mistake, Denfeld declares. For we have been misled about women's true desire for sex with men, and she counters the notion that feminist women no longer desire sex with men with some claims of her own. Women are as interested in sex as ever, she writes — particularly sex they are coerced into having. It must come as a relief to the *Hustler* reader to find a self-proclaimed "feminist" woman endorsing "grudging yet consensual exchanges of sex for drugs" and insisting that having "sexual intercourse when you didn't want to because a man gave you alcohol or drugs" is not rape. Further, without addressing which acts she would be willing to consider rape, Denfeld concludes that a radical feminist overreaction to the events described above has "undermine[d] the real horror of rape" (43). Again, editorial context magnifies Denfeld's slick treatment of violence against women. Hustler interrupts the article with a one-page satirical ad, featuring a close-up image of a woman's thonged buttocks, feces running down the inside of one leg, with the accompanying text: "If pretty girls weren't meant to poop, why do they have that tiny hole between their cheeks?" The model holds a bottle of "Buttwiper" beer.

An open letter to President Bush printed in *Penthouse* in November 1992 and espousing an aggressively pro-woman politic helps to demonstrate the dramatic shift in favor of anti-feminism in this period. While the piece is impressive in its attitude to the president's treatment of women, by the time it is published such statements have become the exception in popular discourse (and pieces like Denfeld's the rule). Regarding the status of working women, the author, Marianne Goldstein, frankly observes:

> All of these women are not entering the work force because they want to have careers. These women are working because of *your damn recession* and the fact that one salary can no longer support the average family [56; my emphasis].

This letter accompanies a scathing, potentially scandal-inducing article detailing the then-president's obsession with sex, blatant womanizing, and contempt for women generally, his wife specifically. Entitled "George, How Could You?" the article contains accusations very much like those made against Bill Clinton only a few years later.* The point here is not that a magazine marketed to men would publish salacious gossip about a sitting president, but that it would include along with that gossip a feminist indictment of his policies toward women. Not only, the piece argues, does the president demonstrate a dismissive, sexist attitude toward women in his personal life, but this attitude is also reflected directly in his politics. Goldstein's letter, published just before the 1992 general election, follows a recognizably liberal feminist line; she criticizes the hypocrisy of Bush's Family Values agenda, cites rape statistics, underscores the problem of domestic violence, and condemns his beloved "gag rule" approach to reproductive rights — precisely the line of feminist thinking that would drive women to vote for Clinton in record numbers and move Bush out of office. Further, Goldstein accuses Bush of insulting women's intelligence, of making draconian demands upon their sexuality, and of ignoring the real needs of actual women.

Now, I am not suggesting that one follow *Penthouse* exclusively to understand trends in American politics, least of all gender politics. The fact of Goldstein's letter accompanying the essay on George Bush may have had more to do with Bush's then-perceived weakness and an effort to revive his own political potency than the editors' interest in any version of feminist politics. (The public persona of George H. W. Bush did not retain Reagan's manly, emphatically heterosexual quality.) It's worth noting, however, that very few of these openly liberal feminist documents will appear in magazines like *Penthouse* during the 1990's, and shortly the anti-feminist female voice will begin to proliferate. We find that women claiming the feminist label writing for these magazines are simply no longer interested in discussing policy. They are now thoroughly engaged in a politics of personality and accommodation. Within three years of the Goldstein piece, *Playboy* will feature an interview with a woman calling herself an "anti-feminist feminist," Camille Paglia, who will level accusations against the women's movement which are virtually identical to those leveled against Bush by Goldstein. Feminism, she will argue, insults her intelligence, makes Puritanical demands upon our sexuality generally, male sexuality specifically, and ignores the realities of women's lives.

---

*This article, however, was not accompanied by the *sturm und drang* exposés of Clinton's lifestyle would later bring — precisely due to the media's lack of a liberal bias and Clinton's association with feminist causes and women, but that's another chapter, or even another book.

In this *Playboy* interview, Paglia wages an anti-feminist, hyper-conservative argument under the guise of new feminist thinking. Paternalistic and avuncular in tone, Paglia's argument, significantly, emerges from an incongruous identity position. That is, her own publicly stated lifestyle and career choices contradict her proscriptions for other women.* An aggressive, self-promoting careerist, a lesbian, and without children of her own, Paglia insists that the biggest problem with feminism is that it has freed women from domestic life, with the promise that such liberation might make women happier. According to her own experience, she argues, "The happiest women" have been those who marry right out of high school, avoid college and "never question" their religious beliefs. These women do not, she adds, "regard the house as a prison" (52). They do, however, swallow received ideas whole, according to Paglia. In a world where there are still limited — often underpaid — spaces for ambitious female academics, these happy women must come as a relief to Paglia. She identifies a group of women who, she believes, not only prove her point (that straight, church-going, baby-making is best for them) but also will ensure less competition for her identity position and career choices. Following her idealizing fantasy, it is legitimate to inquire why she herself hasn't lived this life. Perhaps because these ideal women were not (and are not) in fact leading the seamlessly satisfying lives she alleges; and they are neither rich nor famous.

In an effort to render the anti-feminist editorial strategy comprehensible, Erica Jong writes in the *New York Observer*: "Find a woman to attack other women in the hopes of establishing her byline, and the status quo will remain untouched.... The thing is," she adds, "it usually works." A more generous read of anti-feminist politics as practiced by women (other than securing a byline) might be to understand the rhetorical stance as a defense against the backlash. The anti-feminist announces herself to be emphatically unlike Susan Faludi or any woman who can identify the oppressive nuances of patriarchy; rather, she embodies patriarchal ideology. By curling up comfortably within masculinist status quo, the anti-feminist shields herself from the criticism leveled against women-centered politics, maintains her political cache and (as Jong correctly observes) earns her byline. While she is "alert to the wounds of race and class and gender," Ruth Shalit reminds us, this feminist has learned "that feminism is

---

*We will find such double standards of behavior and lifestyle choice to be typical of the class politics behind the anti-feminist movement.

[only] safe for women who love men and bubble baths and kittenish outfits"; to safely call herself a feminist she must display the accoutrements of male fantasy and female surrender. In other words, "agreeing to men's terms" allows one "to pre-empt disappointment" in discovering just what those terms mean; despite the brief success and momentary sense of safety this strategy provides, as the realities of women's lives makes clear, it is "a very bad deal that post-feminists [have] struck with *Maxim*-like men" (Goldberg, "Ask Buffy"). Moving in reverse, away from political advancement for herself and other women, the anti-feminist instead pulls the parameters of masculine authority tightly around her, blinding herself to political disappointment and guaranteeing she'll have a conservative argument to sell within the post-backlash, anti-feminist marketplace.

In February of 1994, *Esquire* (*The Magazine for Men*) featured a now-famous piece that enacted the ideological trade-off described above. According to the magazine's cover, that month's issue was devoted to "The 21st Century Fox," defined in the cover art as the topless Drew Barrymore. The issue promised further revelations about women in articles like "'Does No Mean No?' And Other Nosy Questions," "The Future of American Womanhood," and "*Esquire*'s Poll of the American Woman."* As the centerpiece of the issue, an article entitled simply, "Yes," celebrated the arrival of a new brand of feminism: "'Do Me' Feminism." In this piece, rock star feminists, like Patty Califia, Camille Paglia, Katie Roiphe, and Naomi Wolf, argue that it's time for a wholesale reconsideration of the feminist project. This new feminism would organize itself around two goals: preserving patriarchy's access to the female body and "saving the penis" from the castrating effects of old fashioned feminism (48). This article served as a kind of crescendo in anti-feminism, and I will treat it extensively here.

According to *Esquire*, women might better achieve power in American culture by embracing and enacting male-defined fantasies of female sexuality. (Paradoxically, then, this is a political movement in favor of the status quo.) The article opens with a brief summary of the message coming out of this new feminist camp: "Yes." Friend thus provides a one-word gloss on what this "new generation of women thinkers" is thinking about; which turns out to be "sex (and men!)" (48). To begin: "women thinkers"? The phraseology belies a prejudice behind the term. That is, for example,

---

**Interesting tidbits gleaned in this poll include the fact that 54.3 percent of women would rather "Get run over by a truck" than "Gain 150 pounds"; 75.4 percent would rather increase the size of their incomes than the size of their breasts; 60.1 percent would choose Elizabeth Taylor over Gloria Steinem for their mother; and when asked "Are you a feminist?" 61.4 percent said "No" (65–67).*

"nurse" always indicates a female subject, and so any exception to that rule requires the modifier "male," giving us the awkward phrase "male nurse." The same is suggested above; "thinker" is assumed to be male, and so a reference to women who think, the exception in this case, requires the modifier "women," giving us "women thinkers." In order to defuse concern triggered by the image of women thinking, the author, Tad Friend, tethers female intellectual activity to the absurd dialogue found in the most benign forms of film and print pornography—"Do me, baby." (Remember the *Hustler* ad for phone sex mentioned earlier?) Thus, he channels anxieties regarding female power into an optimism over what smart women are now thinking about: "sex (and men!)."* Still, Friend pauses to fret over the question of whether these Do-Me's really can "save the penis."

Labeling this new brand of feminism with an allusion to pornography makes a kind of sense, for what better way to reattach ("re-member") phallic prerogative than through recourse to this genre? In straight pornography, female sexual identity serves the penis, underlines its presence as the first, last and only site of female sexual pleasure. Similarly, within the Do-Me ideology, female identity serves patriarchy, underwrites it as the first, last and only site of female political advancement. Wolf underscores the point in the interview when she declares that what women need now are "sluts for the revolution" (56). Highly anxious regarding masculine virility, pornography tends to repeatedly and insistently enact female sexual surrender and the utter necessity of male prowess for female satisfaction. Similar anxieties regarding masculine cultural, political and intellectual potency provoke Do-Me† notions of feminist politics. Within the parameters of patriarchy, feminism is too much about women, too visible an acknowledgment of women's connections to each other, intellectual, cultural, political—and erotic. The notion introduced by feminism that women serve themselves and each other in these ways threatens masculine prerogative at the deepest levels. Cast in a supporting role in this political drama, the Do-Me feminist props up masculine authority by subordinating politics to sex, substituting titillation for viable political goals, identifying herself according to her sexual availability to men, and replac-

---

*I am talking exclusively about straight pornography, here. For the "Do-Me" movement is an emphatically straight phenomenon, which, despite the presence of gay women like Susie Bright, a "lesbian sex guru," and Camille Paglia, honors the needs of straight men.

†Tad Friend did not at first capitalize the term "do me," but in the years since his article first appeared and the term entered popular culture, it is generally written as a proper noun. I will capitalize the term here.

ing a concern for the material realities of female experience with the less taxing concerns of attracting men, pleasing them in bed, and being found conventionally attractive.

> *Lock up your sons — the 21st-Century Woman is in the building.*
> — Esquire Magazine

If much of patriarchal culture derives from the masculine anxiety that women don't really like sex with men, that women merely use sex with men as a tool to secure food, shelter and markers of class status, like a "big house on Long Island," as Friend postulates, then magazines like *Esquire* are the natural place for the declaration of a compliant political agenda. Such publications concern themselves obsessively with female sexual availability and the women featured in them function merely as foils to masculine power (erotic and economic). Friend further explains the masculine fear that as women achieve economic progress and potential parity (feeding and sheltering themselves) then they will no longer seek out sex with men. Not to worry; the Do-Me feminist offers to service patriarchal ideology through a political surrender packaged like a sexual one. Rather than "anti-" or "Do-Me," I am tempted to attach the prefix "fellatious" to this brand of "feminism." For it is absolutely disingenuous in its claims to being pro-women and is emphatically centered instead upon satisfying masculine desire. Lorena Bobbitt was having none of this feminism, when less than a year earlier the angry Mrs. Bobbitt castrated her husband, got into her car and unceremoniously tossed his manhood along the road. (It was recovered sometime later in a field.) Reacting to her husband's sexual indifference* with a terrifyingly symbolic act of violence — "he always has an orgasm and doesn't wait for me. It's unfair," she told police — Bobbitt embodies the masculine socio-sexual dread Do-Me feminism promises to ease. Apparently oblivious to the Lorena Bobbitt story, Camille Paglia assures Tad Friend, "Every man should go for it — that's what women want" (55). Perhaps appealing to the 51 percent of college men who told *Ms. Magazine* they would rape if they could get away with it, Paglia argues elsewhere that "no" does not always mean no; indeed, "'No' has always been and always will be," she says, "part of the dangerous, alluring courtship ritual of sex and seduction" (*Sex, Art*, 5). Paglia does her part to "save the penis" from a castrating

---

*Lorena Bobbitt did not claim "sexual indifference" as her legal defense. She accused her husband of rape and domestic battery.

feminist ideology, one that supports women's right to say "No," and frighteningly embodied in the memorable dis-membering of Mr. Bobbitt (48).

Rene Denfeld, whose book, *The New Victorians: A Young Woman's Challenge to the Old Feminist Order* (1999), was forthcoming at the time of the *Esquire* interview, enacts the magazine's ideal woman: the empowered, fully voiced woman who rejects the movement that won her that voice and moves every conversation quickly toward a discussion of male-identified sex. She envisions the Do-Me philosophy as a need to recover the terms of feminism for women like her, women for whom the wage gap, workplace parity, childcare and sexual violence are significant concerns, but for whom "pornography just isn't an issue" (52). In Denfeld's litany of political concerns, the reference to pornography might come as a surprise, but the Do-Me ethos relies on sexual non sequitors and the tired false dilemma that says to embrace female-centered politics is to hate men and renounce sex. Offering this new feminist philosophy as an antidote to the older version of feminism, Denfeld embraces the sexual objectification of women, and implicitly accuses the feminists who came before her of (a) failing to enjoy full erotic lives and (b) sharing a monolithic intolerance to pornography. By collapsing feminist concerns around pornography, Denfeld encourages the notion that feminists are prudish and discounts the more serious issues of which she is clearly aware but seems less interested in addressing. Bringing up pornography is a rhetorical cheat, I would argue, a cheap shot, a deflection from genuine debate about the material concerns of real women. Feminist efforts to raise awareness about the sexual abuse and degradation of women have frequently been obscured by a distracting fluster around pornography and sex work. How many more times must we see Andrea Dworkin misquoted or Catherine MacKinnon accused of disliking sex, before we acknowledge that such accusations merely distract from the real issues of how pornography and sex work genuinely function in women's lives? Piggybacking the mainstream, shorthand, version of the pornography debate — that any objection to pornography or sex work stems from a misguided, rabid, feminist aversion to all things male and erotic — the Do-Me rhetoric uncritically embraces both sex work and pornography as liberating choices for women.

A recent article in *Details* (a men's fashion magazine) echoes this regressive optimism regarding sex work. The cover promises the following tantalizing discovery: "Exclusive: Buy Your Own Eastern-European Sex Slave for $800 (Illegal Visa Not Included)." In the Contents the editors gloss the article (entitled "Slave Drivers") like this: "In America, the sex trade means a few bucks for a hooker. In Eastern Europe, it means owning a human being" (Jan.–Feb. 2003). The flippant treatment of both the sex industry in America and sexual slavery in Eastern Europe underscores the misogyny so prevalent within men's glossies. The totality of the American sex work industry and its effect upon women is summed up in the glib phrase "a few bucks for a hooker." Men's role in the sex industry is fully elided here; "hookers" make a "few bucks" in a rhetorical vacuum, leaving the sex worker entirely responsible for and profiting from what is a market largely serving men. Moreover, the cover features a man whose public image enhances the flashy misogyny of the magazine. Poised perfectly casually, Colin Farrell leans forward, all leather jacket, white t-shirt, jeans and stubble, subtly biting his lower lip.* Both tongue-in-cheek and quite earnest, the text situated across Farrell's chest asks, "Have You Had Sex with Colin Farrell Yet?" In suggesting that sex with this man is unavoidable, the cover presents him as a model of seduction for *Details* readers; anything Colin wants, Colin gets. Expert at massaging his own notoriety, Farrell peppers his interview with consciously sexist tidbits about himself and women. So many, in fact, that within the brief two-page interview there are too many examples to list here, so I will let the following serve. Using the tendency (or not) to shave pubic hair as the measure of the difference between Irish women and American women, Farrell remarks,

> Ya know, I barely saw a vagina until I came to this fucking country. It's like going to a premiere party and being offered champagne. Just 'cause you're getting offered it, are you gonna love it more than you love beer? No [104].†

Realizing that perhaps he has gone too far, Farrell frets, "I'm gonna get drinks poured over my head when I get back to Dublin, aren't I?" (104).

No drinks will be poured on Farrell by Do-Me feminist Katie Roiphe, who argues that such exquisitely crass remarks are the fault of feminism, which "*makes* men into objectifiers" (Friend, 55; my emphasis). A kind of poster boy for the logical end of men's magazine — fellatious — feminism, Farrell is dubbed wistfully by *Details* as the sole keeper of the golden Hollywood tradition of actors who "chain-smoked their way from one drink

---

Now, I do not mean to suggest that the real Colin Farrell would endorse sexual slavery or prostitution; nonetheless, I do intend to suggest that the persona constructed and enacted by him on the cover of this magazine contributes to the sexism of the magazine in general, its lead story in particular.

†*Women's role in this editorial misogyny continues unabated; at* Details, *fully 50 percent of the editors listed inside the magazine are female (four of eight).*

to the next, interrupted only by brief bedroom appointments with the latest starlet" (101). Like the invisible starlets of the author's fantasy movie star life, Do-Me feminists serve male fantasies of guiltless sexual domination and commerce.

Indeed, in Friend's *Esquire* piece, Pat Califia, who writes lesbian erotica, commiserates with her interviewer over the sexual suffering of men under the influence of, not an intolerant patriarchy, but the women's movement. She conducts her part of the 1994 *Esquire* interview fondling a snake (wink, wink). Califia argues that men and pornography are not the problem for women; rather, following Roiphe, Califia blames feminists and their attitude to sex. According to her argument, feminists find sex shameful and as a result men have to pay for blow jobs and "feed quarters to get to see a naked girl" (55). Feminist objections to sex have given rise to strip clubs and prostitution; further, Califia adds, these exploitative industries foster the notion that "men are unlovable" (55). Here, the Do-Me point of view allows a woman to call attention to the condition of female sex workers — who dance naked for quarters or make their living giving $40.00 blow jobs — and completely overlook the potential and often very real victimization such an observation brings to light. Moreover, the slide from "men are not the problem" to "feminists are" traces the same rhetorical axis that moves from rape as violence to rape as sex. This regressive treatment of rape is a hallmark of the Do-Me (and virtually all other) anti-feminist positions. How did we get here? How can the movement that has successfully raised awareness of myriad forms of sexual exploitation and abuse suddenly be considered responsible for those things? Do-Me feminism makes sense only if we understand it as an effort to retain the sexual oppression of women in patriarchy; it's a pro–peep show, pro-pornography, pro–sex work, pro–date rape movement appropriating the term "feminism."

Mainstream objections to the women's movement generally tend to rely upon statements of 70s radical feminism as the a priori model of feminist politics and to assume a monolithic movement populated by women who subscribe to a single vision (men's role in feminist politics is all but ignored). This has never been the case, of course. But if the women's movement is indeed inclusive, why raise objections to a new manifestation of feminism? Precisely because so many of the "feminists" I address here simply do not practice what one can reasonably label feminism, if we define that term as a liberal social and intellectual movement committed to the political advancement of women. One particularly successful strategy for derailing any social movement is to inspire ideological fear as a distraction from the injustices that movement seeks to redress. In this case, those issues most visibly identifiable as "feminist" and attributable to the workings of patriarchy are blamed entirely upon the movement created to remedy them. For example, Rene Denfeld performed this rhetorical move when she deconstructed the "f-word" for Tad Friend. Any negative connotation of the term "feminism," she argues, grows directly out of the movement's insistence upon exposing the bad news for women. That is, asking women to face the truth of rape, sexual harassment and gender disparity in the workplace is depressing. Denfeld further explains that "if [women] listened" to such news they would wind up "feeling hopeless" (52). Bold only in their brazen accommodation of received misogyny, claims like the above foster the oxymoronic notion that resistance produces pernicious social forces, and that if we ignore victimization, if we refuse to listen, then it doesn't exist (particularly if it isn't happening to us directly).

Indeed, Camille Paglia famously declares, in *Esquire* and during many other interviews, "If you get raped, if you get beat up in a dark alley in a street, it's okay. That was part of the risk of feminism," as if rape did not exist prior to feminism's objection to it (*Sex, Art*, 55). The argument, then: If you're beaten and raped, blame the old, liberal feminism; if you're brutishly objectified, blame the kind of feminism endorsed by Andrea Dworkin and Catherine MacKinnon; if you find pornography offensive, blame feminism for making you ashamed of sex. This makes no sense to me and certainly can't really to the women Friend interviews. If "[t]he poor dears think they're furthering the cause of equality by trashing other women," Erica Jong explains elsewhere, it may simply be a temporary chronological condition. She continues, "they [Do-Me's and other female anti-feminists] have to get old enough to realize how deeply unequal our society is." Here, Jong repeats the notion made famous by Gloria Steinem that women grow more radical with age. In an interview for *Modern Maturity* Steinem says,

> Women tend to be conservative when they're young and more rebellious as they grow older. Why? Because young women often haven't been in the labor force long enough to experience discrimination. They haven't been married or had children — and discovered who does and doesn't take care of them. And they haven't experienced the double standard of aging yet. All those things are radicalizing experiences for women [in Dreifus].

Take Susie Bright, for example, a self-proclaimed "sex guru," who like Denfeld complains in *Esquire* that the movement itself has betrayed women and claims to miss the "take-off-your-top-and-smash-the-state" days of the 1970s (52). (Days during which, by the way, her age would have been in the single digits.) And Lois Maffeo, another woman interviewed by Friend with ties to the riot grrrls movement, who reacts to how fatiguing political activism can be: she'd rather make out with her boyfriend and spray paint than "worry about oppression" (53). Writing for AlterNet.org, Michelle Goldberg perfectly describes the Do-Me ethos as grounded in "playful, self-conscious infantilization." Further, Goldberg continues, "This woman is horny, impetuous, tempestuous, sharp-witted, giggly and supremely self-indulgent"; in other words, a fantasy right out of child porn: an aggressively sexual, infantile, passive little girl.

> *When Bryan said I was too black, I straightened my hair. When Ray said I was too young, I added four years. For Miles I was a young virgin. For Jacob I was a self-assured student of modern art. For Robbie I was a club girl. I was Kevin's steady.*
> — Rebecca Walker, in *Listen Up*

While I do not mean to suggest that the young intellectuals profiled in the *Esquire* piece are merely callow, I do want to underscore the way in which the Do-Me position resonates with adolescent insouciance — if we see adolescence in sweeping, generalized way, as a privileged momentary event, where we hold in abeyance the responsibility (and perhaps regret) we can see from where we stand but know we do not have to embrace just yet. Let me use, for an example, Katie Roiphe's explanation of the joys of masculine flirtation, "It's great," she says when men check us out. However, she adds, "they shouldn't stare if you don't want them to" (52). Breathtakingly naïve, she watches from a safe distance the social interaction of men and women and sees only what she wants to see. The comment might also be understood as symptomatic of her own personal experience; apparently, Roiphe inhabits a world where men intuit women's feelings and naturally respond, turning their heads politely away when a woman wills it. Such an assertion exposes not just naïveté regarding the vagaries of social intercourse, but most importantly the writer's own sense of safety in social situations, a privilege many women do not share and cannot imagine. The class privilege of the *Esquire* Do-Me's can be characterized along this model of adolescent privilege, then: they can recognize and speak to political realities, but remain protected from them not just by experience but also by class.

Rock and roll helps render such a position comprehensible. Having been thoroughly appropriated by the mainstream, we find rock stars cozying up to leaders of the very establishment their revolutionary predecessors sang of tearing down. Having discovered that they keep cameras near politicians, rock stars routinely make themselves available on the campaign trail as well the congressional floor. More than sheer publicity-seeking, discovering a political consciousness ties rock stars to the workings of the status quo. It is now a measure of one's hip status to be seen not resisting arrest or protesting a war, but rather testifying before Congress, visiting the UN, or shaking the president's hand. Paradoxically, in their own works these same artists claim an ostensible iconoclasm. Yet, world tours sponsored by multinational corporations, prohibitively expensive concert tickets, and antiseptic music videos featuring choreographed rebellion quickly expose the claim as an ideological pose required by the genre. The same can be said of Do-Me feminists. Rock stars of women's politics, these women claim a counter-culture hipness that is more a marketing contrivance of the mainstream industry their work continuously reproduces and reifies than a genuine political statement.

Naomi Wolf opened the 1994 *Esquire* piece interview with her own brand of in-your-face rock and roll posing by asking her interview the following questions: "Do you want to make love? Do you want to fuck? Do you want me to go down on you?" She describes her questions as a ploy designed to demonstrate to men "how sexual aggression feels" (49). If coquettish invitations mirror the sexual violence against which feminism has been fighting for decades, then the older feminists are perhaps the uptight Victorians Do-Me's often accuse them of being. Through a rhetorical sleight of hand, Wolf discredits feminism by replacing sexual aggression with something no reasonable person would find aggressive and pretending this has been the thing all along. Through slippery indirection, then, she has reframed the political argument about feminism in favor of male *Esquire* readers, even before the interview has begun.

Remember: at the time Wolf sat safely in a bar in Manhattan with her interviewer. As a celebrity author meeting a sympathetic journalist for an interview, this woman could not have been in less danger of genuine sexual antagonism herself and was in no way turning the tables on sexual aggression. Indeed, her questions contain not the mildest demands for action on the man's part. Instead, they offer action on hers: "Do you want *me* to go down on *you*?" (my emphasis). The tone of the first question, "Do you want to make love?" intensifies with "Do you want to fuck?" "Fuck" certainly may be read as an aggressive term, but the question asks the listener what he wants, asks him to state his preference and fails to demand action or to reveal the female speaker's desires. Next: "Do you want me to go down on you?" Wolf asks a man she has just met, who clearly finds her attractive, if he wants a blowjob. Now, our own private interest in this particular activity notwithstanding, the image presented in the context of the *Esquire* interview is instructive. In order to perform this act, the woman must move into a paradigmatically submissive position, lowering herself before the man. As the subject of an interview in a national men's magazine with wide distribution, as an author invited to speak about her work, this offer is neither politically innovative nor in-your-face, but rather politically regressive and sexually accommodating. As with the other questions, Wolf is not aggressing, she's offering. As the subject of the interview, she owned (at least momentarily) a kind of cachet, a certain power that the interviewer does not share; why surrender that position? She was the subject whose image, ideas, and career Friend serves and will publicize through his work as interviewer. But, how could she talk about her latest book, for example, or about her politics of female empowerment, with the interviewer's penis in her mouth?

This bogus come-on merely enacts the familiar masculine fantasy of a strong woman inviting a man to dominate her. Moreover, Wolf herself undermines any claims to her own empowerment when, after delivering her proposition, she looks around, worrying she's been overheard — an apologetic gesture, signaling her own discomfort with the behavior. Having assured herself that no one else in the bar heard what she said, the famous feminist smiles at her interviewer and runs her hand through her hair. Having quietly provoked a benign sexual tension between herself and her interviewer, Wolf stages a playful hair flip, flirting her way into an interview. Wolf enacts the very notions of female identity feminism has interrogated — and sought to undo — for decades. That is, rather than reflecting the intellectual and political progress of a movement about which she claims a public authority, Wolf embodies received ideas of female sexuality and behavior during her interview, and comes across as desperate for libidinal validation from a man. With a fourth and final question, the one placing Wolf in the most active relationship to her listener, Wolf shifts into the masculine position. She asks, "Do you want me to ejaculate in you?" At this point in the piece, Friend takes the time to note for the reader that he votes yes to (a), (b), and (c), but not to (d). No. He does not want her to take an active role. No. He does not wish to be penetrated. No. He does not want to move into a submissive position. In an article claiming to be about female empowerment (and entitled "Yes"), the "yes" and "no" answers of the male author take on a heightened rhetorical resonance. None of the women writers featured in the article are, in fact, saying "Yes" to political and sexual power; but stunningly, the male author is saying "yes" to a blowjob. To what, then, does the "Yes" in the title refer? Quieter women and sex with men. Despite her efforts to the contrary, Naomi Wolf finally enacts the uneven sexual dynamic which typifies patriarchal coupling and threatens female empowerment (and often safety). The offer Friend is fully empowered to reject is the kind of request women often feel less authorized to refuse. It's a striking turn of events when, in an article claiming to be about feminism, the only one saying "no" is a man.

When one considers how race and class inflect the question of female sexual and political empowerment, the claims of the *Esquire* feminists are exposed as manifestly elitist and racist. As Rebecca Walker (who is quoted only briefly and late in the *Esquire* piece) points out, "if you have little exposure to ideas, you're being beaten and you don't have enough money to eat," you've probably no opportunity for sexual autonomy (56). In other words, privilege of the kind enjoyed by Rhodes Scholar and Yale graduate Naomi Wolf shields her and her similarly classed sisters from the kinds of violence Walker describes and the older feminism has struggled to eliminate. Why, then, am I concerned with Do-Me and other brands of anti-feminism, whose rhetoric is so easily dismantled?

I'm concerned because these women, along with others, like the implacable Phyllis Schlafly, Ann Coulter, and Cathy Young, appear regularly in the mainstream media, exacting an anti-feminist (i.e., openly misogynistic) influence that is unmistakable and harmful to women's political progress.* Consider that the conservative Independent Women's Forum (IWF) enjoyed almost instant media visibility upon its formation in 1992; in the *Washington Post*, George Will calls the group "indispensable." IWF representatives appeared in short order on mainstream news shows like *Charlie Rose, Politically Incorrect, Crossfire, All Things Considered*, the *Mac-Neil/Lehrer NewsHour*, and *CNN & Company*. We cannot doubt media collusion in the anti-feminist project when we consider the impressive media presence enjoyed by the IWF in 1995, when its membership was only 550: according to *Extra!*, "*The New York Times* published six opinion pieces by IWF leaders in 1995, the *Wall Street Journal* published five, the *Washing-*

**If one needs material proof of anti-feminism's very real influence over policy, one need only remember that the ERA remains the only amendment passed by Congress but not ratified by the states, or consider the Supreme Court's recent decision (2/26/03) removing the protection of abortion clinics and their workers from violent protestors.*

ton Post three" (Flanders). "[D]uring that same period, those same papers chose to publish *no commentary* on any subject by anyone from NOW (with 275,000 members) or the Feminist Majority Foundation (with more than 60,000)" (Flanders; my emphasis).* Further, eight years after her book's publication, we could still find Hoff Sommers talking about *Who Stole Feminism?* on C-SPAN and arguing against ratification of the Convention on the Elimination of All Forms of Discrimination against Women (CEDAW) in *The Wall Street Journal*. For a time, Camille Paglia regularly appeared as a columnist in *Salon.com*. Naomi Wolf wrote speeches for Al Gore, and Ann Coulter gains notoriety and sells books while making statements like the following: "I'm not too proud of our gender [on political issues]. We're not that smart."

Feminism functions too often in mainstream political conversation as the scapegoat of patriarchy's culture conflicts — as, for example, Cathy Young, Pat Robertson and the Independent Women's Forum (IWF) demonstrated in their strident reactions to the tragedy of 09/11/01. Finally, feminism has become the new "f-word"; students arrive in class ready to reject the label with a litany of misogynous misinformation, not unlike that offered by the IWF's statement on the wage gap:

> The average wages of women are lower than those of men because the average woman has less work experience and is more likely to choose a lower-paying job that provides flexibility to combine work and family responsibilities. This is not discrimination.... These choices often have a negative effect on pensions, promotions, and total wages, but the fact remains that men and women are willing to make these trade-offs [www.IWF.org].

Repeating anti-feminist jargon regarding women's labor in American culture, the above conceals systemic economic inequities behind the language of empowerment and choice. At home with the "socioeducational elite,"† the IWF ignores the realities of the majority of American women's lives. What the IWF calls a willingness to make trade-offs, others might more aptly call the not-so-subtle coercion of the market in favor of stay-at-home moms with sufficiently bread-winning husbands. Other women who do not enjoy this particular situation but choose to have families anyway will simply have to accept reduced pensions, benefits, total wages, and so on. It's a trade-off IWF members like Lynne Cheney can live with. Fur-

---

*According to the same piece by Flanders, "That same year mainstream news outlets ignored two major demonstrations in Washington, D.C. ... protesting federal budget cuts organized by the feminist Women's Committee of 100."

†See the organization's Board of Directors and National Advisory Board.

ther, like Camille Paglia's gloss of the same issue quoted earlier, the above statement reduces all women to the felicitous "average woman," a passive, family-first stereotype who suits the IWF's Family Values ideological agenda — an agenda that only benefits those who are "not being beaten" and "have [more than] enough money to eat."

Shifting the political discussion from sexual oppression, as Friend puts it, "to the paradigm of sexual pleasure," the regressive Do-Me movement conflates sexual oppression with consensual sex and suggests that sexing up more men will advance women's political goals (50). Remarkably, women's magazines provide the ideological paradigm for such a move. The Do-Me argument outlined by Friend, for example, carries all the pernicious markers common to advice typically found in publications like *Cosmopolitan* (*Cosmo*) magazine. *Cosmo* promises and sells an idealized identity position (a rich, happy, sexy wife) and instructs the reader how to achieve it. A preoccupation with the reader's marriageability acts as the red thread binding all of *Cosmo*'s advice. The magazine first convinces women that they need to be married and then warns them of the real difficulty of the task, considering, of course, the readers' inadequacies. You'll need help, the editors explain. You'll need strategies and schemes. You can't do it alone. Considering that you are absolutely not Jessica Biel, you will need the advice contained in articles like, "Acts of Courage for a Mousy Girl," which appeared in the February 1995 issue. The timing of this piece was felicitous and telling, for that same month Camille Paglia told *Playboy* that fashion magazines do not "cause low self-esteem in the women who look at them. Just the opposite." Nearby on the same newsstand, *Cosmo* inquired, "Does a woman who isn't drop-dead gorgeous or so charismatic she stands out anyway have to try harder — do inappropriate stuff to get noticed?" The answer is (big surprise): "Yes." As mousy girls, we must take risks, summon courage; do things we wouldn't normally do. Like, "dress up in a garter belt and spike heels and do 'let me entertain you' for a date" (151).

Or we must stage a mock seduction for an *Esquire* writer, begin and end with our body, as Naomi Wolf does. The typical cover of *Cosmopolitan* visually enacts the rhetorical politics of Wolf's seduction — a woman posed as seductive, strong and submissive. The impact of the images contained on any *Cosmo* cover stems from a capitulation to patriarchal fantasies of female surrender; the fantasy of a fantastically beautiful and powerful woman performing her surrender to a masculinized audience. Why, then, does this image appeal to an overwhelmingly female readership? Tutelage; we buy to learn. The first lesson? How not to be our feminist, unattractive selves. For example, an article entitled, "My Life as a Cow," teaches us how to coerce our boyfriends into marrying us. We have three choices: (1) make him jealous, (2) withhold sex, or (3) issue an ultimatum. The author assumes a straight, single, female audience fed up with life as a "cow," a moniker borrowed from the misogynist saying: "Why buy the cow, when you can get the milk for free?" The author and her friends ("walking cows," she calls them) seem to be otherwise reasonable women who want nothing so much as to be married, otherwise reasonable women who will refer to themselves as "cows" when discussing the charged subject of securing a ring and a man and devise sophomoric ploys to ensure they get both.

> *I warn you that your programming is intact.*
> Ellen Neuborne, in *Listen Up*

Like declarations of most prefix feminisms of the post-backlash era, the discourse of the Do-Me movement quivers with the kinds of anxieties *Cosmo* encourages; the ideology offers a simple strategy for securing masculine validation. As if tainted by the myth of feminists as "lustless, cookie-baking, June Cleaver[s] in drag" or "fat ugly dyke[s]"—political cows, social outcasts—Do-Me's present themselves as ideologically more attractive partners than earlier feminists. For example, only within this discourse do we find such remarks as, "Preaching these antimale, antisex sermons is a way for them [feminists] to compensate for various heartaches—they're just mad at the beautiful girls" (Friend, 55). The antidote to the perceived failures of feminism forwarded by both men's and women's magazines, then, amounts to a return to regressive notions of relations among women as defined through angry competition for (1) prom queen status, (2) the handsome prince, or (3) rank as least feminist of them all. Do-Me feminism not only diminishes the seriousness of any incarnation of the feminist movement, but also diminishes the cultural space in which all women can comfortably exist. That is, given women's limited access to power in patriarchy, the Do-Me habit of seeking access to cultural authority for certain women while denying it to others strikes one as particularly distasteful. Preaching a politics of exclusion, these anti-feminists offer political viability only to women sufficiently attractive to men, and sufficiently willing to fellate the patriarchal project.

A political *Cosmo* girl, the Do-Me feminist will secure a public role and career by declaring herself a servant to masculine desire (political and erotic). For example, according to Tad Friend, a Do-Me will not only "dress like a prostitute," she will also "behave like a prostitute" (55). If we define our politics according to our desire for masculine validation, if we use sex with men as a political tool to increase our own power, are we not now adding the politics of prostitution to the politics of exclusion? This time, instead of cash, we trade our sexuality for the illusion of political relevance and power. Addressing this illusion in a piece entitled, "Ally, Dharma, Ronnie, and the Betrayal of Postfeminism," Ruth Shalit critiques the mid–90s' popularity of television shows that advance "high-powered vulnerability" as the essence of feminist identity. She describes this trend as "the apotheosis of Do-Me feminism" in Hollywood. This "fantasy of feminism" (the "Do-Me" version) furthers the backlash censure of genuine female empowerment; exposing the conservative underpinning of Do-Me television characters like Ally McBeal, Shalit observes how their shows manage "simultaneously to exploit and to deplore, to arouse and to moralize." Plainly, exploitative portrayals of women cannot be characterized as feminist. When they are so named (remember that *Time* included Ally McBeal along with Susan B. Anthony in a line-up of feminist faces) such regressive portrayals argue against women's political advancement, and work to empty the signifier ("feminist") of meaning and the politics ("feminism") of muscle.

If we read women-driven anti-feminism through the lens of the *Radicalesbians* quote with which I began this chapter, it becomes clear that women working to undermine the women's movement have at least in part absorbed the misogyny of American culture in general, and the backlash era in particular. Contrary to its ostensible goals, anti-feminism (particularly the Do-Me incarnation) constantly demonstrates the continuing need for a feminist movement. As a political statement, anti-feminism reveals the need for more safe spaces (literal and rhetorical) for women in patriarchy. As a career move, it demonstrates the public appetite for the politics of misogyny. And as a rhetorical gesture, it reveals itself to be an ideologically disingenuous pose. Co-opting the language of female empowerment, Do-Me feminism turns its back on all but a very few women and embraces the patriarchal structures that ensure fewer and fewer female voices more and more public influence, authority and bylines.

2

The Vexed Body Politic: Ms. Lewinsky, Mr. Clinton and the Feminist Establishment

"Here is the beginning, where we learn who we must be, as well as the moral of the story."
Andrea Dworkin, *Woman Hating*

"It helps that the President is attracted to women with big-cut hair and low-cut dresses. It makes it easier to slander them later."
Maureen Dowd

Once, a young woman with the right connections landed her dream job in the house of the powerful and handsome prince. For a time, he prefers her above all others and lavishes the young woman with attention, gifts, and false promises. Betrayed by the hateful suburban witch and pursued by the jealous horde, the princess stays true to her man through the crucible of unfortunate love: slander, ridicule, FBI interrogation. Alone in her room, she awaits her rescuer. But the story is not what it seems, and the prince does not come. Bereft of her plot line and her man, abandoned to witness and corroborate her own irrelevance, the would-be princess makes her way through momentary romantic hope into permanent notoriety.

The American media love this tale, not the boy meets girl, girl wins boy with beauty and smallish feet story, but the one about a powerful man and a profligate woman. Once the mainstream has passed its judgment — that she is too available, too sexual and, therefore, dispensable — she becomes a mere prop in the man's story, and fodder for all manner of public misogynist musings. As a prop, she is far from unnoticed, though; on the contrary, her body is exposed to vigorous, invasive scrutiny and her attractiveness as seriously debated as the implications of her relationship to the man. Who can forget Fawn Hall, Donna Rice, Jessica Hahn, for example? Yet, do we recall much beyond size, shape and hair color? Think of the many women associated with Bill Clinton, like Paula Jones, Gennifer Flowers and Kathleen Willey, all of whom became notorious irrespective of anything they may or may not have actually done and a few of whom landed in jeans commercials or inside the pages of *Playboy*. Still, nothing could have prepared even the most jaded observer of American culture for the obsessive, sustained torrent of sexist news and misogynist commentary that attended the Monica Lewinsky–Bill Clinton affair. Nor would one have anticipated the vexed, ambivalent response to the woman herself from some of our most recognizable feminist voices.

If men's magazines supply the test market for the "fellacious" (or Do-Me) brands of feminism during the 1990s, discussions of the Lewinsky-Clinton affair demonstrate the turn feminist politics had taken generally away from interventionist debate and protest toward a more protectionist rhetorical stance. During the sweeping, years-long scandal, the conservative press demonstrated its nearly wholesale appropriation of the terms of feminist discourse. From the moment the scandal breaks, well-known feminist authors and pundits struggle to defend Clinton and find themselves endorsing a politic not unlike conservative anti-feminisms with which they would not ordinarily align themselves. If it were a stamp of feminist conviction, for example, to stand behind Anita Hill, a few years later it became a sign of political savvy to disparage Monica Lewinsky.

The scandal itself must be considered a feminist issue, for it brings together issues of sex, power, politics and the media. The scandal centered upon Ms. Lewinsky's sexuality, physical appearance and powerlessness; further, discussions of the affair belie an overarching sexism in public discourse — and mainstream sexism ought to concern those of us calling ourselves feminists very much. If we ever doubted that the personal was indeed political, consider how this particular exploitative sexual relationship invited and sanctioned a general rush to publicly humiliate the woman involved. Lewinsky was repeatedly portrayed as an oversexed, unbalanced opportunist; the effect such rhetoric continues to have upon political discussions of women's issues is quite real. The ease (and willingness) with which the American mainstream reduced Lewinsky to the cruelest stereotypes of female sexuality indicates that there is much feminist work yet to be done within American culture and just how much ideological ground has been lost in the post-backlash era.

To appreciate how thoroughly the scandal dominated the media at the time, consider that between news of the affair breaking in February of 1998 and September of that same year, "network evening news shows ... aired 1,053 stories" on the scandal ("Sex, Lies").* Print media were just as prolific, taking every opportunity to indulge in gleeful voyeuristic coverage. In all venues, a regular dose of male fantasy was enacted at Lewinsky's expense. For example, Watergate survivor John Dean explains that if Lewinsky were his daughter, he'd want to warn her about a few things. He does so in a *New York Times* OpEd open letter to Ms. Lewinsky. Like an avuncular Sam Spade, he warns that she is in real danger, just as he once was himself, and recommends she read Gavin de Becker's *The Gift of Fear*. "It could," he counsels, "save your life." Dean finally ducks back into the shadows with an unhelpful, "Good luck." In the main, however, stories about Ms. Lewinsky tended toward the prurient, emphasizing not only her naiveté but also her sexual availability. Signs of harassment and abuse — like age differences between the players and overtly uneven power relationships — were all but ignored, or used to further impeach the woman's moral character. For example, *Time* reports as reliable the opinions of a man who admitted sleeping with Lewinsky while he was her high school teacher. The affair began when she was 19; yet, *Time* takes this man at his word that Monica Lewinsky behaved badly. She was, he reports, "obsessed with sex" (Ratnesar). (Had a high school teacher admitted sleeping with, say, Chelsea Clinton, would not the press have been up in arms, charging harassment or worse?) One late night comedian describes Lewinsky as "Deep Throat," and Joan Rivers labels Lewinsky, "The world's luckiest chubbette." The *Wall Street Journal* labels her "that little tart." *Time* magazine calls her "flirtatious and pretty and willing," and treats her "fondness for tight, chest-hugging outfits" as news. John Leo dismisses Monica Lewinsky thusly: "Big Hair, bigger mistakes" in *U.S. News & World Report*. A week earlier, the same publication teases with the following headline: "Starr puts 'another squeeze' on Lewinsky." Finally, taking Lewinsky's hardship about as seriously as the rest, Madonna tells *Elle* magazine, "Monica Lewinsky should shut up and get a life." The rush to publicly define Lewinsky within mutually exclusive, misogynist extremes — hyper-sexual, ravenous manipulator or needy young flirt looking for attention — demonstrates why this affair reasonably serves as a study of the misogynist heart

---

*According to "Media Monitor," September/October 1998, Lewinsky coverage totaled 29 hours of air time and this coverage totaled "nearly as much coverage ... as all White House scandal news combined from 1993 to 1997" ("Sex, Lies, TV News").

of American politics and the media. Moreover, the events surrounding this affair serve as another key moment in post–Reagan-Bush anti-feminism, bringing together the various threads I've identified and enacting their pernicious and very real effect upon mainstream feminist discourse and politics.

> *Please fasten your seatbelts: we are about*
> *to encounter contradictions.*
> Laura Kipnis, *Against Love*

Before I continue addressing this media event, however, I should clarify my own reading of the scandal. I have to admit, throughout the scandal my sympathies lay with Ms. Lewinsky — the reasons why should help expose the rationale behind much of my argument. From the very beginning, the young, inexperienced woman was unprotected and betrayed in every conceivable way: let down by a notoriously dishonest lover, secretly recorded by a back-stabbing, self-promoting friend, and pushed around by a loose-cannon independent counsel. She naïvely linked her future to the most powerful man in the world, who has been revealed to be an inveterate and reckless seducer. Women looking for fame, notoriety, or (perhaps especially) love, approach such men at their peril. What could the 21-year-old have been thinking when she got to the White House? I wish she had known better. No doubt she does now. We cannot overlook that Lewinsky engaged in a sexual relationship with a man she knew to be married, nor should we ignore our own disappointment with yet another woman tossing her body into the stew of public debate over female sexual behavior (think Gennifer Flowers here) — a debate which ever since abortion politics went public cannot fail to implicate all of our bodies. Still, even if an undeniable carelessness on Lewinsky's part contributed to this backlash event against women, I find my sympathies bend in her direction. This young woman, who sadly became infatuated with the wrong man, was certainly more sinned against than sinning.

To see my point, consider the media images of Ms. Lewinsky in comparison with Clinton's earlier accusers. Gennifer Flowers and Paula Jones appeared on the evening news standing behind podiums, surrounded by serious-looking handlers; Monica Lewinsky appears in *Vanity Fair* draped in a feather boa. (Where were her handlers?) Paula Jones accuses the president of sexual harassment; Gennifer Flowers calls a press conference to announce doing what Monica Lewinsky is publicly castigated for doing.

Ms. Lewinsky's arrival on the public scene effectively disinfected Ms. Flowers' image. To be sure, both Jones and Flowers endured their share of the media's invasive gaze, but unlike Lewinsky they were taken seriously at least some of the time. For my part, Lewinsky appeared not as a sexually voracious climber, but as an emotionally starved young woman who lacked the skill, sense or talent to conceal her emotions when most grown-ups understand this to be the socially responsible thing to do. She was not terribly good at taking care of herself. And in her lack of self-consciousness, she holds the mirror up to our sexist society, our media cruelty, and exposes American culture to be unapologetically callous toward female sexuality generally, female sexual vulnerability specifically. Fully empowered to do their worst, the media created a notion of "Monica Lewinsky" larger than the sum of her zealously eroticized parts: an appetitive monster, she stands as a monument to the horrors of untrammeled female sexuality, feeding on the unsuspecting president, eating cookies and ordering out for mousse cake. Editorialists accuse her of being too heavy, too talkative, too enamored of her lover, too willing to discus the affair, too trusting, too fond of email, too this, too that. At the mercy of this hostile media, Lewinsky was subjected to the indignities American popular culture reserves for the wrong kind of woman. Once consigned to this category of woman, then, Lewinsky became fodder for myriad anti-feminist denunciations not only of her role in the affair, but also women's issues generally and, more significantly for this study, feminist politics specifically.

Lewinsky was coerced into public silence by Starr's investigation and could only watch as her character was shredded and her image exploited in the testosterone drama playing out daily in the press between Kenneth Starr and the White House. The press subjected the president to his own share of humiliating images and turns of phrase, but he benefited from the distraction of being leader of the Free World. No matter how high the salacious gasbag index rose, folks had to finally report on the actual news and the affairs of state. Clinton consistently appeared in serious, contemplative poses and came across as juggling the weighty, twin responsibilities of being commander-in-chief and world famous womanizer. For example, in the same February 1998 *Time* announcing the affair with Lewinsky, the magazine also covered at length Clinton's handling of the economic crisis in Asia. Clinton got a new dog, and for two days we were awash in pictures of the family pet. He danced on the beach with his honorable wife. And he chewed his bottom lip with dramatic intensity on the covers of just about every available news weekly. Ms. Lewinsky, on the other hand, enjoyed no public relations diversions, and had little control over her own image. She lacked a good husband and distracting public service. While Bill Clinton staged Family Values photo ops and the press ate them up, Monica Lewinsky supplied anti-feminist pay dirt: a woman even feminists wouldn't defend, who embodied the vulnerabilities of a movement built on concern for individual women.

But why pillory this particular woman? Adultery? Nope. American culture has routinely tolerated such behavior in the right women — like Elizabeth Taylor or, for example, Marilyn Monroe, or Princess Diana. Sex with a more powerful man? Wrong again. American fondness for this particular fairy tale is undeniable. Think here of the VH1 channel celebrations of "Celebrity Wives" or Hollywood films like *Working Girl* or *Pretty Woman*. Must be sex in the White House, then? Not so much. John Kennedy, anyone? Indeed, Eleanor Clift quipped on MSNBC, "I think [with] past Presidents, Lyndon Johnson for one, certainly Jack Kennedy, these things went on, you know, libido and leadership are linked." Gene Lyons makes the following congratulatory observation: Clinton's charms tend to make women "act batty around him." Finally, Katie Roiphe "cooed," as Elizabeth Austin puts it, at a panel discussion sponsored by the *New York Observer* that "[t]his virile President is suddenly fulfilling this forbidden fantasy of this old-fashioned, taboo aggressive male." So, what is the problem? I would argue it's that Lewinsky is the wrong kind of woman; her sins reside not in an unrestrained sexuality, but rather in her open emotional vulnerability and her resistance to crippling requirements of female beauty reserved for the famous. She was in love, a bit giddy, not thin, and not Marilyn Monroe. Neither is she narcissistic à la Gennifer Flowers in a manner that allowed the public to first voyeuristically enjoy her public exposure and just as quickly turn the page, looking for the next disposable female image.

Adriene Sere perfectly describes the gray area in which a 21-year-old White House intern might find herself when entering into a sexual relationship with the president of the United States: "consensual sex but not necessarily empowered consent." The Lewinsky-Clinton scandal was the first to genuinely threaten to unseat a feminist-friendly president, and did so based on the slippery and tortuous issues of sex and power. Conveying the nuance and ideological import of different levels of consent in the Clinton White House was nearly impossible in the media world of shorthand political pronouncement, as well as the politicized "he said/she said" tone dominating media conversations at the time. This political reality alone might prompt the feminist establishment to turn away from a woman who plainly needed its help — for Lewinsky was a woman left at the mercy of the systemic sexism ordinarily offensive to feminist sensibilities.

> *I voted for the lyin', cheatin', cutie pie twice, in line with the "lesser evil" theory of electoral politics, and I'm not sorry I did, but you won't catch me apologizing for him in public.*
> Susan Brownmiller

Standing behind Lewinsky would have meant throwing the force and political capital of the already-embattled movement behind an icon troublingly susceptible not only to personal attacks, but also public missteps. Indeed, Monica Lewinsky was a walking reminder of the difficulty of founding and maintaining a political movement dedicated to the sociopolitical concerns of individual women and what happens to them; she embodied the uncomfortable truth that a woman-centered ideology requires us to suspend many of our own prejudices regarding, for example, the very behavior in which Ms. Lewinsky apparently involved herself. And it requires that we grow more comfortable with the ambiguities surrounding issues of sex, power and consent. Lewinsky engaged in a sexual relationship with a man she knew to be married, demonstrated little restraint in discussing the affair and less skill in protecting herself. Further, she naïvely and recklessly entrusted her future to a very powerful man protected by a machine designed to preserve not only himself and his cultural position, but also the ideological framework which supports that position. She was sometimes embarrassingly untrained in the skills of public life; yet, I would argue that is precisely what made her vulnerable to Starr's machinations and the media's virulence — and precisely why more of us should have spoken on her behalf. Yet, even today, Lewinsky continues to symbolize the difficulty of doing precisely that and the importance of protecting women from sexual exploitation. Her situation, then, further reminds us that sexist aggression (physical or rhetorical) happens to actual women with visible weaknesses, whom we may not like very much. But we need not like one another to work on one another's behalf, to identify the political issues at stake within the muddled morality of gender relations, power and sex.

Further, the intense media focus at the time on the personal, on the details of the players' desires, behaviors and fashion missteps, exposed the difficulty of waging a serious political argument in the larger public domain, as politics is utterly personal in the American mainstream. So when Gloria Steinem refuses to condemn Bill Clinton, she did so through a personal confession: "I am not blameless. How can I require a leader to be blameless?" (in Herbert). She further admitted a personal wish that Clinton were, in fact, "blameless." Such declarations strike me as utterly unsatisfying, non-committal and perfectly meaningless as a statement about Bill Clinton's treatment of women. This is especially true when we consider Steinem's usual willingness to speak candidly and in frank defense of women. But while unsatisfying, this hedging-and-hoping strategy was not uncommon at the time. As Bob Herbert helpfully realized then, the strategy was about waiting out the news cycle for better news. "[L]ike other staunch Clinton supporters," he explained, feminists were deflecting, redirecting and laboring to change the subject, banking on an "improbable" turn of events — the "improbable" being that Clinton hadn't involved himself in further sexual misadventure. Herbert was right about this and one other thing. As self-identified feminists were buying time, they were doing so largely by allying themselves with "the man against the woman." In this *New York Times* piece, "The Feminist Dilemma," Herbert quotes a leader of a "national feminist organization" who preferred not to be named. Confirming his conclusions and reflecting the public bind in which many feminists found themselves, this feminist leader told Herbert: "I hate the stories that are coming out" about the president; and she could not help but believe that "at least some of them must be true." It appears, she admitted, that Clinton was "in the habit" of objectifying women and treating them dismissively. But when this feminist leader looked around for alternatives, she acknowledges that, well, there are none.

Surely, one alternative was *not* to turn feminist principals on their heads and attack the woman featured in the Clinton Sex Scandal du Jour. Nor abandon long-held beliefs as if they had suddenly become passé. Susan Faludi did just that when she accused feminists who worry over workplace groping of acting like shocked Victorian maidens, for example, and Katie Roiphe insisted that "the phrase 'abuse of power' could apply equally to the President and the 24-year-old former White House intern" ("Career Woman"). The first claim relies upon that worn fiction of female oversensitivity to the slightest masculine advances; the second upon the fantasy of female sex as the seat of female power. Both contribute nothing to the work of feminism and reduce women to the most common stereotypes of femininity.

Political and discursive compromises made by Clinton-era feminists do nothing to stall the Reagan-era lurch toward the Evangelical Right within American political life or to counteract that movement's appalling effect upon the lives of women, minorities, the poor. Nor do these compromises help reverse the erosion of feminist credibility within mainstream discourse. In taking Ms. Lewinsky and the scandal more seriously, feminists with access to the mainstream media might have encouraged pundits, politicians, perhaps Clinton himself, to take us and our politics more seriously. Of further concern, of course, is that years later we are still living with the legacy of Clinton-era feminist hedging, which manifests (at least in part) in declarations of each new media event somehow revealing feminism to be obsolete. Take for example the news surrounding 09/11/01, the Abu Ghraib prison abuse scandal, and the invasions of Afghanistan and Iraq. A year after the twin towers fell, conservative columnist Cathy Young declared that those attacks on the U.S. indicate how "the feminist movement, already at low ebb, has slid further into irrelevancy"; further, she argues, feminists ought to have learned from the subsequent U.S. presence in Afghanistan "what real oppression looked like." The goals of my study are to reverse this kind of anti-feminist prejudice dominating the media and to reclaim feminism as a pro-woman movement. More to the point of this chapter, as we moved through the second Clinton administration we saw the battle for control over the terms of feminist debate intensified. Each side of the political divide struggled to fend off the finger pointing of the other: the Right defended against charges of sexual hypocrisy and general prurience; the Left fought off accusations of moral laxity and political expediency. Generally ignoring the glaring discrepancy of power existing between the two players, feminists publicly deny any harassment issues, and instead attempt to define Lewinsky as an autonomous woman, fully in control of her own sexuality and workplace circumstances. The unfortunate result of this conflicted — and a bit defensive, if not reactionary — stance was that in clinging to the hopeful feminist fantasy (equal protections for women), feminists not only colluded in the public humiliation of Ms. Lewinsky (and other of Clinton's accusers) but also damaged the movement's political credibility.

Unfortunately, this damaging tone was introduced early in the scandal by the brittle, legalistic statements coming from the then president of the National Organization for Women (NOW), Patricia Ireland. For example, in response to the Starr investigation, NOW issued the following legalistic, largely meaningless press release:

> The information available publicly regarding Kenneth Starr's investigation leaves the National Organization for Women unable to comment respon-

> sibly about the validity of the allegations of obstruction of justice or suborning perjury by President Clinton.
>
> Based on public reports, it appears that Monica Lewinsky gave different versions of her relationship with President Clinton in a deposition and on tape to a co-worker. We will watch the evidence closely as it becomes available to ensure that Ms. Lewinsky is not (and has never been) coerced by any involved party, including President Clinton, Vernon Jordan, Linda Tripp and Kenneth Starr, among others. If credible evidence of wrongdoing by any party emerges, we will speak out and urge women's rights supporters across the country to make their voices heard [January 23, 1998].

To begin, it simply wasn't true that at that time Ireland couldn't "comment responsibly" about Clinton's part in the events leading to the Starr investigation. Abundant public evidence already suggested a pattern of disrespectful and abusive behavior toward women on Clinton's part as well as a tendency toward duplicity regarding this behavior. In NOW's tiptoeing around Bill Clinton, Ireland evinces an impulse to shield this president and women's issues from yet another scandal, for as Clinton's fortunes went, it seemed, so went the fortunes of feminist politics. Feminists like Ireland, who rather than seeking rock-star status and bylines, works full time to promote women's rights, seemed caught in a rhetorical double bind. The impulse to defend Clinton and to paint his accusers as unreliable speaks to the great hopes women placed in Clinton politically; in the wake of the Reagan-Bush era, women and other minorities had reason to cling to Clinton's liberal promise. Unfortunately, this defensive impulse backfired and resulted in more of the ideologically self-defeating rhetoric I define earlier as "anti-feminist" or "post-backlash" feminism. In this press release, Ireland's response to tortured political needs and realities — as opposed to a conservative or misogynist ideology — coerces her into this conflicted voice.

Still, the damage was done, as this voice corroborates anti-feminist ideology, and even women like the president of NOW maintained that voice for too long. Note that the dearth of evidence, used to avoid censuring Clinton, didn't prevent Ireland from calling Lewinsky's credibility into question; before suggesting the possibility of harassment, she insinuated Lewinsky may have lied. This trend repeated itself over and over. Patricia Schroeder similarly warned against a rush to conclusions about Clinton and hastens to implicate Lewinsky: "somebody," she offers, "may be overstating the case." She counseled patience, because, "A week from now we could find out this was a fantasy" (in Herbert). Potentially reducing the affair to a mere fantasy of the woman's imagination, Schroeder gave credence to the sexist "sluts or nuts" defense of offensive masculine behavior. If the complaining woman could be demonstrated to be either overly sexual (a slut) or mentally unstable (a nut), then the harassing behavior, and therefore the harassing man's culpability, would be rendered moot. That a woman would publicly defend a powerful man known to habitually offend individual women in this way demonstrates the continued need for the feminist movement. Clearly women still lack the political muscle, political equality, to freely practice pro-feminist politics; our position as a marginalized group compels us to cling to even the most distasteful (and not altogether committed) supporters, like Clinton. We find ourselves willing to trade a Freedom of Access to Clinic Entrances Act, or the appointment of a Ruth Bader Ginsburg, for example, in exchange for a few free gropes. It seems redundant to note that this trade constitutes an emphatically un-feminist move. For, in cutting Lewinsky (rather than Clinton) loose, feminists argued implicitly that some misuses of masculine power were beyond our interest, certain female victims of that power not worth defending. As an example of misuses of power, I refer here not only to the probable manipulation of Lewinsky by her superior, Bill Clinton, but also the exploitation of Lewinsky by an out-of-control independent counsel, and an aggressive media machine.

When women argued that Lewinsky was a fully empowered woman, the arguments tended toward the patently regressive and were often contrary to feminist politics. For example, Katie Roiphe argued in a *New York Times* OpEd entitled, "Monica Lewinsky, Career Woman," that Lewinsky's situation was "the opposite of sexual harassment." The unpaid intern was simply honoring "a time-honored female tradition," of using "sexual power" as a means to "improve one's position in the world." She further explained that the power difference between and unpaid White House intern and the president of the United States benefited not the most powerful man in the world, but the unpaid intern; "a person of less power," she contends, can use "her sexual attractiveness or personal relationship with a person of greater power to get ahead." Again, Roiphe ignores the facts in the case. Lewinsky did not "get ahead"; neither her professional nor private life finally were improved by her connection to Clinton. She became, as Austin reminds us, "housebound and unemployable," while Clinton continued "to decide which women [were] Secretary of State material and which [were] merely potential humidors."

When NOW finally does address power issues in a January 1998 press release, the organization was still plainly uncomfortable with directly addressing Bill Clinton's behavior:

> While we do not know the truth of the allegations made against President Clinton, we want to state clearly our belief that it would be a misuse of power for any public official to have a sexual relationship with an employee or intern.

At this time it is common knowledge that Clinton has at the very least attempted to "have a sexual relationship" with an employee, Paula Jones. A reasonable assumption would be that Clinton and Lewinsky were involved sexually, that he in fact *did* engage in "a misuse of power." NOW's press release continues:

> Whether the boss is a county supervisor or the President of the United States, no public official should take advantage of the aphrodisiac of power. We must demand that public officials, at all levels and in all branches of government, pledge to reject sexually intimate relationships with employees/volunteers.

Sliding into policy issues, and thus avoiding criticizing Clinton's specific behaviors, NOW allows itself to avoid coming specifically to Lewinsky's aid. As early as February 9, 1998 (one week after the scandal made news), Barbara Ehrenreich writes in *Time Magazine* that feminists will have a hard time "explaining their stammering and mostly inaudible performance during Week I of Presidential Sex Crisis III." It's time she says, "to cut Bill Clinton loose." Unfortunately, most of us stuck around. A month later (March of 1998), Joan Beck, a columnist for the *Chicago Tribune*, further noted the obvious, that feminists had "shed [their] principles to back Clinton" (azstarnet.com). Maureen Dowd reminded feminists of this failure even less diplomatically in The *New York Times* where she joked that "Ms. Lewinsky must die so that the women of America can have better child care, longer maternity stays, toll-free domestic violence hot lines and bustling mutual funds." Obviously, in their continued support of this man, too many feminists came across as alarmingly complicit in the exploitation of Ms. Lewinsky, as if they saw this particular woman as dispensable, a noisome blip on the feminist radar screen.

> *But feminists should call it as it is. If feminism is to count for anything beyond a mere interest group, we must vigilantly guard its vision.*
> Susan Brownmiller

It is perhaps understandable that feminists would resist denouncing the president himself; yet, the media coverage of Lewinsky described above offered ample opportunity for a feminist response. Indeed, it demanded such a response. One could not have invented a situation bent more in favor of feminist anxieties regarding (and objections to) patriarchy's abuse of women and the female body. How, then, does one explain feminists' hesitation to stand behind Lewinsky against Ken Starr's invasive investigation, or the general lack of feminist outrage regarding flagrantly misogynist treatment by media pundits, and so on? One answer might be that staging and maintaining a strong feminist political movement presents a complex of material difficulties and political vulnerabilities. Succumbing perhaps to a ubiquitous anti-feminism plaguing American media and political dialogue, women calling themselves feminists seemed to agree to indulge misogynist profiling in service to a greater good, or a larger, more urgent, political agenda. In the case of Monica Lewinsky, the conditions of the Starr investigation (compelling her into silence) made this especially easy to do. Another answer might be that at this time feminists occupy a vexed position within public dialogue. For example, unless you were Ellen Goodman, Anna Quindlen, Maureen Dowd, or a mouthpiece for the extreme right, it was nearly impossible to be heard on opinion pages in major urban newspapers — precisely where political analysis enjoys widest access and influence. In 1995, for example, pieces by members of the Independent Women's Forum (the Family Values love child of Lynne Cheney, et al.) appeared six times on the OpEd pages of both The *Wall Street Journal* and The *New York Times*. No OpEd pieces by members of NOW or any other feminist organization appeared in either publication that year. At this time, women were writing only 26 percent of all opinion pieces (Faludi, "Conspiracy?"). If conservative writers, like Rene Denfeld and Cathy Young, appear continuously in places like *The Philadelphia Enquirer* (where Young's byline appeared 26 times between 1995 and 1996), that doesn't leave much room for liberal feminist analysis. Additionally, despite all evidence to the contrary, the myth took hold that American news demonstrates an unqualified liberal bias* and that feminism exerts too strong an influence upon U.S. culture and politics. Therefore, the conservative story goes, the liberal feminist voice must be "balanced" by conservative voices. Predictably, the conservative press uses this scandal to launch a new wave of anti-feminism, which, rather than balancing what

---

*If the conservative voice hadn't dominated public debate, how could the alarm enjoy such a widespread audience? The ploy is genius (and not without historical precedent); as soon as the myth of liberal saturation enters the nomenclature, any liberal foray into public debate constitutes overkill. The effectiveness of the claim demonstrates its fiction.

feminist voices could still be heard, works to marginalize liberal feminist discourse even further.

When liberal feminists do speak about Monica Lewinsky and Bill Clinton, the results, as I've said, are quite disappointing, and politically unhelpful (with the noted exceptions). The story broke at a time when American feminists occupied the uncomfortable position of supporting a man who repeatedly demonstrated a grotesque lack of respect for individual women, but seemed committed to our most important political goals; he appointed the first female secretary of state and attorney general, in addition to putting other women on his cabinet, he named more women as federal judges than any other president in history and appointed a second woman to the Supreme Court, he supported affirmative action, abortion rights, and child care initiatives. Feminists received the news of the affair between Bill Clinton and Monica Lewinsky under the weight of these political realities. Questions presented themselves: how do we continue to support a man politically who personally involves himself in one careless affair after another, this time with an intern? Feminists demand that government stay out of our bedrooms, so shouldn't we stay out of the president's? Yet, if the personal is indeed political, should we not have demonstrated some concern for the young woman, particularly as it became increasingly obvious that the press and White House had virtually unlimited resources and she was quite on her own? As a result of feminists not coming to her aid, we left Ms. Lewinsky to face the enormous financial, political, and cultural forces at the disposal of the media and the White House without a public feminist voice speaking consistently on her behalf. With few notable exceptions—Pollitt, Ehrenreich, Goodman and Dworkin, for example—a tacit strategy emerged: without irrefutable evidence of harassment, the affair was none of our business, and feminist silence would stand as monument to our level-headedness regarding charged (and politically volatile) issues like sexual harassment. How unhysterical of us.

The problem, of course, was that in ignoring the individual woman involved, and putting a brave face on the larger political issues, feminists themselves appeared to collude in Clinton's mistreatment of women, as well as turn their backs on the very category of women they would be expected to defend. I will use examples from two of the most recognizable feminist names of the period, Susan Faludi and Gloria Steinem, to illustrate my point. Both are well known even to those who know next to nothing about feminist politics, so their mainstream comments on the Lewinsky-Clinton scandal packed perhaps a stronger political punch than commentary by other equally credentialed and well published feminists. First, let me offer a (perhaps unnecessary) reminder regarding the work of the first, Susan Faludi. *Backlash: The Undeclared War Against American Women* (1991) established Faludi as a feminist icon. The backlash Faludi identified was not an organized movement, but rather a media trend which argued that feminism's success rendered it no longer necessary. This trend simultaneously insisted that the success of the women's movement was responsible for all female unhappiness (as opposed to systemic sexism, for example). Importantly, Faludi's work initiated discussions of the mainstream class bias evinced by Reagan-era anti-feminism, a bias in favor of privileged groups for whom feminism could be said to have succeeded, and demonstrated that these groups within which the lucky few are fully empowered to make personal and professional choices — choices which are often underwritten by wealth, powerful husbands, and staffs of assistants — represent the smallest proportion of American women. Finally, Faludi's *Backlash* revealed that women for whom these luxuries are out of reach (that is, the vast majority of women) still suffer under the weight of patriarchal restrictions against women and that many powerful, privileged women contribute to the backlash attempting to dismantle the successes of the women's movement. While the value, validity and significance of Faludi's book remain a fairly contentious subject within feminist circles (and elsewhere), from my point of view *Backlash*'s most significant contribution to feminist studies resides in its exposure of women's role in anti-feminist behavior and politics.

As the backlash proliferated through the 1980s and early 90s, a miracle occurred: at the height of the Reagan-Bush era, feminists coalesced as a voting force and visibly influenced the election of a President for the first time in history. In helping to stall the momentum of Reaganesque conservatism and elect Bill Clinton, women demonstrated feminism's promise as a political movement. In fact, Faludi's *Backlash* ends with this hopeful prediction, which at the time of Clinton's election seemed rather prescient: "there really is no good reason why the '90s can't be [women's] decade" (460). Fast forward to that 1998 feminist nightmare: the first president feminists help to elect engages in an affair with an intern 30 years his junior, lies about it, and (the catch for the women's movement) remains in control of the political agenda with which feminists entrusted him two years earlier.

Stunningly, rather than calling Mr. Clinton on his offensive behavior, the author of *Backlash* issued a convoluted attack on the women with whom he was involved; even more troubling, she argued that the scandal somehow revealed the failures of feminist politics. Faludi's "All the President's Flings: Let's Separate the Women from the Girls," appeared in a number of places, including The *New York Observer* and *L.A. Weekly*, the week of February 20, 1998, just weeks after the scandal broke. In this piece, Faludi did not call for better protections for women vulnerable to powerful men like Clinton; rather, she denounced some women — "the girls"— as beyond the interest of what she calls "authentic feminism." Moreover, echoing the prevailing anti-feminist impulse to lay responsibility for the affairs springing from the Clinton White House at the feet of the women involved and to categorize those women according to class, Faludi privileged the experiences of women of wealth and influence over those of less attractive, less sympathetic character. When Paula Jones sought to clear her name, she was attending to a name no one had heard before, Faludi reminded us. Jones "sidled up" to the podium, according to Faludi, accompanied by her handler Susan Carpenter-McMillan like a "Victorian lady-avenger" ready to take on all "sexually voracious" comers. The elitist sarcasm here is unmistakable. Jones "sidled up" to a podium — such language implies that she was undeserving of such exalted attentions as the common press conference. Further, Faludi attacks Jones' lack of celebrity as though that alone argued against her credibility. While hyperbole does characterize much of Carpenter-McMillan's rhetoric, she was not wrong to suggest a link between Jones' media fate and "men of power."

"The real divide," in the White House sex scandals, Faludi continues, was not between the genders but rather between "girls and grown-ups." Ignoring how American culture enables precisely the brand of sexist behavior practiced privately by Bill Clinton and how such behavior harms individual women, Faludi argued that "girls" define themselves through their injuries, or "[gain] power by talking about what was done to" them. Isn't an enormous measure of feminism's work done in the hope of exposing "what was [and *is*] done to" women? Surely, women do not defend themselves against abuses like domestic violence, rape, employment discrimination and sexual harassment by *not* "talking about what was done to" them. Abuses against women largely motivate the women's movement; therefore, exposing (and talking about) these abuses constitutes a crucial aspect of its work.

I would argue that the real divide in these public cases is and was between women and patriarchal power structures; indeed, the rhetoric surrounding these cases underscored systemic gender inequity and the role class divisions play in creating inequality in American culture. On the contrary, Faludi insisted, the women talking about Bill Clinton were simply tattletales. Speaking up, she argued, granted unearned power to "girl[s] whose only recourse is [to] tattle." Again Faludi missed the point: women's limited access to power, particularly in the face of men like Clinton. "[A]uthentic feminism" ought to have taken an interest in the women associated with and criticizing Bill Clinton for this very reason. If women have always enjoyed limited recourse to power (and they have), then women who depend for their livelihood upon a governor or president of the United States enjoy even less. These so-called tattles, then, have no power of their own; it's entirely borrowed from the larger authorities around them. Troublingly, Faludi's rhetoric in this piece echoed the ad hominem attacks characteristic of Camille Paglia's rhetoric that I discussed earlier. Paglia defends the masculinist status quo by reducing feminist women to shorthand (often, flatly inaccurate) versions of their ideas. She then dismisses the ideas and with them their apologists. Effectively de-personalizing feminist politics, an oppressed class now exists as a mere idea, rather than actual bodies suffering under material conditions. Once a human concern has been disguised as an idea, a term of art, or a miscalculation, that concern (and the actual women it describes) becomes much easier to denigrate, dismiss, or simply to ignore.

The concern also becomes easier to lionize, as Faludi did Hillary Clinton, whom she argued represented "grown-up" feminist behavior. Such behavior weighs the public good, takes personal offenses in stride, and keeps things in proportion — all of which is code for, of course, keeping quiet. Faludi exposes her keen prejudice against Jones and company at this point in the piece when she dismisses Jones' public statements as a mere "temper tantrum." Hillary Clinton's defense of her husband constituted, for Faludi, an example of "authentic feminism" precisely because she did not seek the spotlight, and resisted the infantilizing behavior exhibited by "girls." Instead, she would contend, in her *Today Show* appearance "Mrs. Clinton" "tr[ied] to inject some perspective from a woman who knows what's at stake." Again and again Faludi returns to the seriousness of the "political context" and "what's at stake," congratulating Clinton for putting feminist politics above personal pain. I would argue Clinton did something quite different. The rhetoric of the title "Mrs." reminds us precisely whose political survival drives the argument. As a marker of possession which speaks to man's privilege and power over women, "Mrs." subsumes Hillary's identity entirely within Bill's. The feminist "Ms." was created to deny man's possession of women and allow women to assert identities separate from the marriage contract. Faludi allows Gennifer Flowers this feminist marker, referring to her as "Ms. Flowers" in the piece. In fact, Faludi attaches "Ms." to the name of every woman in the piece *except* Hillary Clinton. Bill's wife is stuck with "Mrs." throughout.

In fact, in terms of feminist politics, Hillary Clinton's defense of Bill Clinton was emphatically regressive. I would argue that on *Today*, Hillary Clinton played the betrayed wife who nonetheless stands by her man, staging that quintessential act of female masochism: self-sacrifice for the greater good. Feminism has always sought to liberate women from this role in both marriage and politics. Feminism isn't about women endorsing their husbands' abuse of power against other women. One of the few women to publicly come to Lewinsky's defense, Andrea Dworkin, found Hillary's defense of Bill deeply disappointing because feminist politics demand, she reminded readers, that we refuse to "protect a man's exploitation of women" no matter who that man is (in Horn). Feminism is not about women shielding abusive men from criticism; nor is it about consolidating power for those women who already have it at the expense of women who don't. (Remember: not only were the final chapters of Bill's administration "at stake" during the Lewinsky-Clinton scandal, but also the future of Hillary's political career.)

[T]he women's movement has been neatly pincered.
Katha Pollitt, *The Nation*

At stake for my argument is the opportunity to dismantle the misogynist binary classification of good wife/bad mistress, which effectively shields the man's role in any adulterous affair and pits the two women against one another, reducing one to an impossible standard of goodness, the other to an extravagant fantasy of transgressive sexuality. These reductive categories of female identity obviate any opportunity to discuss issues that might empower women and move to end harassment, like powerful men exploiting their positions to harass and seduce female subordinates, for example. I do not suggest that the women Faludi criticized were not fully responsible for their behavior, or that generally men bear more guilt in romantic or illicit affairs than women. I do suggest, however, that Faludi deployed sexist categories skewed against women in her discussion of Ms. Lewinsky and her defense of Mr. Clinton. Under what rhetorical circumstances would the feminist who famously disassembled the lies used to undermine feminism in the 80s have made the regressive argument above? Faludi answers this question herself:

> As the backlash has gathered force, it has cut off the few from the many — and the few women who have advanced seek to prove, *as a social survival tactic*, that they aren't so interested in advancement after all [Faludi, *Backlash*, xx; my emphasis].

Like conservative women in the Reagan era, feminists in the age of Clinton found their position under attack and sought to secure their own political advancements — too often through the divide-and-conquer strategy Faludi mentions above. An examination of anti-feminist rhetoric from the 1990s demonstrates the power and sway of backlash politics. Therefore, post-backlash anti-feminism should not (indeed, cannot) be explained away as the product of conservative misogyny; in the case of feminists themselves, rather, it's an insidious, defensive response to a media culture generally hostile to women and specifically hostile to feminism. This period in feminism, then, brings one surprising feminist's compromise after another.

My next example comes from Gloria Steinem, who argued in a *New York Times* OpEd piece dated March 22, 1998, that women resist pressure from the right to turn their backs on Clinton. Feminist support of Bill Clinton makes sense, according to Steinem, if we remember "the commonsense guideline to sexual behavior" invented by the women's movement years ago: "no means no; yes means yes." Of the Kathleen Willey story, for example, she suggested that even if her claims were true "the President is not guilty of sexual harassment." Willey's allegations described a foolish pass, nothing more, she says. What's more, the behavior wasn't repeated; after her rebuff, the president didn't try again. No harm, no foul. Since "Clinton took 'no' for an answer," Steinem explains, his behavior should raise no sexual harassment alarms or concern feminist supporters too terribly much. Steinem went on to draw a comparison with the Paula Jones case; in both instances "Mr. Clinton ... accepted rejection." Steinem proposes that as long as a man takes no for an answer, a woman's will has not been violated. The proposal is counterintuitive; it suggests that Clinton is somehow entitled to one freebie from any woman he encounters. If the targeted woman resists and he desists, then he has not violated her will or even transgressed generally accepted standards of decent behavior. Yet, even a single *uninvited* embrace violates the other's will; the nature of the embrace, its invasiveness, determines whether we call that embrace harassment or merely "clumsy." In both the Jones and Willey cases, Clinton is accused of offensive, sexually invasive behaviors. Willey claims he moved her hand to his genitals, and Jones says she was summoned to a hotel room and invited to perform oral sex on the then-governor as he stood with his pants around his ankles. Still, Steinem pressed the point; Jones' story should not distress women because when Jones refused his offer, Clinton told her that he didn't want to "make" her do "anything [she didn't] want to do." First, here Steinem confuses harassment with rape. Had Clinton *made* Jones do something she didn't want to do, that would have been rape. Second, by any reasonable measure, a superior exposing himself to a subordinate must be considered at the very least offensive, if not harassing, behavior.

Perhaps believing that the best offense is a good defense, Steinem made a point of distinguishing the Willey and Jones situations from the harassment suffered by Anita Hill. "[T]he offensive behavior" in the Anita Hill case went on for years, even as Hill issued constant "no's." Further mitigating Clinton's guilt was the fact that this other harassing behavior took place in the workplace, where it was nearly impossible to avoid. Again, the argument is untenable. Paula Jones was working at the time she was summoned by the governor, her superior; there is no reason to think she believed she had a choice under those circumstances. And Willey reached out to hug a man she trusted when he suddenly moved her hand to his zipper. In neither case could the women have avoided the assault. Physically and psychically invasive, such acts move well beyond mere caddish behavior.

Further, Steinem claimed that Monica Lewinsky's relationship with Clinton exemplifies "Yes means yes." A month into the investigation, Steinem demonstrated no skepticism regarding the story being told about the woman's role in the Lewinsky-Clinton affair. Lewinsky herself considered the affair consensual. While Steinem admits that the "power imbalance" between Clinton and a White House intern might amplify "the index of suspicion," she maintains that "Welcome sexual behavior is about as relevant to sexual harassment as borrowing a car is to stealing one." Now, to argue that an intern could seek out and initiate a relationship with the president ("something she sought") is wishful thinking at best, sheer ingenuousness at worst; surely, it is clear that the president need suffer no one he does not care to. (Remember how quickly Ms. Lewinsky was whisked away to the Pentagon?) Monica Lewinsky had access to Bill Clinton because Bill Clinton wanted access to Monica Lewinsky. Further, even if Clinton's attentions "were not unwelcome," why ignore the fundamental feminist notion that within patriarchy, women frequently collude in their own oppression, that oppressed populations can be trained — that is manipulated (or duped) — into self-destructive behaviors that leave them vulnerable to exploitative individuals who hold power over them? Why would Steinem encourage us to rearrange the feminist furniture in our heads? Clearly, Steinem was struggling to find ideological traction. In order to depict Clinton's troubling behavior as optimistically as possible in service to what she considers a greater political good, Steinem demonstrated the near impossibility of both defending a feminist faith in female autonomy and standing with Lewinsky. Given the prevailing anti-feminist media culture, doing the latter risked undermining the former by painting Ms. Lewinsky as yet another woman hurling herself into the arms of a powerful man and inadvertently validating yet another damaging stereotype of female sexual behavior.

Significantly, a male writer from *Time* magazine captures the fundamental feminist objections to Clinton's behavior, in "It's the Sex, Stupid." Andrew Ferguson asserts that in the age of White House sex scandals, the radical feminist deconstruction of sex "as purely a matter of power and exploitation ... seems not so radical." Certain power relations argue against intimate relations, he explains. This is why it's a very bad idea, for example, for college professors to date students. "Immaturity and infatuation make you vulnerable," he explains, "even if you yourself aren't aware of it." In a society defined by gendered hierarchies, women (and others who occupy minority positions) may collude in their own exploitation, but, as Ferguson recognizes, "decent people in positions of power do not exploit the vulnerable for kicks." Simple declarations of alarm and disapproval like this were missing from so much public feminist commentary on the scandal. Feminists twisted themselves, their ideology and their rhetoric into knots attempting to rescue Clinton's image and perhaps earn his further support for women. That the most common sense response to Clinton's behavior — "decent people in positions of power do not exploit the vulnerable for kicks" — seemed unavailable to (or to not occur to) feminists at the time testifies to the difficult position occupied by feminists in the post-backlash age. The tacit alternative strategy revolved around answering one question: How to remain allied to the first president with genuine feminist sympathies as the scandal unfolded?

Susan Brownmiller would argue that I am, in fact, posing the wrong question. Rather, as she argued in 1999, "You're not supposed to be grateful to the President. This is what *we* do; *we* keep the heat on for social change and for equality." She was writing in response to allegations of rape made by Juanita Broaddrick against Clinton and the tepid feminist response, but her point applies to the Lewinsky-Clinton scandal (which overlapped the Broaddrick scandal) as well. Feminists seemed at the time, she argued, "so grateful to Clinton that it [was] clouding their judgment." If feminism is committed to working for equality in the workplace and elsewhere for women, then sacrificing one woman in service to Bill Clinton's political reputation represented the greatest violation against that commitment.

This is a feminist's hell.
Kim McCarten, Merge.com

Public feminists at this time were tasked with salvaging and defending an already embattled political agenda while at the same time fending off misogyny aimed both at themselves and Ms. Lewinsky. This problematical position grows out of the double bind in which women in general but feminists in particular find themselves in mainstream discourse. Like all women, feminists must be level-headed, exceedingly reasonable creatures to avoid being dismissed as emotional in the male-dominated world of politics. Yet, the women's movement itself grows out of an impassioned interest in the rights of oppressed groups (single mothers, rape victims, women seeking abortions, the poor, etc.); it is a movement founded on, among other things, care; it's a politic driven in equal parts by the emotions of sympathy and compassion as well as an intellectual engagement with power structures, systemic injustice and political ideology. The link between the personal and the political manifested in a literal, material body (of Monica Lewinsky) as perhaps never before in the history of feminist politics; coming to ideological terms with this body became, for many women calling themselves feminists, a rhetorical impossibility.

Ordinarily, I would be the first to argue that private relationships between consenting adults, even when one or both of those adults holds public office, ought to remain private, and that such relationships are none of the public's business, but Bill Clinton's affair with Monica Lewinsky is a feminist issue of public import. Its political significance becomes increasingly obvious as time passes and the two key players move into the next phases of their very public lives. Relatively free of the scandal's taint, Bill Clinton launches a second career as a highly paid public speaker, author of a best-selling autobiography, and statesman. Under the weight of the notoriety still clinging to her, Monica Lewinsky, on the other hand, struggles to begin a normal life and remains a public punch line. Of course, Bill Clinton is a skillful politician, a gifted speaker and an ex-president; one would rightly expect his post-presidential life to develop the way that it has. Moreover, given her own gifts and weaknesses, we might expect Ms. Lewinsky to move unsteadily into her thirties. Perhaps my own interest in Ms. Lewinsky might have faded, had Clinton's success not been consistently (at least to some extent) at her expense, had she fallen off the misogynist media radar screen, or had she simply been allowed to fade into private life. But none of these things has happened; mainstream media continue to pound away at her image, her character, her appearance. For example, recently a biography of John F. Kennedy revealed that he had an affair with a 19-year-old intern, and headlines teased that JFK had "a Lewinsky." Monica's last name has been transformed into salacious code; one is "a Lewinsky" when one's "only skill [is] to provide sexual release for" one's boss (Meek). The *Chicago Sun-Times* announces Lewinsky's doomed foray into reality TV by asking, "So who do you have to do to get a show on Fox?" Indulging in sexist frat-boy humor, the *Sun-Times* author Phil Rosenthal quips, "Talk about giving lip-service to propriety," and goes on to suggest that it's "tough to swallow" that Lewinsky is qualified to host such a show. One possible qualification, he suggests, is that "she's still that zippy go-getter with a thong in her heart and a cigar at the ready."

Because as Jennifer Wicke argues, "the celebrity zone is the public sphere where feminism is negotiated," because cultural texts produce political change and because material consequences for actual people result from such change, it is the responsibility of engaged feminists to examine our role in the public conversation we call the "Lewinsky-Clinton scandal." What was said, what becomes history, the official story, and the language deployed to that end teach us how and why our culture endorses and produces the myriad injustices, brands of suffering, and punishing and privileging identity categories it does. Consider the term "intern." Before any of us met Ms. Lewinsky, "intern" referred simply to ambitious young men and women fresh from college working in their chosen profession for a short time and no pay strictly for experience and connections. We knew that internships were generally competitive positions won through either influence or luck. In the wake of the scandal the term takes on emphatically gendered connotations with scandalous suggestions attached. "Intern" now connotes a young woman, oversexed and ripe for abusive office politics. She is an unsophisticated climber, occasionally dangerous to the careless superior, but more likely good only as eye candy and erotic distraction.

That this linguistic transformation took place within mainstream media conversations about Monica Lewinsky's affair with Bill Clinton demonstrates the media's power to influence how we think and speak — and the misogynist bent of that power. Terms like "commander-in-chief" remain unchanged, and no salacious connotations attach to "Office of the President" or "leader of the Free World."

As Miriam Horn notes in *U.S. News & World Report*, this scandal publicly revealed the complexities of practicing a feminist politic in the age of anti-feminism as well as in the wake of events taking place in the Clinton White House. She argues that certain issues raised by the scandal "cut to the heart of feminism." For example, "How power relates to sexual consent; what responsibility women have to one another; when the personal is (and is not) political." To my mind, feminism had already answered these questions, and a feminist response to the treatment of Monica Lewinsky by Bill Clinton, Kenneth Starr, and the press was pretty obvious. Given the grotesque discrepancy of power and age difference between the two, sexual consent had to be called into serious question; as Andrea Dworkin points out, Clinton's "fixation on nonreciprocal oral sex puts women in states of submission." Remember: this is nonreciprocal oral sex with a 21-year-old unpaid intern (in Horn). Further, once the relationship began playing out in public, it was undeniable that Lewinsky was in over her head and that Clinton was at the very least an exploitative user and at the very worst emotionally abusive.

Women have a responsibility to one another to expose this behavior for what it is; women calling ourselves feminists have a further responsibility to consider and announce the political and personal consequences of such behavior. Writing for *feminista!* Juliette Cutler Page reminds us of the value of feminism's historic focus on what happens to individual women: "The personal was truly political in that what each woman experienced independently was part of a larger picture. These women were not alone, although their abuse happened in isolation." The personal is highly political in this case, then, since Clinton's behavior and popular responses to it reflect a distressing and dangerous tolerance for the sexual exploitation of vulnerable women. Clinton invited a naïve young subordinate into a world he certainly knew to be beyond her control and capable of inflicting extreme suffering upon those who are inexperienced and undefended against its power. His crude exploitation of Lewinsky was underwritten by the very mechanisms of patriarchy which concern feminism most, like class, gender and power. Clinton possessed the class status and all that implies to protect himself from whatever scandal or fallout resulted from the affair; he entered the relationship fully cognizant of his cultural privilege and position, not just as a wealthy American man, but as president of the United States. He knew full well that the same protective apparatus shielding him would fail to protect Ms. Lewinsky. A Pentagon official quoted in *Time* magazine seemed to understand this very well; Ms. Lewinsky was "an attractive girl," he notes, "but a *girl*" (Cohen; my emphasis). Regarding gender, we should ask ourselves: can we imagine such things happening to a young unpaid male intern? A boy? The possibility simply wouldn't occur to us. And if we are honest with ourselves we'll see that it's nothing to do with the truth of Lewinsky's sexual appetites or women's attraction to power generally, but rather the sexist foundations of our culture.

Public enactments of cultural sexism require public objection, invite feminist disgust. Those feminists with direct access to mainstream discourse would have served women better by denouncing sexist language in the press than by standing behind Bill Clinton or marginalizing Monica Lewinsky. Moreover, I wished at the time for more nuanced considerations by public feminists of who Clinton's accusers were and how they came to be involved with him. When Katha Pollitt observes that Paula Jones seems pushed around by her mouthpiece Ms. McMillan and despite a new nose and a Mercedes rarely leaves the house, I see feminist politics at work. When Pollitt goes on to conjecture that perhaps Jones might be more than just Clinton's victim and McMillan's gravy train, but also an "abused wife," we see the connection between personal and political opening the possibility of meaningful action. That is, opening the possibility of conversations that might result in an individual woman receiving help. When James Carville characterizes Paula Jones as "what you get when you drag hundred dollar bills through a trailer park," we see the need for feminist objections to sexist, elitist stereotyping, as his glib characterization reinforces myriad brands of class and gender bigotry. The post–Reagan-Bush era was not the time when aggressive defenses of women or attacks on conservative notions of masculine entitlement were especially welcome in the media; of course, that time has yet to come. Therefore, I maintain that it is an emphatically feminist gesture to say that men of power like Bill Clinton ought to behave, ought to know better than to approach, seduce or otherwise romance openly vulnerable (and much younger) subordinates like Monica Lewinsky. And to further state that women calling ourselves feminists ought to act on such women's behalves when the full power of the media are brought to bear against them in specifically gendered and misogynist ways.

3
"A Gaggle of Dutiful Daughters": Feminism Does the Waves

> *By claiming the label feminist, we announce our interest in understanding and undermining gender inequality.*
> Estelle B. Freedman, No Turning Back
>
> *Rather than subordinate our differences in the service of the flabby populism* Manifesta *promotes, I would like to see contemporary feminism embrace contention, ... and strengthen its analysis.*
> Michelle Jensen, in The Nation

As we know, the Reagan era created media hostility to feminist goals and welcomed all manner of conservative critiques of the women's movement. The market niche opening at the time for conservative commentary generally served anti-feminism and contributed to concerted attacks on feminist politics.* Women writers willing to criticize feminism were especially welcome and as an indicator of their disaffection began calling themselves post-feminist.† This term seeks to mark the end of feminism, or the feminist era, and suggests that American culture now proceeds without need of this particular political movement. As the term tends to be used, it suggests not so much that feminism has succeeded (and therefore come to its natural end), as that it has either fallen into irrelevance or become a destructive influence upon American culture. During this period,

---

Which is not to say that the media welcomed all women's voices with open arms; those who were courted and allowed a voice did not add to women's media presence significantly.

†*See Linda Chavez, Cathy Young, Rene Denfeld, Camille Paglia, Phyllis Schlafly, Katie Roiphe, Christina Hoff Sommers, Maureen Dowd and anyone representing the Independent Women's Forum.*

feminists tend to be defined in the mainstream media as a bit precious, oversensitive to the merest slight, mirthless, and unsexed. Further, conservative mouthpieces take the opportunity their dominance in the mainstream media affords them to write various histories of the movement, all of which cast feminists as out of touch with cultural trends, behind the times historically (feminism was a success, we can all sit down), or inclined to petty turf wars. Two claims underwrite these histories: Second Wave feminism continues to define all women as victims; and in order to retain relevance, the next phase of feminism must declare women to be uniformly empowered. Often, these assertions appear as categorical and uninterrogated as I have presented them here. Objecting to this portrayal of contemporary feminism, Rebecca Walker declares in *Ms. Magazine* in 1992, "I am not a postfeminist feminist. I am the Third Wave." The term stuck. The media love of shorthand, highly recognizable and therefore repeatable, phrases propelled the phrase "Third Wave" almost instantly into the media nomenclature.

Like the conservative anti-feminist media stars I discuss earlier, Third Wavers argue that the work of the Second Wave is generally done and turn their attention toward women's sexuality as the natural next ideological frontier, championing female sexual autonomy as an untapped source of personal and political muscle. Unfortunately, the defining assumption — that women's bodies are ideologically entirely their own — is false and based in the experiences only a very few women can claim. Here the class privilege upon which this wave relies presents itself. As I have argued elsewhere, only the most privileged women, those with wealth, access, free time, and safety, enjoy the kind of autonomy implied by this turn toward the body. This turn differs from the provocative display of "Girlie" feminism or the locker room talk of Do-Me feminism in that Third Wave feminism tends to celebrate all things personal, including but not exclusively sexuality, to define itself as a kind of confessional politic, and to ground itself in the lived experiences of young women. The documented lived experiences of members of the Third Wave, however, tend not to include the kinds of hardships with which feminism traditionally concerns itself. The work of feminism is not done — women and children still make up the majority of the poor and underinsured, for example, are more likely to be abused and homeless than men — yet, the spokeswomen for this wave insist that feminism must turn its attention not toward issues of social justice but toward the personal concerns and disappointments of women like them.

A movement serving the needs of such individuals, who occupy the most privileged positions in our culture, cannot serve the needs of women being beaten, starving, raising kids in poverty, or just struggling to make ends meet. When the Third Wave emerged in the early 1990s, as Michelle Sidler observes, "real wages dropped for people at all levels of income except those in the top 20 percent" and women were losing as much as $.21 per dollar in some industries ("McJobdom," 31). Under these social stresses a group of self-described "young" feminists announce their intent to battle generational prejudices against youth present within the upper echelons of the movement and create their own brand of feminism. Yet, in terms of class, connections and cultural status, these women cannot represent the majority of women or their experiences, for this movement relies not only upon membership within the upper reaches of the feminist machine, but also within the upper strata of American culture.

> *Roiphe's and Denfeld's impassioned critiques are often uninformed and somewhat appalling....*
> Deborah L. Siegel

As the next big thing in media-generated feminism, the Third Wave bridged the worlds of public and scholarly feminist debate. It produced, for example, a number of single-author books which directly attack contemporary feminist work and numerous collections of personal essays by varied authors. The collections tend to contain more confessional pieces. In both, women claim academic status while singling out academic feminism as responsible for sending feminism off-track. We found this same tendency in works by anti-feminists who at the time were laying the groundwork for the kinds of mainstream critiques we see in Third Wave and other post-backlash iterations of the women's movement. Katie Roiphe, Naomi Wolf, Rene Denfeld and Camille Paglia appear regularly as titular correctives to liberal feminism and largely define the mainstream voice of this moment in post-backlash history.* Indeed, one might say that these personalities and their political identities provided the Right political voices at the right time. As opposed to transparent and considered political critique, anti-feminism served and still serves as a product

---

*As I am using this term throughout the work, post-backlash refers to the period after Reagan-Bush during which backlash politics were in full swing. Further, the term acknowledges Faludi's important work and is not intended to suggest that the backlash against feminism has ended, but rather refers to the period after which the backlash was identified and established a presence in feminist nomenclature.

line or a brand name — one that enjoys considerable demand, if not by consumers themselves, then certainly by editors. This brand-name approach to politics reveals itself in catchy labels, like "Do-Me" or "Sex-positive" feminism, "Girlie" or "Third Wave," labels sure to grab headlines and provoke controversy; this moment in media history transforms the impulse to lay claim to one's political identities and affiliations into a marketing strategy. Political affiliation now places folks within a publishing niche. While folks calling themselves Third Wave claim a political identity grounded in their placement in feminist history, this wave also claims ideological tenets all its own. While both Roiphe and Paglia often position themselves as apologists for Third Wave politics, Third Wavers tend to define themselves as young women; that is, in terms of their generation. In broad strokes, over the last 25 years publishing about women has reflected a return to conservative notions about gender and class in America; we have moved from works addressing the dangers and stresses of women's lives and urging feminist intervention, like Kate Millett's *Sexual Politics*, or Susan Brownmiller's *Against Our Will*, to works celebrating American women as the safest, most free and most equal women on the planet, and urging an acceptance of the status quo. Think here of not only *The Morning After*, but also *The New Victorians, Fire with Fire, to be real, Manifesta, Listen Up,* and *Catching a Wave*.

Like most iterations of post-backlash feminism, the Third Wave isolates academic theory as the signal indicator of feminism's fall into irrelevance and its general misapprehension of the real world. While folks like Paglia and Hoff Sommers deploy theoretical language consistently in their popular critiques to imply the uselessness of such language and single out theoretical abstraction as the root of feminism's problems, a less rancorous relationship to academe characterizes much of the Third Wave. However, writers like Paglia must be included in any discussion of Third Wave feminism, for ideological if not chronological reasons. Third Wavers tend to call themselves and present as "young" women, and certainly Paglia and Hoff Sommers do not. Still, all share a commitment to rejecting an "older" feminism in service to defining a newer one. The works listed above make this same rhetorical move at some point in their arguments, and all appeared within five years of one another (1993–1998). The authors share skepticism toward academic feminism and see supposed ivory tower elitism as leading feminism astray (that mythical academic indifference to real life, which assumes academics don't read the paper, watch reality TV, pay electric bills or wash their own socks).

For example, in her Third Wave anthology, *to be real*, Rebecca Walker outlined the book she chose not to write, the book that included an "incisive critique of patriarchy" (xxxix). "I prefer," she explained, "personal testimonies" to cultural critique; in fact, her "requirement" for contributors "was that the pieces be personal, honest, and record a transformative journey taken" (xxxvii). "Many pieces didn't make it" into the book due to a failure to disclose; the "writers were afraid to expose themselves," she explains (xxxvii). Academic feminism simply cannot appreciate ordinary women, Third Wavers argue, and has nothing to offer them, common sense least of all. Katie Roiphe famously compares an undergraduate literature seminar to the "Mad Hatter's Tea Party" in *The Morning After* and relates the following anecdote in support of this characterization. Roiphe's critique is paradigmatic of how the modified, prefix feminisms of the time characterized academic (that is, theoretically inflected) feminism. In a discussion of Edith Wharton's *The Age of Innocence* a fellow classmate disagrees with her reading of a female character from the novel. The student challenges her claim — that one ought to resist "looking at literature for well-rounded characters" — with a claim of his own: "within the hegemonic male discourse, it is impossible for the female voice to be empowered" (114). The challenge apparently silences Roiphe, and she describes seeing herself for the rest of class as "Alice listening to the Mad Hatter tell riddles without answers"; indeed, her "head is spinning" (114).

The post-backlash critique of academic language does not lead as we might expect to a considered interrogation of that language, or a study of its history and sources, its usefulness or limitations. No. The next step in the post-backlash era is away from feminist concerns altogether and toward individualistic and emphatically conventional (pre-feminist, if you will) conceptions of female behavior. For example, Roiphe's negative encounter with liberal education led her to the following insights about sexual harassment. Responding to an article in *Ms. Magazine* saying that "experiencing sexual harassment transforms women into victims and changes their lives," Roiphe worries that a college student who had been harassed herself might read this and misidentify the "lecherous professor"— the harasser —"as the agent of [her] transformation" into victimhood (111). The student's victimization should not be attributed to the man's harassing behavior, she would insist, but rather to the very notion of harassment itself. Roiphe explains that the author of the *Ms. Magazine* piece, Mary Koss,

> does not see that it is her entire conceptual framework — her kind of rhetoric, her kind of interpretation — that transforms perfectly stable women

into hysterical, sobbing victims. If there is any transforming to be done, it is to transform everyday experience back into everyday experience [112].

In this case at least, Roiphe appears quite at home with academic language; she writes of "agent[s] of transformation," critiques a "conceptual framework," sees the meaning of individual experience as contingent, that is, permanently open to and dependent upon interpretation. She further argues that the language in which an experience is rendered, the "kind of rhetoric" used to describe it, is constitutive of that experience. Roiphe has studied well and uses her liberal training to produce a post-structuralist "reading" of Koss' argument. Nevertheless, she marshals her own utterly academic, theoretical analysis in an effort to pillory others who do the same — and in service to disturbingly regressive ideas. Women should expect to endure harassment as an "everyday experience," she argues; and if they do not, if they are troubled by sexual harassment, then they are "hysterical" and, further, rendered that way by the other women who recognize their misery, women like Mary Koss. Roiphe's own rhetorical skill couches a conservative, ugly idea as progressive, even interesting: harassed women are responsible for their own suffering, harassment is treatment we ought to shut up and take.

Camille Paglia makes a similar rhetorical gesture in *Sex, Art and American Culture* (1992) when she complains that feminists misunderstand rape in their failure to "see what is for men the eroticism or fun element in rape, especially [she continues, almost unbelievably], the wild, infectious delirium of gang rape" (51). Roiphe and Paglia's claims foreground feminism as responsible for harassment, rape, and most of all women's sense of their own suffering; the argument continues, paradoxically, that feminism has failed to protect women from the very things they argue we ought not fear.* For example, in a chapter from *Sex, Art and American Culture*, called "Rape and Modern Sex War," Paglia explains how "on our campuses far from home, young women are vulnerable and defenseless. Feminism has not prepared them for this" (50). In order for Paglia and colleagues to have a rhetorical product to sell, women must continue to be seen by the market they serve as essentially helpless, unchanged over time and badly served by feminism. So, characterizing women on campuses as young, vulnerable and defenseless allows Paglia to forward a notion of women's position in society as fairly hopeless, and women therefore must be in need of

---

*There will be more on takes on rape culture by post-, anti-, and Do-Me feminists in a later chapter.

not only male intervention, but also the insights she offers in recognizing and celebrating this intervention. Her rhetoric, then, reveals the lie of her claim to practicing a feminist politic. Indeed, Paglia's accusations against feminism are most alarming, for she seems to be arguing that nothing, really, can protect women against rape, least of all the first social movement to take violence against women seriously. The solution offered in this piece is by now very familiar: a return to the good old days, where we sought comfort and shelter in the arms of strong men, when the "old double standard protected women" (51). As a plank in the Third Wave generational platform, Paglia's argument is a perfect fit, for she proposes that moving forward was feminism's mistake — not only has feminism failed to protect women, but the movement has itself created many of the situations that endanger them.

Her aggression toward feminism cannot be overstated: Paglia insists that if feminists fail to embrace the patriarchal "truths" (like harassment and rape) fixed within American culture, then they will never speak to real women's lives. If feminists can't speak the plain language accessible to us all, if they can't avoid academic convolutions, how can they expect to enjoy cultural relevance? Timing contributes to the momentum of the argument, for around the time Paglia's *Sex, Art and American Culture* appears, women began refusing the moniker "feminism" and the chestnut, "I'm not a feminist, but..." was born.

Significantly, at this time conversations about feminism's evolution and development continue to take place inside the academic community as well. The 1990s brought visible reconsiderations of feminist scholarship in the university by scholars in other theoretical branches of the liberal arts for being "white-centered" and unresponsive to issues of race, class and alternative sexualities. Writers like Chela Sandoval, Judith Butler, Angela Davis and bell hooks have offered stark critique and genuine remedies to such omissions and in so doing have expanded the reach and relevance of feminist literary studies and cultural theory. Too often "woman" in feminist discourse did not mean women who were poor or black, transgendered or living outside the United States, for example. While academic women were self-policing, doing the hard work of challenging the intellectual institutions around them (which many had helped to build), the American media was making a home for women willing to wage anti-feminist arguments. As I've argued, many of these critiques take the university as the source of all the trouble, and as a result, the link between academic feminism and mainstream anti-feminism is nowhere as powerful as in Third Wave feminisms. For example, like Hoff Sommers, feminist graduate student Jo Trigilio worried about the reach and relevance of academic feminist ideology: "Feminist theory is becoming the product of the privileged few who hold academic positions," she writes in a scholarly journal article in 1997, "a product to which non-academics do not have access" (11). While many works of the Third Wave are written by young academic women like Trigilio, most engage a decidedly popular audience. Academics are not the representatives of feminism who make it to the mainstream, however; when one reads the *Wall Street Journal* or the *New York Times* OpEd pages, for example, one finds Katie Roiphe, not bell hooks, Maureen Dowd, not Judith Butler. In these venues academic third wave concerns with diversity become media fodder, serving as evidence of academic feminism's descent into abstraction and the arcane.*

For instance, Christina Hoff Sommers insists that to fail to recognize that "by any reasonable measure, equity feminism has turned out to be a great American success story" is just silly (22).† Consider her gloss on "radical, Second Wave doctrine": "women, *even modern American women*, are in thrall to 'a system of male dominance' variously referred to as 'heteropatriarchy' or the sex/gender system" (22; my emphasis). To begin, such notions are far from radical; calling attention to obvious cultural norms is no more "radical" than misrepresenting them. To balance her contention that "women can join with men on equal terms to contribute to a universal human culture," one might call Hoff Sommers' attention to the few basic statistical truths to which I refer earlier: 15 percent of Congress is female; while white women make around 73 cents for every dollar a man makes, African American women make 65 cents for every dollar earned by a white man; Hispanic women make only 53 cents; the U.S. remains the only industrialized nation not to ratify CEDAW (Convention on the Elimination of All Forms of Discrimination against Women); half of families living under the poverty line are headed by single mothers; every six minutes a forcible rape occurs. And on average three American women are killed per week by their intimate male partners. Hoff Sommers' appositive, "even modern American women," provides the tell here. The phrases Hoff Sommers highlights with quotation marks call the very assumptions

---

**As I have been arguing, the race and class prejudices at the heart of conservative attacks on the women's movement are obvious here.*

†*Christina Hoff Sommers defines "equity feminism": "A First Wave, 'mainstream,' or 'equity' feminist wants for women what she wants for everyone: fair treatment, without discrimination"* (22).

into question — our culture is ruled by men and privileges heterosexual identity — and isolates them as vaguely ridiculous. (Think here of a speaker making the bunny ears gesture for quotations marks when carefully enunciating "heteropatriarchy" and "a system of male dominance.")* While the quotation marks single out the language she finds troubling ("heteropatriarchy"), the parenthetical reveals the foundational politics of the statement: modern American women enjoy a free and equitable state of existence, to say otherwise is unreasonable and, well, academic. To actually face these realities is even less wise.

> *...it has become increasingly apparent that students are feeling a disconnect between feminist theory and feminist activism.*
> Statement from the Alberta Women's Studies Association

Third Wave rhetoric, then, moves along this post-backlash rhetorical continuum, attacking academic vocabulary and embracing that movement's assumptions about feminist history. Still, popular Third Wave feminism addresses many issues also addressed in academic feminist theory, and they do share some issues of concern. Indeed, there is often an identifiable, meaningful transfer of ideas across the popular-academic divide as academics study the media and popular culture, and popular commentators dabble in academic discourse; however, I will in the main insist on the distinction between popular (Third Wave) and scholarly (third wave) feminism. Within the mainstream, representations of academic feminism tend to be limited to celebrity academics making careers out of arguing against feminism, like Hoff Sommers, Roiphe, Wolf and Paglia; therefore, despite academic appointments and degrees, these writers are emphatically part of the Third Wave.

Academic considerations of feminist generations, or waves, tend to concern the more flexible and self-contradictory category of "young feminists" working to find "their place and [create] their space in the political landscape" as Amber Kinser explains. For example, in an article appearing in the *Journal of the National Women's Studies Association*, Kinser

---

Certainly academic language can sound strange, off-putting, even supercilious. Spend any time in a university English Department and one will find a few folks encrusted in jargon, more enamored of the sound of their vocabulary than interested in the ideas it may convey. English and Women's Studies are not unique in this, however. Every discipline, from Accounting to English Studies, Art History to International Relations, uses language specific to that area of study and quite foreign to the general public; we call this language "jargon" when we seek to denigrate the scholars in the field, "terminology" when we don't.

considers the value of the term "third wave" and concludes that embracing the name helps feminists of her generation to differentiate themselves both historically and ideologically from what came before. She identifies the "conceptual leverage" of the term, or, the ease and power with which the term conveys what young feminists mean about themselves; the value of naming for Kinser, then, resides in the way the right terminology can "articulate a feminism that responds to the political, economic, and cultural circumstances that are unique to the current era" (Kinser 1). As an academic feminist, Kinser turns a critical eye to the language of her movement and conveys the value of not only its convictions, but also the manner in which it articulates them.

Further, in an article entitled "Surfing the Third Wave: A Dialogue Between Two Third Wave Feminists," two graduate students, identifying themselves as third wave feminist philosophers, enact a sustained scholarly critique and interrogation of the very ideology they put into practice. These students, Rita Alfonso and Jo Trigilio, discuss third wave feminism via email and publish the exchange in a special issue of the feminist academic journal *Hypatia* in 1997. Both position themselves generationally, as women who grew up with the internet, who routinely exchange ideas with other feminists via email, and who encounter feminism primarily as academics. They also hold that their political identities reflect the "changed political conditions" of their era (11). For example, Alfonso claims membership within "the first generation to have the good fortune to learn, in an academic setting, from the lived experience of women, and to have female role models in nearly all the traditionally male-dominated fields" (11). Indeed, within academe, scholars and students study the lived experiences of other women, and cultural studies and theory have opened academic discourse to considerations of the material conditions and cultural realities faced by women inside and outside of the university. Here Alfonso makes an important and helpful observation for understanding the evolution of mainstream Third Wave feminism, then; that the ideas of feminist academic discourse have migrated into the mainstream via email and the internet, mainstream media, and been largely misunderstood there. These ideas are often mocked as irrelevant to the real lives of women, just as academics are often mocked as speaking an idiosyncratic, jargonistic language incomprehensible to ordinary folks.

When feminism entered the academy in the 1970s it did so as a previously undertheorized political movement, one concerned with the political issues facing women, not the study of the aesthetic conditions of patriarchal dominance or theoretical interrogations of the very terms of our culture, like "power," "feminine," "empowerment" and "patriarchy." The coupling of academic intellectual work, which is often highly theoretical, abstract and generally safe, with real world activism, which is often heartbreaking, concrete and sometimes dangerous, has been an uncomfortable one from the start. In the best cases, these fields mutually reinforce and strengthen one another; in the worst, each seems at odds with the other. Unlike academic feminism, I would argue, Third Wave feminism takes up the points of departure more often than the moments of support and mutuality between these constituencies. In general, these points of disconnect are defined as generational.

The women who constituted the post-backlash establishment in the mid–1990s were indisputably the benefactors of women who came before them; they are the daughters of privilege. For example, Katie Roiphe appears in the *New York Times* magazine and OpEd pages while still a graduate student, benefiting from her mother's twenty-year relationship with that publication, and the co-authors of *Manifesta* (perhaps the best known work in the Third Wave canon) remind the reader of their status repeatedly. For example, in her "Introduction to Jennifer" Baumgardner drops names and establishes her cultural credentials in the guise of righteous political anger. She fumes that she was paid only $1.50 a word for a "Condé Nast Magazine" while a male friend was paid $2.00; walks out on her "job as an editor at *Ms. Magazine*" at twenty-six; relates an anecdote about a disappointing experience she had interviewing the pop-star Bjork for *Bust*. Finally embracing their privilege, she explains, she and Amy decided "Why suffer?" Opting not to lock themselves "in a tiny apartment for a year" chain smoking cheap cigarettes, they instead "went to Cuba, organized intergenerational readings, attended sample sales, and wrote a fucking book" (xx). All, she explains, in service to "keeping joyful" while doing the hard work of "figuring out what's wrong with the patriarchy and the movement" (xx). Perhaps it is understandable that vibrant, brilliant, committed women whose careers depend (at least in the beginning) on the work their mothers and mentors have done take the confrontational and sometimes dismissive tone of so much of the Third Wave rhetoric. Don't we all seek to carve out our own space separate from our parents? Outgrow our mentors? Create identities and accomplishments outside their shadows? Such understandable impulses explain much of Third Wavers' insistence on separating from their feminist "mothers"; it is less understandable that they would parade their relative privilege vis-à-vis the other women of their own generation. Nonetheless, the rhetoric betrays no small investment and pride in their political lineage. Jennifer Baumgardner writes, for instance, that she loved her job at *Ms.* "more than anywhere since the womb" (*Manifesta*, xvii).

Richards and Baumgardner argue in *Manifesta* that the major battles of the women's movement have passed, and that the movement's objectives have become more subtle, more subjective; having secured concrete privileges like the vote and choice, we now face more abstract challenges, like gaining the prerogative to be "girlie"—even, it seems, the prerogative to describe our choices, no matter what they are, as empowering. The Third Wave argues for a feminism tailored to individual desires, whether those desires involve social justice, sexual autonomy or "taking back the color pink" (Gilbert-Levin). Problematically, the mainstream enactments of Third Wave feminism smacks of the very behaviors, beliefs, identity politics these young activists complain they have been accused of exhibiting. Demands for personal disclosure imposed by Walker as editor of *to be real* and found elsewhere in Third Wave literature, harkens back to the days of consciousness-raising, perhaps, but finally fails to produce a meaningful "to do" list, an agenda for the empowerment of women, or even a plan to address perceived Second Wave failures. Walker insists instead, for example, on a confessional politic, one too easily dismissed as a bit careless in its analysis, a bit self-important in tone: "I hope the journeys in this collection," she writes in the Introduction of *to be real*, "encourage you to reach into the spaces of yourself where you are most afraid to go, to create a feminist space in which you can be real" (xl). Myriad ideological problems present themselves, not least of which are notions of how we define "real." To be "real" in this work seems to be to serve oneself, one's personal journey; to be real within a movement for social justice, however, demands a larger vision, one directed toward the experiences and needs of other women. Walker herself noted in *Ms. Magazine* that feminist conviction "must translate into tangible action."

When Baumgardner describes writing a "fucking book" we witness a similar appeal to the personal, as well as a faith in one's own experience of feminism sufficing to represent one's generation. The tone further belies a confident, almost glib, security in one's publishing and political cache. Slick language and rhetorical arrogance explains many of the negative associations clinging to the popular Third Wave—whose most well-known proponents come off as a bit self-important, prone to superficial analysis, and disappointingly oblivious to their own privileged positions. The generation of women to whom Baumgardner and Richards' work reacts (that is, the upper echelon of the Second Wave) have done similarly difficult things, like writing books, traveling, experiencing the world and thinking hard about women's issues. Still, Amy uses the following anecdote to explain a faith in her own ability to produce a book:

> The idea of writing a book wasn't so daunting, since I had quite literally lived through Gloria Steinem's writing of *Moving Beyond Words*. I knew the process — the sleep deprivation, the blurry vision, the familiar delivery person who brings a can of Coke or a pint of ice cream at odd hours, and the endless yellow stickies [xxviii].

The notion that having watched someone write a book prepares one to write a book exemplifies the red thread of generational ease and prerogative running through this movement; these women have lived through much of the Second Wave as privileged witnesses and call attention to that privilege as a kind of entitlement program. Naturally, they seem to suggest, the next "wave" belongs to them. Amy, for example, parades the privilege not only of spending endless hours with one of the most important political writers of our time, but also of sharing the mundane intimacies of a close working relationship, such as groceries delivered "at odd hours." The delivery (like references to sample sales in Cuba) betrays the urban setting and the wealth required to live in such a place; the understatement betrays the humdrum portrayal of such privilege in the life of the writer. It's disturbing to imagine a movement for social justice distributing political and activist credentials based entirely upon class status. Women like Chela Sandoval, Alice Walker, and Gloria Steinem have repeatedly argued against just such a hierarchical construction.

In the shelter of her own status, Jennifer relates the following exchanges with her mentors as evidence of the generational divide plaguing the feminist community and its mistreatment of young feminists like her. Regarding the publication of *Manifesta*, co-written with Amy, Jennifer endures the following indignity:

> A mentor of mine, who has yet to write any book, congratulated me ... this way: "Here's to your next book, which you'll be ready to write alone" [xx].

Later, when faced with "[a]nother Second Waver" whose advice was a bit unkind —"Important books aren't co-written, you know"— she congratulates herself for being "too polite to mention the eight unread books she wrote after the one groundbreaker" (xxi, my emphasis). These are young women, twenty-somethings, whose book deals allow them the freedom to vent in this way, exhibiting not only a lack of appreciation for their good fortune, and the older women whose friendships have assisted them, but also a desire to denigrate these older women in print. Surely, having written just "one groundbreaker" is more than any of us might hope for. As Steinem writes in another Third Wave collection of the same period *to be real*, many women in this Wave too often make older feminists feel like "sitting dogs being told to sit."

> *My feminism wasn't shaped by the antiwar movement or civil rights activism. I was not a victim of the problem that had no name.*
> Barbara Findlen, *Listen Up*

The Third Wave emerges and comes to popular attention during the second Clinton administration, so its development is inflected by the political events of that period. It follows, then, that many of the differences between Second and Third Wave might stem from the political difficulties of the period — a president practicing situational feminism and a pervasive post-backlash media misogyny. Third Wave feminists tend, as I have said, to wage a generational argument and to contend that their feminist mothers (Second Wavers) have stripped the fun out of women's lives and thus rendered feminism uninteresting to and out of touch with the younger generation of activists. It follows, then, that the Third Wave would work to recover what the Second Wave ostensibly rejected, like beauty, fashion, heterosexual coupling, and celebrations of female sexuality. When Third Wave feminists forge identities differentiating themselves from the generation before them, the younger women begin expressing frustration with not only the failure of the Second Wave to reflect their experiences but also the heavy shadow cast by earlier feminists. Popular Third Wave feminism, then, is obviously a claim to a culture and historical position as well as a response to shifting cultural realities. Unfortunately, those changes have moved mainstream conversations, indeed American politics, away from the goals of the feminist movement and the needs of American women. One of those changes has been a media ossification, increasing control of the flow of information in the main by fewer and more conservative forces, as well as full blown media anti-feminism.

According to a piece by Laura Flanders for Fairness and Accuracy in Reporting, a media watchdog group, the mid-nineties saw an infusion of conservative women into American mainstream media. The efforts of the ultra-conservative Independent Women's Forum (organized in 1992) "to get conservative women's view heard in the media" resulted in quick and resounding success. In 1992, for example, "television's most visible female pundits," speechwriter Mona Charen and Civil Rights Commissioner Linda Chavez, came from the Reagan administration. In 1995 only 21 percent of syndicated columnists were female and half of them gave advice; "19 women columnists" covered such topics as "nutrition, interior decorating, sex and family psychology, recipes, travel tips or entertainment reviews," leaving the policy issues to the men. At the time when Roiphe, Paglia, Denfeld, et al., are publishing their works, women writers were turning back toward the-angel-in-the-house ideal in the most widely available media venues, like magazines, newspapers, and Sunday talk and news shows. Indeed, in the first half of 1995, "93 percent of all the columns on the nation's most prestigious op-ed page" were written by men. But this is no surprise to academic feminism. Indeed, Kinser warns us that feminists must embrace change beyond the personal, must embrace collective change and in a hurry, she warns, since anything else can and will be "outrun" by "the patriarchal social order" (1). Leading this race were publishers like John Brewer, then-president of the *New York Times* Syndicate, who commented in 1995 that even with increased competition among a shrinking number of newspapers, "conservative columns by minorities or women" were still highly sought after. By the end of 1995, in fact, the *New York Times* had replaced the strongly political, feminist Anna Quindlen with the very anti-feminist Maureen Dowd, who, according to one media critic, "writes as if she were William Safire in drag." Unfortunately, things are no better a decade later. Terry M. Neal reports in the *Washington Post* that "women and minorities are still too often unrepresented in the punditry class." For example, in 2000 and 2001 women made up only 11 percent of all guests on Sunday news shows and only 7 percent of repeat guests on Sunday talk shows (Neal).

I argue in the previous chapter that in order to serve the larger principals of the women's movement, feminists must sometimes stand in defense of women whose actions we may not approve, whose characters we may not particularly admire, even in the face of widespread anti-feminism. I argue for a politics of liberality, care and intellectual engagement, one that includes the careful critique of cultural power and its pernicious gender bias. I further argue that this was especially necessary in the case of Monica Lewinsky, who engaged in behaviors many would find morally repugnant, distasteful, or just plain silly yet who suffered in ways disproportionate to her personal choices or failings. Just such an egalitarian and inclusive impulse seems to motivate the Third Wave feminist movement, characterized as it is by a willingness to embrace all things female as markers of feminist identity and signifiers of female empowerment; however, when we look closely at the Third Wave response to Lewinsky's relationship with Bill Clinton, we see that perhaps the opposite is true.

Indeed, as practiced or described by the major — that is, best known — practitioners of Third Wave feminism, such inclusiveness actually results in watered-down politics. For example, the Introduction to *Listen Up* argues:

> We [Third Wavers] know that what oppresses me may not oppress you, that what oppresses you may be something I participate in, and that what oppresses me may be something you participate in [3].

But if all behaviors are markers of empowerment, then no behaviors are. If we can accept that sometimes our own pleasure might contribute to other women's oppression, then for whom are we fighting? Merely ourselves? The right to practice a politics not of the personal but of the individual? When Heywood and Drake argue that such a feminism is a beast demanding "a different name altogether"; I couldn't agree more (3). Even more important than this obvious logical failing is the fact that such politics obviate the possibility of political action. For example, in the case of Monica Lewinsky, Third Wave feminists generally discussed her affair with Bill Clinton as ideologically unproblematic, identified Bill Clinton as seductive, not shifty, and defended Lewinsky as entirely in control of her own choices. The cranky Second Waver inside me wanted to rationalize this trend as symptomatic of the great pressure under which the Clinton sex scandals continually were placing feminism, to explain it away (the fantasy continues) as a resulting impulse to preserve whatever is left of Clinton's second. Clinton made us do it; women, including feminists, were coerced into political and moral relativity in their struggle to retain political hope. I wanted to attribute the above notions to the power misogyny wields within American culture, which can bend even strong feminist women away from their most deeply held principals. Of course, I was wrong. Alas, just as acknowledging oppression fell out of fashion, it became fashionable to value female sexuality as a source of political authority and personal empowerment — and the glee with which this notion was embraced and propagated within popular culture exposes the depth of my mistake.

That is to say, while academic feminists recognized that "the goals and strategies that some third wave feminist elect do not always coincide with the goals and strategies associated with the second wave," the only "goals and strategies" to get much press were those concerned with female sexuality (Alfonso and Trigilio, 11). For example, both scholars in the *Hypatia* email exchange claim that the "Second wave has been marked by strands that appear prudish," and "It seems that second wave feminism has put up more restrictions than green lights when it comes to sexuality" (12). They go on to make two apparently contradictory but important observations: (1) that "Second wave feminism seems to say no to [alternative] forms of sexuality," and (2) that the wave has also successfully and "seriously challenged the institution of compulsory heterosexuality and sex defined as male-centered intercourse" (12). The second observation rarely makes it into popular discourse; the first gets all the press. So, when Amelia Richards and Jennifer Baumgardner write in defense of Monica Lewinsky at the time of the scandal, they quickly dispatch "classic feminist concerns," like workplace behavior, abuses of power, and so on in favor of what they called Lewinsky's right to the sexual life of her own "based on [her] own morality" (Richards and Baumgardner). Indeed, they concede that according to the terms of the older feminism Lewinsky was certainly exploited; yet, they insist, according to the Third Wave political paradigm, the exploitation was not sexual. Her privacy was violated, she was ambushed by the FBI, abused by the Office of the Independent Counsel, and publicly ridiculed by the press (all events that would concern the older feminism); however, since "the relationship [with Bill Clinton] was consensual," these other issues do not concern these practitioners of Third Wave feminism so much as her right to sleep with whomever she likes.

In their article, "In Defense of Monica," published in *The Nation* (1998), Amelia Richards and Jennifer Baumgardner argue that feminists can best support Monica Lewinsky by considering her not a victim but rather "a young woman with a libido of her own." To see Lewinsky in this way, they argue, would benefit the movement in general; when we endorse Lewinsky's decision to involve herself with Bill Clinton, the argument goes, we defend all young women's right to chose their lovers freely and without the assumption that they are easily "used or duped." Further, women ought to avoid infantilizing Lewinsky and presuming to speak for her; indeed, they remind us that Lewinsky never "said that Clinton 'victimized' her." Richards and Baumgardner see themselves defending not only Lewinsky's choices, but also young people, who often fight to be heard. As an autonomous young woman, then, Lewinsky is both free to choose her lovers and entitled to define her experiences as she sees fit. Which, of course, one would not want to dispute; Lewinsky owes no one a critique of the affair's cultural influence or political implications for women. Those of us calling ourselves feminists, however, owe ourselves and each other this critique.

In fact, Lewinsky's own statements belie the seductive sway of the very conditions of the affair that most concern me, like the extreme power difference between the lovers, as well as between herself and the other official organs in play around her, like the Office of the Independent Counsel, the FBI, the media. Clearly, a significant measure of Lewinsky's attraction to Bill Clinton must have been the apparent power she possessed over him; to think that as an intern she could initiate and prolong an illicit affair with the president of the United States had to be potent stuff indeed. But as I've already argued, this is the alchemy of seduction; Lewinsky had access to Clinton because he wanted access to her. Perhaps these dynamics represent the dangers of the aphrodisiac of power Steinem and NOW warned us about but have overlooked in this case, for under its influence we feel ourselves to be more seductive, more protected, more fully empowered than ever before and, therefore, more likely to place ourselves in harm's way.

> *I long for a militant, argumentative feminism — one that would abandon the personal essay ... and get on with elaborating a political program.*
> Michelle Jensen, in *The Nation*

None of this is to say that women are inherently more susceptible to seduction and bad choices; it is to say that because power is available disproportionately to men, its seductive sway is also disproportionately at their disposal. Yet, Richards and Baumgardner reject the hazards of aphrodisiacal power, finding it "not coercive but seductive." Feminists who object to Clinton's involvement with Lewinsky risk reducing her to a "violated naïf," they argue. Further, they suggest, such an objection would contradict the feminist notion that "an adult woman can take responsibility for her own desires and actions." A profoundly optimistic faith in women's sexual empowerment and freedom, like that demonstrated above, underwrites Richards and Baumgardner's description of the affair. However, the insistence that to suggest Lewinsky was not fully equipped to protect herself at the time of the affair is to label her "a naïf" exposes the contradictions inherent in building a political movement which presumes we have achieved female sexual empowerment in this culture, as does remembering the rest of Lewinsky's story, or perusing rape statistics, sexual harassment cases, or abortion law. Now, before I seem like a cranky Second Wave killjoy,* let me reiterate that my argument is not that women should not have the sex lives of their own choosing or that we shouldn't listen to what they say about those lives if and when they find themselves in harm's way. What I am arguing is that a faith in female sexual autonomy should not blind us to the realities of gendered discrepancies of power inherent to patriarchy nor to the potential and very real harm so often resulting from those discrepancies — harm like abandonment by one's lover, FBI interrogation, media aggression, threat of prosecution, or public humiliation. I am further arguing that an ideological critique of the affair, its media vagaries, and possible meaning for women in general (Lewinsky in particular) is not the equivalent of claiming Lewinsky was powerless, a mere "naïf," or not accountable for her actions.

Third Wave feminism tends to embrace an egalitarian optimism that promises equal access to the successes of the movement so far and argues that those successes now guarantee women greater choice in their lives and greater levels of power culturally — hence the insistence that Lewinsky was equally empowered in her liaison with President Clinton. One consequence of this optimism is a turn away from the discussion, analysis, and acknowledgment of systemic oppression, the kind of discussion, I would argue, that is precisely necessary in this case. So it is here we part ideological ways, as I see the political argument fall away in service to another, generational and more subjective agenda. Essentially, Richards and Baumgardner maintain that the affair was whatever Lewinsky said it was, as if her role as an unpaid female intern in the White House were not ideologically fraught, or somehow failed to place her at a disadvantage when faced with the leader of the Free World. To insist that one can talk a wish into existence — that if we say we are empowered then we are — strikes me as a bit naïve, indeed, childish. It also suggests a point of view of safety and privilege; all the talking in the world won't grant power to, say, a poor, undereducated woman being beaten by her partner. And so, regretfully, through the lens of this scandal, the generational argument does make a

---

*In discussing the Lewinsky-Clinton affair, representatives of the so-called Second Wave, like Barbara Ehrenreich, Katha Pollitt, Susan Brownmiller and Andrea Dworkin, tended to highlight Bill Clinton's cheating ways and well-documented tendency toward duplicity, to worry over issues of consent and workplace harassment, as well as to dissect the misogynous and gratuitous media coverage.

kind of sense to both Second and Third Wavers. I was born in 1964, so (as with Baby Boom dates) I reside at the outer limits of the historical phases of feminism as they tend to be defined; I am either a very old member of the Third Wave or a very young member of the Second. And I acknowledge sounding like someone's (rather cross) mother when I call a position "childish." If I respond in this way, then, in fact, are feminist politics not diverging along generational lines? Or is this generational argument a distraction from what is actually an ideological one? My own chronological placement argues against the generational position, however; that is, I reside on the boundary of these generations and would contend that my response to comments like the one quoted above are driven more by the identifiers of race, class and cultural status, than by age.

Paradoxically, the Third Wave began with a very Second Wave gesture: a cross-country "down-for-the-feminist-cause" voter registration drive which seemed destined to create a movement continuous with what came before (Walker, xxxii). However, the market demanded other female voices and plot lines, and did not solicit stories reflecting the totality of women's experience or the real reach of feminists working for change. It did not solicit the unpublished stories of unglamorous feminists, those not appearing on Oprah, writing books in Cuba, or appearing on the OpEd pages of major newspapers; in other words, those whose revolution was not being televised fail to make the news. Women serving dinner in city missions, distributing clean needles, escorting women through picket lines outside abortion clinics no longer seemed newsworthy, and so no longer served as visible representatives of this movement for social change. Instead, every time Oprah cheered "You go girl!" or Naomi Wolf recommended earth tones for Al Gore, or another women became CEO of a Fortune 500 company* the feminist ground shifted a bit beneath women. Faced with such overwhelmingly soothing evidence of women's advancement, and confronted with so few female voices contradicting this evidence, how could media fail to reproduce the notion that feminism has succeeded, is perhaps even passé?

As I have noted, Third Wave arguments begin and end with a kind of generational disaffection, as well as a conviction that as a chronological whole women identify as Third Wave due to the lived experiences that bind them. As Rita Alfonso explains, "the experiences that led [her] to iden-

---

*In 2005 there were only eight female CEO's in the Fortune 500; of top corporate officers, 8 percent are women.

tify as a feminist were significantly different from those that inspired the previous generation" (9). Further, she describes differences between the waves as "a consequence of changed political conditions" and warns that some Third Wave goals "go against some perceived second wave feminist positions" (11). Their own experiences seem to have taught them that within the larger movement they are undervalued as a generation. As a liminal member of both waves, I have witnessed and personally experienced these political realities. Baumgardner and Richards recount such events as the time in 1999 when Kate Millett stormed the stage, disrupting Elizabeth Wurtzel's reading of Millett's *Flying*. The event, organized by Jennifer and Amy, was intended to celebrate International Women's Day. Contravening the unity of the event, however, Wurtzel commented to a noisy audience that perhaps their inattention was not a problem, since the text she'd selected "wasn't Millett's best work anyway"; she then proceeded to denigrate from the stage Millett's relationship to her former husband, Fumio. Quite understandably, I would argue, the older feminist had had enough and took matters into her own hands; Millett took the stage and demanded to read her own work (*Manifesta*, 221).

Manifesta's analysis of this event enacts the glibness I refer to earlier. In defense of Wurtzel's comment that Millett's marriage had been "complicated," Baumgardner and Richards explain:

> Wurtzel was probably referring to the fact that Millett had had quite a few female lovers during her ten-year marriage, which, to the reader, qualified as complicated [221].

It seems to me perfectly obvious that this turn of events had nothing to do with politics, generational conflict, and especially not "International Women's Day." No. This event was about one woman being terribly impolite and disrespectful, publicly, to another; the insult made all the more indefensible, when we consider that feminists insist that women be left to make their own relationship decisions, to make those decisions free from compulsory institutional notions of proper behavior. Wurtzel here tacitly suggests that as a wife, as a married woman, Millett had somehow transgressed; "complicated" served as none too thinly veiled code for other, more critical terms. Baumgardner and Richard's role as spokeswomen for the Third Wave — see Amy's wildly popular feminist advice column "Ask Amy.com" — is troubling in this case, particularly when we consider their defense of Monica Lewinsky, who they insist simply acted according to her own moral compass and libido when she slept with a married man. Similarly, they report that in the crowd, "many of the young women yelled out that they were pissed that Millett took over when a younger woman had the stage" (221). Drawing a generational lesson from this event, they argue that "[s]ubconsciously or not, Second Wavers often deny that they could benefit from younger feminists' knowledge and experiences" (222).

Alfonso evinces the generational defensiveness one might expect to grow out of events like the one described above. Below she clearly anticipates very specific objections to her politics.

> ...it may seem that what characterizes my "political generation" is a general lack of cohesiveness or continuity, as well as a lack of political conviction in the face of a more politically conservative environment [11].

I would like to argue that something other than generation and birth order makes sense of this ideological and stylistic break evidenced in Wurtzel's treatment of Millett. That has to be the manner of critique, the critical framework deployed by each generation; clearly, the so-called Waves do not necessarily share the same goals when examining and interrogating events affecting women at this time. For three of the most famous and influential individuals in the Third Wave, Wurtzel, Baumgardner and Richards, all share the same interpretation of Wurtzel's treatment of Millett. Clearly, the pissed-off crowd of younger feminist demonstrate that this is not a community seeking to create generational continuity or to learn from those who came before. This Wave is about burning bridges to the past, establishing new celebrity feminists, and leaving the past entirely behind. Indeed, in discussing the challenges facing their generation of feminists, editors of *The Third Wave Agenda: Being Feminist, Doing Feminism*, Leslie Haywood and Jennifer Drake, acknowledge a shift away from ideological critique when they call for the creation of "a coalition politics that acknowledge the existence of oppression" and then remind their reader, "even though it is not fashionable to say so" (*Agenda*, 3). This saying so seems to be what they seek to avoid as an unhip leftover of what Princeton University Professor Christine Stansell calls "their mothers' dusty old feminism." Yet, as Haywood and Drake make clear, such analysis propels the movement forward, motivates the work of the feminist movement, which would not exist had women not thoroughly analyzed their cultural circumstances and announced what they found.

> *It's a dangerous thing to assume that just because we were raised in a feminist era, we are safe. We are not. They are still after us.*
> Ellen Neuborne, *Listen Up*

The analysis that is so often missing leads us to recognize what most would agree is a vital element of feminist politics: aiding women who suffer under the sexist mechanisms of patriarchal culture and identifying sexist abuse of women, whether in the press or in everyday existence, or both. For example, once connected erotically with Bill Clinton, Monica Lewinsky's body parts ceased being her own. Within the cultural debate and political fallout, the body belonging to the individual woman, Monica Lewinsky, became an idea of the body erotically involved with the body of the president; this body, then, came to be known as the fantasy, "Monica Lewinsky," and suffered abuse after abuse within the mainstream media. Because public treatment of this fiction (Monica's body) produced cultural repercussions and very real personal anguish, a politic which strictly privileges individual sexual choice over the larger cultural event fails finally to consider either the totality of Monica Lewinsky's experience or the political significance of the affair.

As these daughters step out on their own, they struggle to find ideological traction and create their own distinctive voices. I am drawn to adolescence* as a metaphor in that it accounts for generational conflict based in the younger generation's need to separate and differentiate itself from the older, often through subtle and overt rejections of what came before. But the privilege of the world of most Third Wave writers presents two challenges: rejecting what came before requires renouncing the very privilege that gains entrée into publishing houses, OpEd pages, elite schools, platforms they need in order to reject what came before; how to reject and embrace one's lineage? And it does not appear to be a world in much need of social activist movements like feminism. As the Reagan era ushered in a flattening of liberalism's public affect, feminist rhetoric softened; that is, popular conversations about women grew increasingly conservative and also impatient with notions of work yet to be done on behalf of women. The Reagan era insistently portrayed American culture as tidy; the family was intact, gender roles were sorted, foreign policy reasoned and minimal, the social order, well — in order. The media welcomed, then, negative portrayals of women seeking change, encouraged profiles of those still spying out the gender inequities in our culture as wrongheaded and perverse. The media welcomed stories of feminist infighting, for example, and favored stories portraying feminism as a pernicious influence on those

---

*A pejorative, dangerously ad hominem metaphor, I admit. But following the generational argument set up by representatives of the Third Wave, I find the metaphor felicitous and fitting.

things Reagan had finally sorted out. The story that took hold, that was convenient, expeditious and in line with misogynist social roles endorsed by Reagan et al., was the story of turf wars and generational conflict. Perfect: media-constructed feminist cat fights sold, multiplied and became a prevailing truism within popular culture.

Conservatives rail against feminism and its supposed alliance with political correctness and yet they tend to use questions about feminism as a kind of litmus test in the media. That is, feminism has since Reagan been elevated to a singular position in American culture; it functions popularly as the predominant signifier of female opinion or conviction. In a kind of perverse turn of events, conservative efforts to disabuse audiences of feminist influence have resulted in feminism's elevated media status. For example, every woman who comes to public notoriety or fame, it seems, must declare her views on feminism, each female image must be rationalized in terms of women's politics. Whether she's Halle Berry, Oprah Winfrey, Sarah McLachlan or Courtney Love, any woman who gains a public voice will be asked to identify herself in term of the women's movement and rationalize what she does accordingly. Often she's asked without provocation, as in Sarah McLachlan's well-known comment on the first Lilith tour: "The tour isn't a soapbox for extremist feminism," she said in a *New York Newsday* interview. "This [all-female tour] is not at all about dissing men," she would add. Similarly, films about women, particularly women who lay claim to physical power, as in *Thelma and Louise*, *Aliens*, even 2004's *Catwoman*, are judged as if the directors and performers were explicitly addressing feminist issues. For example, Mick LaSalle calls Halle Berry's *Catwoman* "A feisty, feminist feline with a taste for sushi, leather and, most of all, revenge," while Robert K. Elder describes the same film as a "vacuous lingerie show posing as feminism." I would argue that it's a film about a sexy female superhero — ripe for feminist interrogation and analysis, perhaps, but not addressing feminist politics specifically.

The politics of female performers like Madonna, Cher, and Courtney Love have been thoroughly commented upon, as they have invited scholarly and ideological critique through their self-consciously controversial performance styles. More to my point is the fact that even the most mainstream performers are constantly asked to describe their personal brands of feminism, not because their work touches upon things political, but simply because they are female and famous. For example, Shania Twain's answer specifically addresses criticism of her sexy image and costume choices. "I think a lot of what's being stripped from us these days is the fact that we need to be more masculine to fit in in the world," Twain says. "And that pressure is not coming from men," she adds; indeed, "[t]hat pressure is coming from women. Not everybody has to go out there and downplay their femininity or their sensuality to be taken seriously."* Such sentiments echo the woman-beware-woman misogyny we see in Do-Me feminism, where women accuse other women of failing to enjoy their own sexuality properly, and cite feminism as the source of all that ails women, including the repression of that very sexuality. We find in our classes and in our everyday lives that women generally feel obligated to position themselves and their choices vis-à-vis the women's movement. I'm thinking not only of the familiar, "I'm not a feminist, but..." that we so often hear from our students, but also the tendency of women to explain choices, like whether to use daycare or stay home with their children, work full-time or part-time, take self-defense or belly dancing classes, in terms of what they imagine a "feminist" would say.

Although I recognize the limits of the generational argument and would like rather to endorse a kind of impressionistic notion of political experience which might more accurately reflect our lived experiences of political change, it's clear that the anti-feminist events of the mid–90s helped to create the political environment that would welcome the particular manifestation of feminism called Third Wave. And it's clear that the spine of Third Wave thinking is generational identity. The pervasive assumption that the study of women's issues, particularly those that seem particularly female, like beauty, fashion, and so on, leads to a reactionary prohibition of those things undermines adequate analysis. I would argue that Third Wave overcorrects, too often insisting that we see any and all choices made by women as empowering (a new litmus test) or risk being labeled avuncular, Victorian, or worse, old. But biology is not political destiny; to be female is not necessarily to be feminist. One practices feminism irrespective of gender the way one works for civil rights irrespective of race. Estelle B. Freedman makes this same argument in *No Turning Back*:

> While women may participate in a variety of social movements — civil rights, ecology, socialism, even fundamentalism — those movements cannot be feminist unless they *explicitly address justice for women* as a primary concern [8; my emphasis].

To deny this simple claim strips the politics from the movement. So, when Nomy Lamm argues in *Listen Up* that "If there's one thing feminism has

---

*Jim Patterson, Associated Press writer. "Twain Preaches Feminist Message," South Coast Today, http:\\archive.southcoasttoday.com

taught me, it's that the revolution is gonna be on my terms," she reflects a troubling trend in this new brand of feminism, a turn away from social issues and toward individual rationales for individual life choices. She further adds,

> And I know that a hell of a lot of what I say is totally contradictory. My contradictions can coexist, cuz they exist inside me, and I'm not gonna simplify them so that they fit into the linear, analytical pattern that I know they're supposed to.... The fact that I write like this cuz it's the way I want to write makes this world just that much safer for me [85].

Freedman reminds us that social movements like feminism work toward a collective goal — "justice for women," as she says — and that a politics of the self is incongruous with that goal. Making the world "that much safer for me" does not guarantee the world will be "that much safer" for any other woman. If Third Wave women feel unfairly criticized by Second Wavers, if they feel put down or condescended to for "lack[ing] a knowledge of women's history," for example, the kinds of self-centered rhetoric illustrated above might explain why. Lamm's piece appears in one of the foundational works of Third Wave literature, *Listen Up*, where she is not alone in her autobiographical politics. And as intransigent as such reactions may sound, I have to admit that such language strikes me as bold only in its audacious focus on the self, adolescent, to continue the generational metaphor, in its lack of concern for historical context (and others). Moreover, in its use of the first person and, as Catherine M. Orr observes of the same piece, its "degradation of anything that resembles intellectual labor," Lamm's defensive tone tends to alienate her audience, making the strengths of her position very difficult to recognize (34).

If all activities and choices are gestures of female empowerment, then none are. We face rather, as Michelle Jensen says in her review of *Manifesta*, "the dubious politics of generality." To carry a Hello Kitty lunchbox, for example, is not to make a feminist statement any more than engaging in cultural critique of such items is to suggest individual women fail the movement by carrying them. It's time to stop defining the movement through either extremes or ephemera. The extremes, like early feminism, radicalism, separatism, strict mothers, and disaffected daughters, have often moved political progress forward, but never represented the totality of feminism; ephemera like fashion do very little for political progress and tend to divide, rather than unite, women. In her foreword to *to be real*, Gloria Steinem addresses the differences between her political experience and that of the contributors to Rebecca Walker's anthology:

> In my generation, we came to feminism as adults. Our revelations came from listening to one another's very different lives, discovering shared themes, realizing we were neither crazy nor alone, and evolving theories as peers.

As a result of this 1970s' consciousness-raising coming together, Steinem argues, 1970s feminism evolved in "a long and organic process that felt like rebirth, as if we were inventing ourselves and feminism" (xviii). The much younger contributors, on the other hand, did not discover feminism but "were born into a culture with many images of feminism, or they came to it via the media and books, existing groups and women's studies, teachers, parents, and siblings" (xviii). In other words, these young writers were born into a world in which feminism already existed, was already practiced, imagined, commented upon, written about, already in the water. The line dividing these two points of view turns out to be impermeable. As with Steinem's argument, within discussions by members of the Third Wave, feminists necessarily stand on either side of this line. In a kind of feminist birth order, one cannot but reside where one is deposited chronologically; as if chronology were destiny, this position supersedes all ideological or political considerations. Perhaps this helps explain the turn toward the personal, then, in that many of the women and feminists under discussion here take their politics quite to heart, their move into feminism as a kind of political birthday.

It seems appropriate to address the question of privileging one iteration of feminism over another and the potential accusation that my argument tacitly places the Second Wave above the Third. Certainly, the Second Wave has come under many of the same criticisms I have leveled against the Third in terms of class and race; the conventional critique argues (not incorrectly) that much of American feminism in general has failed to adequately serve poor women and women of color. If popular Third Wavers seek to differentiate themselves from their political mothers, then, this might be an appropriate area to examine more closely within their own movement. Further, while we might agree that the feminism of the 1960s and 70s largely served a middle-class, white constituency, any examination of the actual political record of those decades reveal lasting, valuable changes made by the movement on behalf of women in the areas of workplace discrimination, access to contraception, abortion, education and inclusion in the armed forces, for example.* A similar examination of later

---

Between 1960 and 1980 women's activism produces remarkable results, among them the marketing of the birth control pill, passage of the Equal Pay Act, election of first black woman (cont.)

decades does not produce the same result. Indeed, since the age of Reagan, feminism and women have lost considerable ground in each of these areas.

The Third Wave employs the vocabulary of feminism to validate particular kinds of experiences and choices, to identify a narrow array of personal choices as politically empowering. The familiar feminist notion that "the personal is political" haunts and defines post-backlash feminism; from "Do-Me" to "Girlie" to "Third Wave," all tend to center on women's personal experiences. However, refusing any ideological interrogation of the roots and consequences of these experiences leaves us without a political agenda; in the Third Wave, then, the personal is, well, merely personal. I would argue that the turn toward the personal and confessional requires an attendant (and very careful) apparatus for examining the cultural implications of the uses of the female body one promotes. Most importantly for the future of feminism as a movement for social justice, the move toward politics of the individual potentially reduces all women to a metaphor of feminine achievement and ease and erases all traces of women's suffering under patriarchy. This is an erasure that would find a happy home within the anti-feminist media; however, any movement struggling against race and class prejudice would suffer immeasurably from such a development.

(cont.) to congress, Shirley Chisholm, the first Women's Studies courses, founding of National Abortion and Reproductive Rights Action League (NARAL), passage of Title IX, passage of the ERA, Roe v. Wade, opening of the first battered women's shelters, passage of the Equal Credit Opportunity Act, ordination of female priests in Episcopal Church, opening of U.S. military academies to women, training of female astronauts at NASA, passage of Pregnancy Discrimination Bill, birth of the gay rights movement.

4

Booby Traps and Botox: Putting the Fun Back into Politics

> *We argue that young women's primary expression these days is a joy and ownership of sexuality and that's a form of power, a type of energy.*
>
> Jennifer Baumgardner

Whereas Do-Me feminists will claim an erotics of political empowerment, Girlie feminists tie their political identity to elitist ephemera like shopping, gossip and latte. Taking Do-Me ideology to its consumerist extreme, the Girlie feminist would prefer not to "worry about oppression"; instead, power shopping and political indifference characterize this trend for the privileged. The rhetoric of ideological assertion backs this movement; in fact, it is a largely rhetorical movement, one which requires its adherents merely to assert female empowerment and lay discursive claim to women's political status. Take, for example, the following declaration of Girlie philosophy:

> We, and others, call the intersection of culture and feminism "Girlie." Girlie says we're not broken, and our desires aren't simply booby traps set by the patriarchy. Girlie encompasses the tabooed symbols of women's feminine enculturation — Barbie dolls, makeup, fashion magazines, high heels — and says doing so isn't shorthand for "we've been duped" [Straus 6].

Note the uncritical acceptance of "enculturation" and the slip from "desires" to "booby traps." If one's socialization can be described as a booby trap, how can it simultaneously represent one's "desires"? Rhetorically untenable, the above claim exposes the disconnect between enculturation and desire, while suggesting that cultural manipulation reflects precisely what women want. Like Do-Me feminists, Girlies engage an ideology based in a paradox: one that argues enculturation acts as a boon to women. Further, as in many Third Wave arguments, in the statement above empowerment means simply asserting that those things that work to undermine women's political status actually enhance it. If we say we are empowered, then we are. The argument, then, comes down to categorical assertions, like "Feminism got it wrong." And to prove it? Reverse the terms of the feminist position: feminism is the problem, not patriarchal culture. Sorted thus, feminism becomes the bogey against which women must defend our less noble acts and desires. If feminism has failed women within popular discourse, this way of thinking suggests, it is in allowing itself to either ossify around impossible standards of female behavior or to be defined as if it had. Either way, the mainstream critique of feminism consistently takes the notion that feminism has become brittle and dowdy as its a priori assumption regarding the women's movement.

While the Girlie trend can't really qualify as a stand-alone movement, it possesses depth and breadth enough — that is, popular representation — to merit a chapter of its own. Further, the Girlie position draws attention to the troubling class issues which have always vexed the women's movement, and that I argue appear especially conspicuously in the Third Wave in particular, post-backlash in general. Serious critiques of Second Wave feminism have taken place in academe for years, raising issues of race and class and reproaching the women's movement for concentrating its efforts too narrowly upon the needs of white, middle-class women. The importance (and, sadly, accuracy) of such critique cannot be overstated, and my earlier criticism of the Third Wave should not be mistaken for a blanket endorsement of Second Wave or naïveté about the weaknesses of earlier feminism. Indeed, I seek to resist any either-or construction of feminist politics; we are not limited to either one notion of the movement or another. Identifying fickle voices, injurious gestures, and regressive convictions within feminism (or any political movement) must always be seen as a necessary act of self-correcting. This is precisely the project academic (versus mainstream) third wave feminism has undertaken: to identify and theorize the weaknesses of the movement, indicating where it has served and failed to serve particular populations of women, and where it has failed to address the needs of certain women under patriarchy, namely the poor and women of color.

Consider as another example of this brand of anti-feminist argumentation, Christina Hoff Sommers' declaration that "[t]he belief that American women are living in thrall to men seems to suit some women more than others. I have found that it does not suit me" (26). Hoff Sommers' statement crystallizes the philosophical spine of Girlie ideology: the supposition that one can talk (or write) one's political desires into existence. Hoff Sommers ignores the political realities in which she lives and argues that ignoring them will make them go away. Wouldn't it be nice if patriarchy were an abstraction, a "belief," and in order to escape its inequities and abuses one need only assert in writing that such things no longer "suit" one? More to the point, I would argue that "living in thrall to" patriarchy suits Sommers right down to the ground, as well as other Girlies like the first author quoted above, for their arguments reveal an endorsement of the patriarchy around them and suggest that an overly sensitive feminist movement is the real problem for women. If one identifies with Barbie, for example, or enjoys "makeup, fashion magazines, high heels," that is not inherently a political statement — neither is it an overt rejection of any type of feminism. And this is my position. Too often, women publicly claiming the feminist label portray themselves as angry girls in petty competition over who has the best toys. In this way, the political conversation regarding women and politics has been thoroughly diffused, reduced to questions of "booby traps" and Barbie, shoe selections and fashion magazines.

The argument repeats what has vexed the women's movement from the beginning: the myth that feminist resistance to patriarchal demands upon their time, labor and bodies turns them ugly, unfeminine and intolerant. The earliest feminists were accused of behaving unnaturally, later we were "ball busting and unreasonable," now we are over-serious, touchy, prone to turf wars and badly dressed. Feminists are consistently portrayed in popular media as, simply put, no fun. Even Rebecca Walker has this to say about the difficulty of maintaining a feminist identity: "it is tedious to always criticize world politics, popular culture, and the nuances of social interaction" (Walker, xxxiii). But I would ask anyone finding social awareness and political engagement wearying to consider why this might be the case; quite likely, Hoff Sommers, Walker, and those claiming the Girlie title find themselves fatigued not by the act of cultural critique but rather by the realizations about women's status in patriarchy that such critique brings to light. Moreover, any argument about the politics of clothing or the feminist statement one might make in wearing one thing or another — insisting that pink, make-up, plastic surgery or high heels are empowering — *is* a critical argument about "popular culture" and "the nuances of social interaction." Girlies do engage a critique of fashion when they claim to build an ideology of empowerment upon fashion and consumer tastes. To argue the reverse is to wishfully turn away from the realities of female existence to which their own behaviors and choices clearly react.

> *There is a widespread assumption that simply because my generation of women has the good fortune to live in a world touched by the feminist movement, that means everything we do is magically imbued with its agenda.*
>
> Ariel Levy

Generally, women writers attaching a prefix to the term "feminist" or "feminism" are hot these days, marketable and heavily promoted within the mainstream press. These prefixes — "anti-," "post-," "Do-Me," "victim-," "sex-positive," "equity-," and "Third Wave," to name but a few — function very much like brand names, securing through repetition an immediate understanding of what they represent. Further, they stand almost without exception as declarations of feminism's failure or decline and remove the women-centered politics from the term itself. We have yet to see repeated declarations by "Proud-of-the-movement" feminists dominating urban OpEd pages; no claims to the label "Women's Rights" feminist, for example, have shown up lately in *Lip*, *Bust*, *Bitch*, *Cosmo*, not to mention the *New York Times*, *Time*, the *Washington Post*, or *Newsweek*.

Like most of the "feminisms" occurring since the Reagan-Bush era, Girlie relies first and foremost upon a kind of straw feminism, a faux feminism set up to be shot down as the wrong answer, as the mistake that the Girlie movement must correct. Arguing that they have not "been duped" in the passage above, for example, implies that someone or something has accused them of just that and the younger generation finds itself obliged to react. (Members of the post-backlash movements emerging at this time might be best described not as activists but rather *re*-activists.) While Girlie is often associated with the Third Wave, indeed defined as a derivative of that brand of feminism, in fact, ideologically Girlies share more with Do-Me feminists. "In holding tight to that which once symbolized their oppression," a pro-patriarchy, pro-sex-and-shopping momentum carries Girlies to a definition of "feminism" as a movement for young, oversexed, middle-class women who like to shop and talk about themselves (Baumgardner and Richards, 136).

This consumer trend for the privileged, concerned with Barbies, shoes, make-up — consumer items all — makes a full-blown appearance in the mid-nineties, first in zines and then print magazines, like *Bust* and *Bitch*, *Lucky* and *Jane*, and later in books like *Sexual Personae*, *The Morning After*, *Fire with Fire*, *A Return to Modesty*, *The New Victorians*, *Bitch*, *Fresh Lipstick*, and *Are Men Still Necessary?* The Girlie has, of course, historically been a staple of magazines like *Cosmopolitan*,* where one is routinely encouraged to see cleavage and better orgasms as indicators of female political progress. If those embracing the Do-Me attitude were reacting to a no-sex, no-fun feminism they believed prevailed in the late 1980s, Girlies specifically sought to reverse what they see as too serious a turn away from not only sex and fun, but also the delight of female display. This movement embraces the performative aspects of female identity, and, therefore, encourages women to recover conventional notions of female beauty by wearing "girlie" or "girlish" clothing, shopping, educating themselves on the relative value of $30.00 lipsticks and sexy shoes, and asking themselves questions like, "Do short skirts and cleavage still pay off?"* Michelle Goldberg is on to something when she notes, ironically, that the Girlie movement sets itself as proof that women can finally "reconcile beauty and power, fun and feminism." Indeed. This reconciliation removes the politics entirely from the feminism that came before, and the master narrative driving Girlie philosophy rationalizes this mode of reconciliation.

Master narratives are the stories a group or community tells itself about the historical moment or events to which it claims to react. To understand the function of such narratives, think of the evolution of Third Wave Feminism, for example, whose premise begins with the conviction that one's mother's experiences fail to represent one's own. The story of a mythic "Feminism Past" (Second Wave feminism?) establishes a contrast, a failed system, against which to rationalize a new feminist position. By foregrounding and then rejecting this fictional failed past, the next generation of feminists present themselves as guarantors of the movement's natural evolution. Thanks to them, women's politics will progress toward better and better iterations of what came before. So, rejecting the old and

---

I can't resist the observation that Girlie is a perfect homonym for Gurley-of Helen Gurley Brown, the long-time editor of Cosmopolitan *magazine-and that she preferred the term "girl" to "woman" when speaking of grown-up females. Indeed, she urges us into perpetual girlhood. "If you're not having sex," she has said, "you're finished. It separates the girls from the old people" (King).*

†*As the cover of* Jane *did recently.*

embracing the new makes a kind of organic sense, for isn't the hope of progress that the new inevitably serves the needs of both women and culture better than the old? The problem of course is that, in fact, Girlies turn toward the past; that is, toward conventional notions of femininity. Here, then, we see how the Girlie approach to women's politics would appeal to conservative anxieties regarding radical women. Girlie feminism links conventional notions of both female sexuality and political advancement, for the Girlie woman marches with history toward the status quo and away from 1960s' radicalism. Mainstream responses to feminism since the Reagan-Bush era rely uniformly upon an historical notion of Feminism Past, and this narrative has remained virtually unchanged over time.

"But," as Lisa Jervis reminds us, "when was it ever a good idea to trust a master narrative?" (*Ms.* online). We must approach master narratives with care and skepticism, for they tend not to relate an ineluctable truth about the past as much as a foundational set of beliefs about something new. Master narratives are not historical truths; in fact, these narratives serve the ideological needs of the group deploying them. The story of Feminism Past, then, allows the Girlie movement to define itself through what it is *not* as well as what it is; therefore, identifying the master narrative constructed by the Girlie movement reveals much about the movement itself and its implied critique of what came before. The master narrative goes something like this: feminism has grown increasingly anxious about female sexuality and all things identifiable as conventionally feminine, like beauty, sex with men, fashion, shopping, make-up, the color pink. Feminism might be understood as a club which extends invitations only to unfeminine, ball-busting, dowdy types. The story continues: a small but vocal minority has emerged to control the political conversation about women, and this minority insists that feminism function as a monolithic ideology. This minority, which, the myth continues, wields power through key positions in academe, polices female behavior, sifting for violations of the code of proper feminist conduct. Swallowing this notion of feminism whole, the Girlie movement insists that feminism has traditionally required an angry overreaction (ball-busting, radical behavior) to all things that call attention to female beauty; therefore, the narrative implies, Feminism Past proscribes a dress code which fails to flatter. You've heard of consumer therapy? Welcome to the age of consumer politics.

"Feminism is definitely shifting," according to Molly Jong-Fast, "toward consumerism" (Iley). In an interview with Chrissy Iley for the

Daily Mail, Molly Jong-Fast discusses growing up in the Second Wave world of her mother, Erica Jong, who is the feminist author of 20 books, most famously *Fear of Flying* (1973). Jong writes in an identifiably Second Wave idiom, one comfortable with confessional representations of her political and personal journey. Jong-Fast occupies a unique position, then, to articulate the relationships among the master Second Wave narrative, a reactive ideology and consumer culture. She complains that "having to wear overalls and worry all the time that men were trying to humiliate you" was "repressive" as a young woman; now, she says, "All the thrills I need I can get in a department store." Further, she found the feminism practiced by her mother not only fatiguing and dull, but also unconvincing; for she argues that feminist activism is repressive, angry, and also unattractive: "Feminists these days" she explains, "are associated with lesbians and polyester." Jong-Fast's response to her mother's politics draws overtly upon a master narrative, assumes a stable historical idea of feminist politics, and then specifically rejects those politics in favor of their apparent opposites. Jong-Fast's life enacts her critique of the Second Wave, then; she has emphatically embraced a lifestyle she witnessed to be (or now believes to be) antithetical to her mother's politics.

Post-backlash feminisms like Girlie tend toward performative identity politics generally, emphasizing how women look, how they behave; one must be seen to be Girlie. Do-Me's and Third Wavers also tend to describe their lives as highlight films depicting the differences between their lives and those of their feminist mothers. Theirs is a revolution made for 20th- and 21st-century media, a visual movement celebrating "the buzz of retail therapy or bitching and joking with other women over a latte," as opposed to working quietly for political change (Iley). Take the work of the author of *Fresh Lipstick: Redressing Fashion and Feminism*, Linda M. Scott, for an example. She bases her critique of feminist attitudes toward beauty upon her own version of Feminism Past, one that combines the master narrative of Second Wave feminism with what she sees as the Marxist bent of academic feminism. She suggests that worry over class inequities has reduced the efficacy of the women's movement—as plainly demonstrated by its failure to a appreciate cosmetics and fashion appropriately. "American feminism," Scott announces in the first line of the book, "takes a dim view of beauty" (1). She offers the following history of 1980s' campus radicalism as an explanation of how this happened:

> The influence of Marxism solidified in the 1980s, when many campus radicals ended up on university faculties.... A large body of literature was

produced that involved, primarily, a critique of capitalism through an attack on pictures and self-decoration. The result was an ideology that dealt with significant social problem by blaming them on the images of fashion. Child abuse became the fault of cosmetic advertisers, and rape could be blamed on the manufacturers of bedsheets [7].

Scott offers no research to corroborate these rather sweeping claims, neither about cosmetics and child abuse nor the correlation between linens and incidents of rape. Scott further argues that "[c]ampus feminist groups developing under this influence used dress as an instrument of exclusion" (7). A single piece of anecdotal evidence does appear immediately after this claim, in the form of a report from a woman who graduated college in 1990 and was criticized for "her lipstick habit" (7). Scott describes the event: "One 1990's graduate reported that, though she was converted to feminism [and] took classes in women's studies, and joined the women's coalition, her lipstick habit drew fire from her new friends" (7). The student concluded at the time (and Scott agrees now) that the only reason for this censure was that "[the student] was different, and therefore, a threat to their neat, closed, secret, homogeneous community" (7). Surely neither Scott nor this student ever believed that the women's studies classes she attended and the women's coalitions groups she joined existed as "secret[s]" where she went to school. While I sympathize with the student's situation, one cannot be expected to consider this story a reliable indicator of a wholesale feminist attack on cosmetics on her campus. Being criticized by friends or colleagues is not the same thing as being discriminated against; more likely, the student suffered an unfortunate moment of what Scott rightly calls "political pettiness" (7). I would argue that the student had a very unfortunate experience but not one that defines an entire movement; perhaps she needed better friends in 1990, not better politics.

Are you there, Girlies? It's me, politics.
Manifevsta

As in any large movement or organization, those who insist upon utter conformity are generally the exceptions rather than the rule; unfortunately, much of Scott's argument throughout *Fresh Lipstick* relies for support upon the behavior of the former rather than the latter. In order for feminism to recover its role as the political voice of social justice for women, discussion must move away from such extremes. Significantly, the story recounted above represents the kind of anecdotal evidence regularly offered in arguments relying upon a defining, largely fictional, master narrative of feminism that characterizes all feminists as one thing or another (man-hater, lesbian, anti-beauty).

Moreover, works like *Fresh Lipstick* tend to drop in personal anecdotes, unsubstantiated claims, or plain falsehoods — generally, in the form of complaints against an individual feminist or group of feminists — as evidence that the motives of American feminism itself have gone wrong. (We must add to this list works like *Who Stole Feminism?*, *Promiscuities*, *The Morning After*, or *Are Men Necessary?*) This technique has become conventional with popular works of prefix feminism. Indeed, Amy Richards (co-author of *Manifesta*) praises Scott's research style in a brief review of *Fresh Lipstick* featured on the Palgrave website: "Thanks to *Fresh Lipstick* feminism will be fashionable. Linda Scott uses historical anecdotes and strong opinions to make the case for feminism to more honestly approach beauty and fashion." Without aid of statistics, quotations, or even in many cases anecdotal evidence, Scott further insists that in the 1990s feminists cajoled other women into denying their femininity and displaying themselves as masculinized and unglamorous. Such a claim is counterintuitive, though, for during this period we, in fact, witnessed the rise of "feminisms" like Do-Me, power-, sex-positive, lipstick-, and Third Wave. The 1990s were emphatically not the era of "dress correctness," as Scott argues; in fact, this was the era of the riot grrrls, the emergence of zines like *Bust* and *Bitch*, and print magazines like *Sassy*, *Jane*, and *Lucky*, which claimed the feminist moniker and celebrated in their own ways (and to sometimes different ends) the female body and its display. Feminisms of the 1990s embraced highly sexualized notions of female empowerment, communicated through clothing and makeup styles, as I have said; specifically and quite self-consciously eschewing their own perceptions of old-school dress codes.

The tacit Girlie argument regarding female beauty suggests that in a kind of reverse discrimination beautiful women have been punished by the feminist movement. Such an argument reminds me of similarly counterintuitive arguments appearing in the mainstream press at this time, like the insistence that white men were losing power in American culture, or that campuses were overrun with multicultural curricula. On the face of it, the arguments are outrageous. American feminism no more discriminates against beautiful women than American culture does; diversity has no more overrun American universities than Milton and Shakespeare have disappeared from college curricula. Plainly, Linda M. Scott's and my positions are irreconcilable: she sees not only a pervasive "antibeauty ideology" dogging feminism today, but also claims that this ideology (which is merely, in fact, a critique of the beauty industry) "serves the interests of the few at the expense of the many" (2). But it simply does not follow that wearing makeup or Girlie clothing constitutes a liberatory political move, or that *not* wearing those things constitutes a reactionary or unreasonable one, so I reject this master narrative of the plain-Jane feminist and categorically object to any suggestion that we fail to serve the many when we critique fashion markets. "Maybe the real feminist is the one wearing the lipstick," Scott argues, since women head many cosmetics firms and write cosmetics advertisements. Assuming all "women" are "feminists" presents myriad problems, however. For there is no reason to assume one's gender automatically speaks to one's ideology; many women exploit capitalist structures and principles to enrich themselves at the expense of others, just as many men do. But market politics themselves emphatically privilege the few over the many; in order to argue the opposite one must ignore the material and economic conditions under which most women (indeed, most people) live, overlook the realities of who can afford Manolo Blahniks and who struggles to make ends meet, and disregard the difference between the numbers of women running cosmetics firms and those working to pay for their products. The post-backlash shift away from cultural critique hopes to inject some glamour into women's public lives, and that ambition drives this trend more than any other. No matter who heads the firms, tying glamour to political identity creates a market for a particular form of beauty, and makes the right clothes, shoes, bags, and makeup constituents of a political identity one can purchase and consume.

Much of the criticism of feminism appearing after Reagan-Bush and written by women, as Amy Richards points out, relies upon strong opinion, but angry personal sketches comprise much of the evidence presented there. We find such sketches in Richards' own *Manifesta*. Obviously, all critique contains strong opinions, but to rely so heavily upon anecdotes to generalize the political conditions of women is problematic, and leads to wildly insupportable statements disguised as fact. Remember Katie Roiphe's insistence that if "my women friends were really being raped — wouldn't I know it?"; Hoff Sommers' claim that gender feminists "hold the keys to many bureaucratic fiefdoms"; or Scott's own: "'Dress correctness' became the litmus test on campuses in the 1990s." And let's not forget the most famous falsehood in the feminist universe, the allegation that Andrea Dworkin (or was it Catherine MacKinnon?) said "all heterosexual sex is rape." Falsehoods like these multiply expansively in the 1990s as the works of anti-feminist authors hit the best seller lists, virtually all repeating the same dubious research.

Michelle Goldberg explains the appeal of the Girlie rhetoric (and helps explain the lack of research there): "This new shopping-and-fucking feminism is so ubiquitous right now in part because it jibes precisely with the message of consumer society" ("Feminism for Sale"). Post-backlash feminisms largely identify with youth culture, and tend to market the latest "feminism" the way one would market the latest low-rise jeans. The youth market, significantly, is enormous; indeed, "[g]irl power" has, as the authors of *The Bust Guide to the New Girl Order*, remind us, "become a marketer's wet dream" (xii). The largest consumer group of females is aged 12 to 24, and in 2000, for example, they spent $67 billion, mostly on makeup and clothing (Maciulis). According to the U.S. Bureau of Economic Analysis, women account for as much as 88 percent of all retail purchases and control nearly $3 trillion in consumer spending (Kanner). In order to serve a lipstick-and-mini-skirt generation of feminists, someone — man or woman — is going to make a killing selling lipstick and mini-skirts. Moreover, when we purchase consumer markers of empowerment, we enrich the few who design them and explicitly endorse the cultural and political decisions behind them. (Need I say more about low-rise jeans?) None of this is to say folks buying into the Girlie movement have been duped, but it is to say that to collude in a movement away from the social justice goals of the women's movement brings genuine consequences for other women.

> *I got mine, fuck you.*
> Susan Faludi

This leads us to the magazine *Lucky*, whose editor-in-chief is female and which markets itself as "the first magazine devoted exclusively, singularly, and fabulously to shopping." In the inaugural issue we see why this magazine has been describes as the place where "the Girlie ethos reaches its absurd apogee." Kim France launches her magazine with the following declaration:

> On days that are like most days in my life so far, days when I don't settle the conflict in Kosovo, win the lottery, or establish a system of economic and social opportunity that creates true equality for all, I'm willing to settle for the very real joy that there is to be had in finding the perfect kitten-heel pump.

Here the editor articulates the cut-off between politics and Girlie identity, as well as the class imperative motivating that identity. My objection here is not to a woman writer-editor publicly declaring a love of shopping, but to her conflating — indeed, substituting — political consciousness with consumerism. As this Girlie woman discusses the necessity of material indulgence in American women's lives, the real value of the perfect lipstick and a certain style of shoe, she throws into sharp relief the class issues highlighted by Do-Me and Third Wave rhetoric discussed earlier. France blithely conflates issues like rape camps, civilian casualties and other war crimes with a privileged indulgence: shopping. Having called attention to political atrocities, this author not only celebrates her own safety and wealth, but also assumes a female audience who can afford to buy this gesture. A rejection of political consciousness does not constitute a political consciousness; the manifest impossibility of such a position strikes me as obvious. So why do these women work so hard to call their social consciousness feminist? Why attach their way of life to that one?

A contributor to *Moxie* magazine, Kate Epstein, offers a striking confession that goes a long way toward answering my questions. She articulates the biased false-dilemma facing many women in the workforce: "If I shouldn't have to act like a man to get what I deserve, I shouldn't have to be Girlie, either." Yet, she admits that she willingly works this system and can't really see the sense in not working it. While she may not endorse the sexist game she has to play, Epstein will play rather than give up the "privileges" that attach to "conforming to society's ideas about women." Rather than dismissing a world of pain and suffering in service to her own pleasure, as France does, Epstein confronts the position of women in American culture and her own placement within it — and knowingly colludes. She's stuck, knows she "shouldn't have to be Girlie," but can't really see a way out. Actually the way out, as she sees it, would require "abdicating the privileges that come from conforming" to patriarchal demands upon women. These privileges include avoiding harassment at work, for example, or the myriad penalties associated with seeming unfeminine. Other privileges clearly include social status, validation and plain flattery.

In order to gain social power and appeal, the Girlie leads with her sexuality; indeed, the female body and what it's wearing foregrounds most of Girlie discourse. For example, Janelle Brown, who has been a senior technology writer at Salon.com and a co-founder of an online zine, *Maxi*, comes clean. "I love clothes," she says. "I love makeup." Lest the reader draw the wrong conclusion, she adds, "I also don't let anyone step on me.

I hold my own." Clothes and makeup are not inherently disempowering loves, she argues; for not only does she write about fashion, she also covers "geek stuff" (technology). Her fashion and career choices demonstrate, she argues, that "all women" should seek to strike a "balance between consumerism and feminism" (in Goldberg). As a feminist trained in academe, I see Brown's impulse to explain herself as symptomatic of culturally enforced notions of female sexuality as well as pervasive anxieties regarding female achievement. We experience (or witness) this phenomenon all the time in our own lives: in order to defuse the aggression or the simple discomfort of others, women often feel compelled to apologize for our personal successes, to balance indicators of our own power with signs of vulnerability. Hence the "I-love-makeup" preamble to Brown's discussion of her personal choices and professional skills. Such apologetic signs come in many other forms — passive behavior in the face of male desire, performed weakness when confronting people in positions of power, or infantilizing dress.

For example, in her piece for *Moxie* magazine, quoted above and entitled, "Femme Feminist," Kate Epstein also confesses that she has always loved Girlie clothes and won't be persuaded to dress differently by feminism: highly feminine dress just "feels right," she says. "It's not weak or silly to act like a woman. That's sexism talking." She's right, of course, to draw negative conclusions about a woman based on her style of dress constitutes sexism. Yet Epstein's relationship to fashion is obviously not unvexed, nor entirely empowering. For while she sees her insistence upon wearing dresses as "political defiance" in the face of overwhelming feminist pressure, those same dresses also constitute workplace "expedience, too." She explains that men in power find her intelligence "less threatening" if she wears dresses. Dresses put the people around her at ease, she argues, leaving her to get what she wants free of ideological conflict or distracting office politics. This "working the system" works when facing all authority figures, male or female, she continues. As long as any woman feels compelled to wear a dress to diffuse a superior's anxiety about her intelligence and successes, a critique of the politics of fashion is entirely appropriate and necessary. Some of us fret over the semiotics of female display, for example, or the implications of our daughters sifting fashion magazines for role models precisely because of this kind of workplace bullying. Epstein's experience demonstrates that out in the world (within our lived experiences vs. our rhetorical ones) how we look too often directly influences how we are treated; without doubt female appearance is weighted ideologically. For Epstein workplace politics come down to wearing clothing designed for the needs of patriarchy—*this is the definition of oppression.* Embracing such oppression, colluding in subtle (but undeniable) masculine coercion at work, even when we can recognize that we are, doesn't make it go away, or make us feminists.

It does, however, make one the perfect consumer of feminine ephemera. Magazines like *Moxie, Maxie, Lucky, Jane, Bust,* and *Bitch* sell a brand of feminism, in the same way they market cosmetics, bags and clothing. And despite their claims to a feminist ethos, interrogations of markets, economic inequities, or their effect upon women would not be welcome on their pages. Better, rather, to venerate the machine. As the ideal consumer, the Girlie has no desire to "overturn the way society is structured." And why should she? Consumer therapy is a lot more fun than writing to your congressman or teaching self-defense classes. But Goldberg helpfully illustrates the problem with choosing the path of most fun and least resistance: "When consumerism is integrated into feminism," she argues, "it dilutes one of our last bulwarks against full-bore materialism" ("Feminism for Sale"). And materialism disempowers the majority—impossible standards of beauty, expensive clothes—and cannot constitute a liberatory political ideology. The author of "Girl, You'll Be a Woman Soon," Tamara Straus, provides a clue to the Girlie puzzle when she writes in a Silicon Valley weekly called *Metro,* that "in creating a feminism of their own, Girlies are repeating a pattern as old as patriarchy" (7). Indeed, patriarchy is the point. This political trend calling itself "feminist" allies emphatically with capitalism and embraces masculine culture as it finds it. And Girlie rhetoric consistently belies this contradiction; descriptions of their own lived experiences frankly deny their stated politics of female empowerment, as Epstein's disclosures above demonstrate. Esptein does not dress Girlie strictly for her own pleasure, but primarily to keep her boss at bay and other women at ease. Girlie politics honor and repeat punishing notions of female beauty and behavior which serves the culture of harassment many women find in the workplace. Nonetheless, these women clearly feel safely ensconced in—something, perhaps a social identity that seems to provide them with political cover.

Girlies reflect an ideology of female beauty that reminds me of my own mother's concerns for appearing "ladylike" when I was growing up. A contradiction of this movement resides in this return to what came before, even as it seeks to define past notions of feminism as in need of revision, for in their commitment to girlish self-presentation, Girlies move backward toward images of, for example, Breck Girls and Miss America contestants. Take for another example, Wendy McElroy's defense of beauty pageants. After insisting that "society has no one standard of beauty," she argues that feminist criticism of beauty pageants "sounds like envy." Moreover, now is the time for feminists to abandon this jealousy, she says, "to lighten up and applaud beauty, not pathologize it." In other words, uptight feminists wrongly identify a beauty hierarchy damaging to women; yet, McElroy elevates beauty as an individual accomplishment, something we ought to "applaud." McElroy, then, engages in the woman-against-woman competition to which feminists object and which she insists does not exist in the pageant industry. But the argument doesn't hold; for, if "no one standard of beauty" were pressed upon women, then there would be no source of jealousy over feeling slighted or left out. The argument doesn't follow because McElroy couches her endorsement of an explicitly insidious element of the American beauty industry in contradictory language; the industry's harmful effect does not exist, she argues, and if it does, blame feminism. We see a similar convolution when Hoff Sommers argues that academic feminists are "compensat[ing] for various heartaches — they're just mad at the beautiful girls" (in Friend, 55). The argument that feminism overreacts to (or, indeed, *invents*) a beauty prejudice is instantly revealed to be disingenuous as these authors endorse and enact precisely that prejudice. As I have argued earlier, these are the politics of collusion, not a movement toward social justice. Like the Do-Me trend celebrating male attention and female sexual surrender, Girlies strike me as a bit too joyful in their celebration of clothes and shoes; defensive, even.

Take, for example, the rationale for the *Girls Gone Wild* franchise. Female apologists for this phenomenon maintain that young, drunk, college-aged women surrounded by crowds and male camera crews expose themselves entirely of their own volition, free of coercion — social or alcoholic. They further maintain that these women engage in liberating moments of rebellious sexual expression that had previously been denied them. Similar arguments have been waged lately in favor of women sharing Howard Stern's love of strippers, *The Man Show*, learning to pole dance or knit. Perhaps in order to survive in a post-backlash world where men still coerce women into positions of passivity and women still feel compelled to dress the part at work, celebrating that oppression might feel to some women momentarily empowering — or at least less difficult, less tiresome. Candace Bushnell (whose "Sex and the City" column inspired the television series) lays out the post-backlash impulse toward sexual capitulation when she describes the hopelessness with which a successful single woman faces the dating scene in New York City. She can "beat [her] head against the wall" looking for love and relationships or she can just "say 'screw it'" and "have sex like a man" (in Goldberg). Here having sex like a man means having sex outside of relationships and commitment. Like Kate Epstein, who feels she must charm both men and women simply to get by at work, or Rebecca Walker, who admits that social awareness is totally tedious, Candace Bushnell just sounds tired and not a little unhopeful. I can sympathize. Being a woman who resists, who doesn't collude in the patriarchal statue quo is often like banging one's head against a wall. Who wouldn't want to just say, "Screw it. I'll be skinny, teeter around on high heels and have sex like a man?" Why not orient one's life and identity around the small things like lipstick or shopping? Why? Because those small things turn out to be big things, and mere distractions from the larger concerns that simply won't go away if we ignore them. Things like the wage gap, sexual violence, poverty, abortion rights, sexual harassment, and domestic violence.

> *Rather than subordinate our differences in the service of the flabby populism* Manifesta *promotes, I would like to see contemporary feminism embrace contention, ... and strengthen its analysis.*
> Michelle Jensen in The Nation

Its superficial connection to the politics of choice makes the Girlie point of view apparently political. Epstein, for example, clearly sees herself as making informed choices, saving herself the trouble of the hopeless project of resisting sexism in her workplace. Yet the choices are stifling and limited — beauty queen status or "having sex like a man." The implicit argument goes something like this: when we emphasize individual choice, we value the diversity of female experience and open the door to a politics of the personal. But we cannot ignore social influences upon women and the tacit privilege inherent to statements which ignore these things. McElroy argues regarding beauty pageants, that all "the women I know are intelligent enough to make such decisions for themselves," and perhaps this is the case. But her circle of friends cannot represent the majority of women. McElroy narrows the vast category of "women" down to those who share her educational and class status, relative wealth and safety. The argument further assumes that an access to education, ideas and social safety are distributed equitably across American culture. Reducing all political arguments to questions of individual choice, in the post-backlash age, actually generalizes all women into a category of an empowered identity untroubling to the powers that be and compliant with the sexist machinations of patriarchal capitalism.

A politics of the personal is one thing; a politics of shopping is entirely another. None of the choices outlined by Girlie feminism address female political advancement, perhaps and only oh, so provisionally, does it address social advancement. Perhaps that's the point; Girlie feminism is not politics at all; it's a trend, a fashion show masquerading as a political movement. And class (not gender) identification provides Girlie ideological backing. Spending power constitutes cultural power in this case. In this case, the rhetoric of choice results in a consumerist notion of female identity and the choices are either not viable choices for most women or mere rhetorical gestures: the choice to not feel oppressed, not see your society as a patriarchy, to "have sex like a man," or simply claim that stripping for money is empowering. As a strictly wishful political movement, Girlie ideology asks very little political action on the parts of its adherents and we find instead an ideology indifferent to the larger social issues with which feminism has historically been concerned. "[T]he perfect kitten-heel pump," then, is indeed the ideal accessory for the Girlie feminist and her contemporary sisters; one can't canvass a neighborhood, for example, in high heels. If we're asking very little of ourselves, then we aren't participating in a movement for social justice — no activism without action.

I feel it necessary to reiterate that my central concern is not to insist that all women be activists, or that they practice or enact feminist politics. But if I'm honest, I have to admit a wish that women who refuse (or simply don't want) to consider their personal and political choices in terms of other women would stop calling themselves feminists. If the term is to retain meaning, ideological traction, it cannot simply be synonymous with "woman." Which is not to say women should or should not marry men, bear children, wear short skirts, wear long skirts, wear makeup, or high heels, Birkenstocks or the color pink; it is to say that moving through the world in our more or less feminine or feminized personal iterations does not make us all feminists, anymore than a familiarity with the language of class makes one a Marxist.

Let me illustrate with a politics-of-the-personal tidbit: I hate my abs, and I really like my legs. I wear skirts above the knee and Nine West black pumps to work as often as I can. I think I look pretty, and that cheers me. Sometimes it even improves my concentration. On the other hand, I feel genuine sadness when I look at my stomach. Now, as a woman calling myself a screaming feminist, I find this perfectly ordinary and also terribly frustrating. I feel compelled to do crunches at the strangest times and wish both that I could get the stomach of my dreams and that I were immune to this desire. My feelings and behavior reveal my own vanity, my susceptibility to cultural messages about female bodies, and the failure of my politics to inoculate me from such feelings. Most women suffer some version of the self-love and self-loathing associated with standards of beauty. Most of us both love and hate looking in the mirror. As a feminist, my job isn't to attack women who have plastic surgery, wear lots of makeup, love cleavage and low-rise jeans or do crunches before job interviews (that's me). And that is not my goal or intent. On the other hand, as a feminist, I feel obligated to help other women and men see women's value as separate from arbitrary standards of bodily perfection — or any other cultural notion that diminishes women's self-assurance or limits their mobility. I can do this through my teaching and social interactions, creating communities of tolerance and acceptance in my classes, and treating the women around me with respect and equanimity. Critiquing cultural imperatives and received ideas about femininity has allowed me to recognize the need for these things and their value to women. Modeling tolerance and acceptance of other women's choices, then, are political gestures — particularly if we understand politics to concern social relations and how those relations reinforce power structures — wearing or not wearing lipstick is not.

As I have said, my interest is with the continued viability of feminism as a political movement, one committed to social justice and bettering the lives of all women — not creating a dress code for all women. A number of factors have been complicating feminist politics since Reagan-Bush, and these complications are the larger concern of this book. À propos of Girlie feminism, complications include the increased commercialization of ideology for women and girls as well as the emergence of anti-feminist conviction as the next big media thing. While Girlie claims the status of a political (that is, feminist) statement, it is also a fashion statement, an image one purchases. Because consumer culture speaks to class, and class to privilege, safety and consumer opportunity, no movement committed to social justice and to the betterment of the lives of large numbers of people constitutes an object one can purchase, own or wear. Feminism isn't a t-shirt any more than a fish is a bicycle.

The battle for definitional control over the terms of feminist politics began almost immediately with the birth of the movement. The discursive backlash with which this study concerns itself has enjoyed a steadfast presence within an American media largely sympathetic to its misogynist point of view. One mode of resistance to this backlash has been to reclaim language used against women on our own behalf. This strategy does not always result in women's progress, however, for, unfortunately, popular media urges women (indeed, everyone) to see political conviction as a kind of brand loyalty, encourages slogan-rich political discourse. But ideology need not fit neatly on a t-shirt nor be cut to the measure of a prevailing editorial ethos that is increasingly anti-feminist, conservative, masculine and white. Debate within the women's movement has been utterly hijacked by an anti-feminist, often openly misogynist, media dominated by voices that see and spin disagreement among women as "cat fights" or, worse, evidence of the movement's failure. My goal is not to monitor feminist discourse for signs of weakness or transgressions against my own point of view; rather, my concern is with appropriations of feminist language and the label itself which serve to undermine women in general and the movement specifically. So when I complain that a position strikes me as adolescent or that tying the feminist label to certain claims drains the politics from the term, I seek to retain feminism's role as a political movement committed to the protections and advancement of all women, not to control other women's behavior. For example, ostensibly powerful and empowering slogans dominate certain media conversations about women; but they tend toward regressive, even infantilizing, language. Think of the ubiquitous and tiresome, "You go, girl!" or the faux self-empowerment of "Girls Rule!" jewelry, "Chicks Kick Ass!" baby tees and "Work It!" refrigerator magnets. Such language only serves the already empowered, the very rich, the very, very safe. No woman isolated from ideas and opportunity through illiteracy, poverty or violence will ever benefit from cheerleading like this.

While we may acquire our own slogans, for example, and call one another "bitch" or "dyke" as ironic demonstrations of our power over language and our refusal to bow to its wounding blows, the Girlie discourse fails to successfully exploit this strategy. For example, while the recovery of the term "girl" through slogans like "girl power" make perfect sense as a gesture toward reclaiming a term that has traditionally been used to disempower young women, the emergence of the term "Girlie" when discussing issues of feminism makes an entirely different statement. This is emphatically not an ironic movement, as much as its rhetoric may indulge in irony. When we say "dyke," we mean the opposite; we declare we do not think of one another as the unkind image to which the term once referred. On the other hand, even among Girlies, the term "girlie" means what it means: a "nod to our joyous youth"; "if I wear this dress, my boss won't harass me"; "the power of beautiful women is not only over men, but also over other women." Those embracing the term do not seek to reorient our notion of the term, then; indeed, Girlie culture embraces uncritically the very denotation of the term: infantilized young women who like toys, or, rather, consumer goods.

The term also names another regressive image of femininity: women dressed, or undressed, to entertain and titillate a specifically masculine erotic appetite. The term enters the Western imagination with the development of the pin-up; erotic images of women, featuring exaggerated breasts, legs and hair, precursors to magazines like *Playboy* and *Penthouse*. Lest we imagine these images to be lost to a quaint past, Pamela Joseph reminds us that "[p]aintings of unclothed women with unreal dimensions can still be found where men tend to congregate: in auto repair shops, army barracks" (in Lasky). Indeed, the calendar-girl genre was invented specifically to serve and underwrite the most conventional needs of patriarchy; in the era of World War II Girlie models satisfied a masculine desire for submissive, highly sexualized, and above all patriotic beauties. As early as the 1930s Ziegfeld was touting his Girlie shows as "Glorifying the American Girl." The typical pin-up featured women in high heals, shorts, panties, or very short skirts, a bustier or other garment calling attention to oversized breasts, not to mention a winning smile. These were women pleased to, well, please, and happy to strip for the cause. Rear end propped high in the air, smiling face beaming over one shoulder, flag draped in the back ground, these Girlies would recruit soldiers as well as inspire patriotic obedience to the needs of war-time America. In fact, "By the 1940s, the American public generally hailed the 'pin-up girls' not as prostitutes but as patriots who boosted the morale of soldiers" (Meyerowitz, 12). The iconic, highly sexualized female support for the cause of conservatism and patriarchy is plainly still with us, witness NFL cheerleaders on Monday nights; Naomi Wolf calling the male body her "rocket"; the covers of books written by Ann Coulter or Maureen Dowd, or any cover of *Maxim* magazine.

Calling oneself "Girlie," then, is a rhetorical movement devoid of irony. I point this out because I am tempted to see much of contemporary Girlie behavior as a kind of sardonic play, to try to understand this "feminism" as truly turning the tables on sexism by, for example, appearing to embrace infantilizing and hyper-sexualizing markers of female identity, like Hello Kitty, cleavage, high heeled shoes and breast implants, only to reject them. How else can one understand grown women doing and saying the things I have observed in this chapter? When a magazine editor publishes the statement that finding the perfect sexy shoe is more important than the suffering in Kosovo or the devastating effects of economic injustice, I cannot but hope that her actual intent is to point out the regressive, utterly indefensible, nature of such a claim as a means of calling American women to action. I further wish (the dream continues) that such claims are intended to expose consumer culture for what it is— the domain of a small, privileged percentage of women and men around the world—and to take the needs of others more seriously.

However, there is little irony in calling oneself Girlie and failing to contradict the very connotations of the term most damaging to women. For example, within representative Girlie magazines like *Jane*, we find the following kinds of advice. Under the headline, "Jane loves Dirty Dancing," the then-editor-in-chief, Jane Pratt, writes:

> I think more women should call themselves Baby [after the lead female character from the film *Dirty Dancing*]. It would've been sexist and demeaning years ago, but now I like it. I don't know. My 2-year-old daughter Charlotte says it 'cause it's easier than saying her own name [*Jane*, Sept. 2005].

One might wonder about the claim that calling oneself "Baby" was once one thing and is now another, but the reference to the film *Dirty Dancing* provides a clue. In that film, a daughter, Frances, whose family all call her Baby, suffers under an oppressive, fretful father. By the end of the film, it becomes clear that he treats Baby this way because he is reluctant to let her grow up. The hero, played by Patrick Swayze, ushers Baby out from under her father's shadow and into womanly sexuality through a style of dance the disapproving parents call Dirty Dancing. The cinematic father certainly found calling his daughter Baby "easier than saying her own name" as it suited his image of Baby as an unsexed, dependent, and very, very young girl more than her sturdy given name, "Frances."

Think of the times when people call each other "Baby" as an indicator of intimacy. We create our own silly baby talk with our families, friends, lovers, and children as an indicator of safety, closeness, and vulnerability. We indulge in baby talk with a lover, for example, to present ourselves to one another as vulnerable, and the fact of trust and safety existing between us makes the gesture not only possible but also a reflection of those very things. The same can be said of calling our toddlers "Baby," as Jane does, in order to acknowledge the vulnerability we so carefully honor and protect in our children. But women cannot assume that the culture at large will extend to them trust and safety, honor or protection; therefore, I cannot imagine the value (political or otherwise) of advising women to label themselves as infantilized versions of femininity. As personal choices, private nicknames make their own kind of sense, of course, and are absolutely no one else's business. Further, we all are entitled to call ourselves whatever we see fit and women especially ought to support other women's right to make such choices free of ideological pressure. My argument here is that while greater choice is a political accomplishment of the women's movement it should not preclude our study of cultural meaning, and the ideological implications of how we use language. Nor should it encourage us to ignore that indeed some choices we make are more or less empowering, and that women's diminished cultural status still limits those choices.

> *So, what happened? Where has the fury,*
> *the passion, the combat boots gone?*
> Apryl Lundsten

Somewhere along the way, anti-feminist women abandoned their willingness to distinguish among choices, obliging themselves instead to judge all choices as equivalent. At least publicly. And this retreat from critique has resulted in an antagonism to any criticism of choices made by women calling themselves feminist. Too often in mainstream conversations, making these observations is seen as mean spirited or disrespectful toward other women. I would argue the contrary, that such reactions simply reflect the misogynist myth of the cat fight, the sexist assumption that women cannot disagree reasonably. I make these observations in the hope that women would take care of themselves and each other, and carefully consider their choices with this care in mind. Critiques of female behaviors by female writers doesn't have to be catty or condescending; no need for Roiphe's dismissive elitism, Paglia's smug condescension or Denfeld's attacks on rape victims, if our argument remains centered finally on social justice for women.

Think of the riot grrrl movement during which young women announced no expectation of safety, honor or protection, and performed through their Girlie dress both an understanding of that fact and their anger toward it. This dress was adapted unambiguously to express a political critique of where the clothing came from and the damage it can to do girls and women. When riot grrrls initially tore their fishnets, matched micro minis with combat boots and applied make-up heavily enough to conceal rather than flatter their features, they were performing a smash-the-state mindset; they manipulated conventions that disempowered women in order to make those things obvious and to begin to turn the power tables. Riot grrrls wore near-ruined or wildly iconoclastic combinations of traditionally female clothing—sweater sets with bare legs, screaming guitars and DIY (do it yourself) hair—to enact the dissolution of mass market gender commodification. If oppressively body-conscious clothing were not visibly oppressive, and were instead a viable indicator of female power, then the riot grrrl gesture would have been impossible to make, would have had no meaning at all. So, while Girlies often visually reflect riot grrrl affiliation, they simultaneously disavow that movement's most obvious goal—of freeing women from oppressive body, beauty and fashion standards. The divergent trajectories of these movements reveal further their divergent ideological alliances. When riot grrrl sensibilities (musical and fashion) were exploited by the marketplace by faux, "girl power" pop stars from Fionna Apple to the Spice Girls to Avril Lavigne and by fashion marketers, that movement went back underground where it continued to thrive on its own terms. One the other hand, when Girlie hit the mass market, it was home and began residing comfortably within the covers of shopping, fashion and girl-power magazines like *Bitch, Bust, Maxie* and *Jane*.

Taking another example from the same issue of *Jane* cited above, consider the frivolous turn an interview with Hilary Duff takes when she begins discussing her political convictions. When asked if she supports "any environmental or political causes," Duff answers that she "works for the Armed Forces Foundation" and explains the services that organization provides:

> It raises money for families that have a parent serving overseas, giving supplies, clothes, toys.... When I'm in Washington [D.C.], I go to the National Naval Medical Center in Bethesda [Md.] for injured soldiers. Their stories are incredible [140].

In response to Duff's concern for military families and the injured, the *Jane* interviewer asks: "Is it scary? Are there guys with limbs missing?" (140). This interviewer asks Duff the kind of question children ask one another; he might as well have asked if she were "grossed out" by all the sick people in the hospital. Although the founder and former editor-in-chief, Jane Pratt, promised this magazine would blend fashion magazine sensibilities with feminist politics, the publication generally maintains an ironic distance from any issues it may cover and a condescending tone toward its female subjects especially. So when the male interviewer asks if Hilary Duff found a military hospital "scary," he indicates not only his own brand of sexist condescension, but also the magazine's attitude toward women and politics. This representative publication of Girlie feminism undermines the seriousness of politics and activism, assuming such things are *too scary for girls*. The notion of politics as a little scary appears with some regularity in this publication for young women. For example, a "Rant" section of the online *Jane* asks readers to consider if "we should come up with a new word to replace 'feminism' so *women who are scared of that label* will finally join the equality cause?" (my emphasis).

The question posed to Duff about "limbs missing" is similarly outrageous and indeed sexist. The inquiry does not cultivate the hip MTV-style detachment to which the magazine (and interviewer) plainly aspires, but reveals instead a crude disinterest in the face of others' suffering. One does not inquire after "guys with limbs missing" with such bald insensitivity unless one were: first, physically intact oneself; and second, in no danger of losing one's limbs any time soon. Further, one cannot imagine the interviewer asking, say, Johnny Depp or Tom Cruise the same question. As an agent for *Jane* magazine the male interviewer expected no resistance, or strong reaction, from his female subject to his impolite question. He expected no lectures on the impertinence of his remarks or their assumptions about his subject. Whether he got any or not, we cannot tell, for the editors surely tailored the exchange to fit the magazine's larger editorial ethos. Irrespective of what Hilary Duff herself may or may not have actually expressed to the interviewer, the article as it stands models the Girlie approach to politics and reflects not the subject (Duff's) lack of political engagement, but the magazine's itself.

In order to bring the interview to a close, Jones says, "Okay, somehow we've gotten way too serious" (140) and dropping politics altogether since politics are "scary" like the term "feminism" to Jane's readers, shifts into a mocking description of how "Hilary's people" refer to her as a "quadruple threat"; Jones only counts three things his subject does well, singing, acting and producing a line of clothing. The fourth must be "something else I haven't figured out yet" (140). Such an attitude suggests that Duff strikes the interviewer as a mere girl, a weak female subject who offers no resistance to rhetorical aggression or crude questions.

A quick look at the editorial page reveals even more about *Jane*'s Girlie status. The mission statement plainly aligns the magazine with the Third Wave and Girlies in its appeal to young women and a new brand of political engagement:

> Connecting with the under-30 crowd today means ignoring cultural, ethnic and sexual-preference stigmas because they never had them in the first place. Music, frank talk and humor are the common ground with this generation.
>
> Jane Pratt, Editor-in-Chief

In fact, one will find very little "frank talk" in Jane; irony dominates issues of this magazine. Irony is largely a privilege of the relatively well-off; to say one thing and mean another indicates that what one say need not be tied to political realities like violence against women, abortion rights, voter fraud or the wage gap, for example. Being ironic, further, requires a kind of class homogeneity; the body of knowledge to which one refers in ironic conversation needs to be understood by one's audience for the ironic humor or effect to take hold. So, when Jones concludes his piece on Hilary Duff with a list of ironic album title suggestions — for example, "Hilary 'n' Morrissey — Is It Really So Strange?"— he assumes an audience who shares the same cultural cachet. Unfortunately, acquiring cultural cachet takes time and money. And *Jane*'s demographic information demonstrates that its readers have plenty of both: circulation and demographic information reveals youth-culture-class connection within *Jane*'s readership: 87 percent of readers are females whose median age is 29 and whose median household income, $75,284 (*Jane*, online, Sept 2005).

Further, in the mission statement quoted above Jane Pratt articulates the limits of a Girlie commitment to social justice when she claims that in order to connect "with the under-30 crowd today," she and the editorial staff at *Jane* have chosen to *ignore* "cultural, ethnic and sexual-preference stigmas." The language is telling, of course; like Kim France of *Lucky* magazine, Pratt does not seek to overturn or challenge these stigmas, only to ignore them, belying the fact that these magazines contain no authentic political goals. Hip detachment stands in for political engagement, and indeed this constitutes an ideological statement — one that relieves one's obligation to act on any group's behalf besides one's own. It is an ideological statement, then, particularly in its supplementary claim that the under-30 crowd "never had" the "cultural, ethnic and sexual-preference stigmas" the magazine commits itself to ignoring. Consistently, Girlie discourse asserts deeply romanticized ideals of women and culture. Categorical declarations like "never" and "in the first place" indicate not only an entrenched refusal to interrogate nuances of cultural interaction, but also a privileged position from which it is safe to do so

> It's a business. In a perfect world maybe we'd stop and change things. But we know the formula. We know what works.
> Mia Leist, tour manager, *Girls Gone Wild*

It's a gorgeous strategy, seamless, brilliant — and totally depressing. It works because women do this to other women; and in the case of post-backlash prefix feminism, these are very young women. Take the *Girls Gone Wild* franchise in which a woman, Mia Leist, a 25-year-old *Girls Gone Wild* (*GGW*) a tour manager, praises a woman she calls "Crazy Debbie." "I love her," Mia explains in a South Beach bar where *GGW* is filming, "She's like a *Girls Gone Wild* groupie. She gets so many girls for us" (Levy). Lest we imagine her franchise contributes at all to the exploitation of women, she argues that "It's not like we're creating this" ("this" being young, drunken women flashing their breasts, masturbating and stripping for *GGW*'s cameras). In an interview with Ariel Levy, author of *Female Chauvinist Pigs*, Leist continues, "This is happening whether we're here or not. Our founder was just smart enough to capitalize on it"; of course, the same could be said of prostitution, child pornography, price gouging after Hurricane Katrina or stealing signals from your local cable company. Dreadful things exist around us; we expose our politics and characters in how we respond to them.

Of course, if one's neighbor does steal cable, one could always blame feminism, as the IWF does just about everything, including women's sexuality and the exploitation of women in general. According to a report by that organization entitled, "Sex (Ms.)education: What Young Women Need to Know (But Won't Hear in Women's Studies) About Sex, Love, and Marriage," feminism's presence in academe and women's greater access to birth control have combined to drive women into increasingly sexualized behaviors. "It is difficult to escape the conclusion that, at times, the feminist movement is not remedying a lack of information about safe sex," the report argues, "but seeking to entirely divorce it from morality and to encourage more sexual activity" (10). Based on this report Linda Chavez, staff writer for the conservative Catholic Exchange.com, concludes that feminism must bear the blame for sexist exploitations like *GGW*. Chavez asks, "Could baring their breasts be the newest symbolic act of young feminists?"

We see a similarly untenable, yet superficially convincing, argument that claims strippers and *Playboy* models empower themselves by exposing their bodies for money. Indeed, an article in *The Journal of Popular Culture* recently argued that "If a strong, confident woman is willing to pose nude (and stand up to a potential backlash), then she must be very tough indeed" (Beggan 810). This notion aligns perfectly with anything Camille Paglia has ever said about Madonna, for example, or Katie Roiphe's claim that Monica Lewinsky "used her personal power over the President to get results." In their own ways both the conservative and seemingly more progressive responses to women's bodies quoted above ignore the vexed relationship between choice and enculturation. Obviously, *Playboy* presents supposedly "tough" playmates as a standard masculine fantasy of a strong woman gladly submitting to masculine desire, just as Madonna brilliantly markets a similar, though arguably much shrewder, S&M fantasy. None of these things happen in a cultural vacuum; women might be dressed provocatively, dancing and drinking themselves silly in South Beach most nights, but *Girls Gone Wild* fundamentally alters and intensifies the terms of that behavior, moving it toward prostitution and violence and guaranteeing that nearly everyone but the naked, used women will benefit.

An interrogations of the terms used to describe female behavior is missing from this media-generated and approved feminism. When *Playboy* spreads can be said to signify female empowerment, when masturbating in public earns the female performers a t-shirt and the male founders of the video empire $100 million, women are in trouble.

It has become a truism in American culture that women own a unique power in their bodies; that women can gain access to power through literal or rhetorical striptease. Let's define power, then. First, it must be differentiated from simply gaining attention — otherwise anyone shouting "Fire!" in a crowded theater would be politically empowered — and divorced from masculine susceptibility to and distraction by female sexuality. To attract attention and, for example, to con a few beers out of a starry-eyed man is not a sign of power; it's just a few beers. Nonetheless, we frequently hear such scenarios used as evidence that the tables have turned politically and culturally in women's favor, that men are, as one television hunk put it recently in *Men's Health*, "tired of having their balls cut off!" Definitions of power absolutely must be conceived outside of this masculine frustration; just because men find themselves occasionally under the erotic sway of women and don't always like the way it turns out doesn't put more women in Congress, close the wage gap, increase access to abortion, reduce incidents of rape, domestic abuse or sexual harassment. Definitions of power must also be conceived outside of women's pleasure in certain kinds of attention. If women want to attract masculine attention, that's cool. If they want men buying them drinks. That's cool, too, but it's not politics. And it's got absolutely nothing to do with power. When fleeting social validation constitutes our political ideology, when a desire for sexual validation replaces social consciousness, then we are no longer engaged in a genuinely political mission. We're flirting.

Power reveals itself in cultural safety, in having one's choices not limited by threats of sexual violence, reduced wages, harassment or social stigmas; it is involved in enjoying equal access to wealth and positions of influence. Women, then, are disempowered in that our choices, far more than men's, are curtailed by pervasive and prejudicial notions regarding female behavior and proper uses of the female body. Therefore, to strip for a trucker hat, participate in beauty pageants or buy the right lipstick cannot rightly be called gestures of political empowerment. What they actually demonstrate is the durability of the divide-and-conquer mechanisms of patriarchal capitalism: that is, as long as stripping defines women as sexually vulnerable, beauty pageants pit women against one another, and consumer purchases reinforce class divides.

Now, before I am accused of being one of those "Feminist professors ... uniformly hostile to anything market-oriented" (Scott, 8), let me again say that I am not insisting women reject all (or any) of the social ephemera we all enjoy. Indeed, my "feminist professor" friends and I take pleasure in lipstick, shoes, great fitting jeans, the next episode of *The L Word* or *Lost* as much as the next gal. What we also recognize is that none of those things constitutes political statements or the essence of our political identities — and the dangerous ridiculousness of suggesting that they do. Just as Girlies celebrate "that which once symbolized [women's] oppression," Scott insists that the difference between feminist academics and "women's rights-oriented professionals" is in how we dress. Can that really be the case? That our clothing choices define our differences and determine who and what we are politically? As I have argued, such statements drain the politics out of "women's rights" and "feminism," and replace them with images of petty women competing for, in this case, Plainest of Them All.

Of course, fostering regressive stereotypes does pay off for certain famous women, who often enrich themselves through their appearance, through a willingness to expose their bodies to the public gaze. But is wealth a sign of power? It certainly is a better starting place than poverty.

But even more than wealth, I would argue, we must consider control over one's body and its safety. So, when for example, Pamela Anderson exposes herself, she is sober and forwarding the career of her choice; she chooses when and where her breasts, thighs, butt and mouth will be publicly consumed. I would argue that her control over her body, her ability to decide where and under what circumstances she exposes it, does demonstrate a certain empowerment on her part. The same cannot be said of the women in the *GGW* videos, most women in the sex or porn industries, or even *Playboy* centerfolds.

Katha Pollitt laments in *The Nation*, "Eating disorders, breast implants, stripper chic, Queen for a Day weddings, the resurgence of 'girl' and 'chick'—it's not a happy story." And she's right. Even worse, the mainstream media elevate these things to the level of political gestures and empowering choices for women. It's not a happy story, indeed, when we embrace regressive images of ourselves, call ourselves and each other infantilizing names, and dismiss feminism as a tired anachronism clinging to our out-of-date mothers. My hope is to help reverse the trajectory of this narrative, return conversations about feminism to issues of politics, and get back to the business of helping women—whether we do these things in Blahniks or Birkenstocks.

5

What a Wonderful World It Would Be: Feminist Bashing and National Calamity

it seems clear to me that women's liberation did not introduce a feminine humanizing quality into male culture. Instead, ambitious women have taken up traditional male roles, allowing men to move even further into the aggressiveness of macho male behavior.
Georgie Anne Geyer

Few groups have suffered the kind of sustained and generally unearned public abuse that American feminists have since the Reagan era. In the past 25 years, feminism has been blamed for the decline of liberal education, increased divorce rates, false reports of rape on campuses, the failure of young women in school, the failure of young men in school, the Tailhook sex abuse scandal, female sex offenders, violations of the Geneva convention at Abu Ghraib, the feminization and social confusion of American men, the spread of venereal disease, the 09/11/01 attacks on New York and the Pentagon, a lack of sympathy for victims of Hurricane Katrina, increased incidents of rape and domestic violence, the U.S. defeat in Viet Nam, declining birthrates, the deterioration of the American family, as well as the supposed overmedication of children and American culture's preoccupation with "victimhood." Are you a grown woman who, while holding down a job, running a household and raising children, finds herself feeling a bit fatigued? Blame feminism: the movement forced you into the job market. Are you single and would rather be married? Feminism is your problem: it has ruined your fashion sense and rendered you unmarriageable. Are you stuck in an abusive marriage? Feminism, again: without it, you'd never have heard the term "domestic violence." From the patently false to the totally ridiculous, such claims have become a staple of popular culture; and provided fodder for the careers of myriad writers and pundits. Indeed, one journalist recently published a book predicated on the assertion that despite her obvious charms and appeal, feminism has kept her desperate and dateless for years.

> *Gender equality cannot, all alone, bring about a just and peaceful world.*
> Barbara Ehrenreich

Claims against feminism grow progressively more alarmist, increasingly categorical and uninterrogated throughout the period of media conservatism and anti-feminism which is the subject of this book. Early on, the backlash language of the Reagan-Bush era included the skewed use of statistics about women's issues, like fertility rates or female marriageability after the age of forty. For example, "By the end of the 80s," Susan Faludi wrote in 1991s *Backlash: The Undeclared War Against American Women*, "women had become bitterly familiar" with such "'statistical' developments" as: "A college-educated, unwed woman at thirty has a 20 percent likelihood of marriage, at thirty-five a 5 percent chance, and at forty no more than a 1.3 percent chance" (3). The media announced findings like these at every opportunity and constructed news events around them; remember the infamous *Newsweek* issue a decade ago announcing that it was more likely that a forty-year-old woman would be killed by a terrorist than find a husband and the weeks of subsequent coverage of the "man shortage" that story produced.

Anti-feminist conviction turns out to be fantastically elastic; with each media event, anti-feminism modifies itself accordingly. Immediately after 09/11, for example, abandoning feminism became the right thing to do. For example, like the Do-Me feminism appearing in men's magazines a decade before, post–09/11 commentary insisted that the most traditional notions of female identity would best serve the needs of American culture. If we don't renounce feminism, the terrorists win. These attacks on women and feminism are even less subtle than before, generally eschewing the niceties of misleading mathematics in favor of personal attack and the language of crisis management. It has become commonplace to find feminists described as rotten people, petty, malicious, backbiting women who may be even more prone to violence than men. As media-driven anti-feminism has grown, it has also evolved a more, shall we say, organic strategy. News events no longer need be organized around a statistical claim or grain of research flotsam, not that this doesn't still happen. The strategy more common today is the attachment of feminist guilt to scandals which evolve out of issues and events not specifically to do with women or women-centered politics. So, we don't awake to headlines announcing the "Man Shortage" as often these days as we find declarations on the *New York Times* OpEd page that feminist progress doomed Monica Lewinsky to her fate, essays in *Reason* magazine declaring feminism responsible for compassion fatigue experienced by victims of Hurricane Katrina, or articles in the *Wall Street Journal* detailing feminist guilt in Abu Ghraib.

This chapter examines the manner in which critics borrow post-backlash claims against feminism to support American military aggression and violations of international laws in the wake of 09/11, particularly the Abu Ghraib torture scandal. Coverage of that scandal exposed the immensity of anti-feminist sentiment pervading the U.S. media. Post–09/11, we find feminism no longer responsible for such banal disappointments as crises in American education and women's decisions to stay single longer; rather, feminism becomes the very source of the atrocity in question.* In the wake of Abu Ghraib we heard that allowing women into the American military so thoroughly perverted that institution that all moral control was lost, the rules of the Geneva Convention all but forgotten, sexual restraint abandoned.

Moreover, the abuse of prisoners in Abu Ghraib by female soldiers was, according to an editorialist for the *Union Leader of Manchester*, Bernadette Malone, a patently "American" event because "women were among the alleged perpetrators." Another headline taunts: "Abu Ghraib is a Feminist's Dream." In rhetorical situations like these, feminism must function as an abstraction, an idea that has infiltrated and perverted the American social order, and as an abstraction, it remains divorced entirely from actual human beings. Otherwise the above accusations would be too irresponsible, too fantastic to print, and no reasonable person would take them seriously. For, to publicly allege that folks one has never met, has

---

Certain claims regarding 09/11/01 and beyond are obviously screwy, like Jerry Falwell's claims made on The 700 Club *that "the pagans, and the abortionists, and the feminists, and the gays and the lesbians who are actively trying to make that an alternative lifestyle, the ACLU, People For the American Way, all of them ... helped this happen"; and Ann Coulter's venomous barbs: "We should invade their countries, kill their leaders and convert them to Christianity" (*National Review Online *September 13, 2001). Such claims do not seriously interest me here.*

no first-hand knowledge of, condone torture and sexual humiliation is libelous stuff, indeed — unless, that is, one is castigating an already-embattled category. And that is precisely how such aspersions have come to be taken: harmless political hyperbole, authorized by a mainstream willingness to ignore that feminists are actually people working for the betterment of women's and men's lives. Stripped of a human center, the movement functions rhetorically as a mere notion infuriating to its critics; and therefore criticism, no matter how noxious, doesn't seem to touch anyone's actual friend, wife, sister, partner or mother. The politics of abstraction emerges as an effective strategy, then, for it inoculates critics from accusations of taking their ideas too far.

And it emboldens them to speculate wildly. Elaine Donnelly, the president of the Center for Military Readiness, asserted in an interview that American feminism created the environment that resulted in the abuse of prisoners at Abu Ghraib. Regarding the women in the now infamous photos, including the one of Lynndie England humiliating Iraqi men, Donnelly warns that "these women may not have been aware of" the influence feminism exerted upon their behavior and, in effect, uses the insidious influence of feminism to excuse their actions in Abu Ghraib. "[T]hey've been raised in a culture" which discourages "respect between men and women," and therefore, she argues, tormenting Iraqi prisoners "becomes a little bit more understandable even though it's not excusable" (Thibault). Feminism made them do it. In other words, feminist-inflected thinking leads women to abandon their moral consciences; for no feminist would turn down the opportunity to violently humiliate a man. Donnelly tells her interviewer, David Thibault, she has no doubt that many feminists are "quite fond" of the photo of the Iraqi prisoner on a leash because it depicts actions "demeaning to a man" and feminists are all for demeaning "any man" they can get their hands on. The horrifying events at Abu Ghraib, she argues, represent "exactly what feminists have dreamed of." The rhetorical strategy is unmistakably cynical: the American imperialist machine is off the hook if mistreatment of prisoners is the result of a feminist ideology saturating the American military and confusing the female soldiers at Abu Ghraib. Even more importantly so are George W. Bush, Donald Rumsfeld, Condalezza Rice, et al. Reckless foreign policy, unrestrained military aggression, failures along the chain of command in Iraq, violations of international laws are not to blame, the argument suggests; rather, the women's movement — a movement for social justice — must bear the entirety of the responsibility for abuses at Abu Ghraib.

> *Ah, feminism! The perfect fall gal!*
> Michelle Cottle

Feminist political pressure has been largely responsible for the movement of women not only into the American military but also closer to combat; in response to such pressure, President Clinton relaxed restrictions against female involvement in war zones in 1994. In the world of mainstream anti-feminism, what ought to be celebrated as a success is positioned as a failure, and feminism's commitment to social change used as evidence of feminism's wholesale appropriation of women's lives and wrong-headed notions about female ambition and desire. Events that violate the conservative myth of American moral superiority, that threaten to reveal the lie of that myth — in this case, by exposing serious missteps on the part of the Bush administration in Iraq — tend to be recast by the conservative press as the result of progressive politics, often through an attack on feminist politics. While the press consistently turns to feminism as a fall gal, feminists are not alone; the list of other liberal targets includes gays, pro-lifers (also known as "pro-abortionists"), and Hillary Clinton. Images of Lynndie England's gleeful torment of naked Iraqi men horrify, we are told, because women are natural born nurturers, and in all other American wars, according to the same cultural mythology, women tended the home fires under a protective veil of moral righteousness. Before feminism, American men left home to fight the good fight; after feminism that fight became tainted by women's presence. Feminists want things to change; real women want them to stay the same. Once removed from the domestic sphere and allowed into the world of men, women become toxic; therefore, returning home to traditional gender roles is the only answer. And yet when a famous feminist confesses her own long-standing faith in one of those traditional notions of femininity, female compassion, the press calls the very notion of female nurturing a feminist myth. Obviously, the anti-feminist argument collapses under its own contradictions: women function simultaneously as scions of American goodness (at home) and instruments of depravity (in combat).

Barbara Ehrenreich's famous confession of dismay and disappointment over events at Abu Ghraib has been misunderstood and misused as evidence of both feminist arrogance and feminist naïveté regarding female behavior. In a commencement speech at Barnard College in 2004 Ehrenreich discloses the following about the images of Abu Ghraib then saturating the media: "These photos turned my stomach.... But they did something else to me: they broke my heart." She admits she holds no fantasies about the "United States mission in Iraq"; however, "it turns out," she confesses, "I did have some illusions about women." Ehrenreich's admission of personal disappointment and her willingness to examine her own long-held beliefs about women do not square with the likes of Third Wave, Do-Me, Girlie, or most other post-backlash responses to women's issues in general. Those iterations of feminist thought suggest women should beware of other women (not critically examine their own belief systems) and, further, be especially wary of feminist women. These arguments in no way reflect Ehrenreich's hopeful notions of politics, progress and the value of open debate. Mainstream media outlets propelled bits of Ehrenreich's speech around the globe, using it to prove alternately feminist naïveté regarding women's true nature and feminist arrogance regarding women's natural moral rectitude.

What was less well reported was what Ehrenreich *also* said in the rest of that commencement speech. She observed that not only is feminism "in terrible trouble worldwide," but also that feminism is only "minimally about the achievement of equality with men." To her mind the greatest threat to the "feminist project" comes from "fundamentalism of all kinds — Christian as well as Islamic." She urges her audience to recognize fundamentalism within their own society and to embrace "a moral vision that goes beyond gender equality." "To cite," she concludes, "an old — and far from naïve — feminist saying: 'If you think equality is the goal, your standards are too low.'" Tellingly, excerpts like this one, which demonstrates Ehrenreich's reasoned and realistic approach to women and politics, received virtually no attention in the press. Her argument here is about doing the hard work of moving a women-centered ideology forward through the vagaries of new world events. Rather than looking toward mythic better days past, Ehrenreich faces resolutely toward the future and the work left to be done in the name of feminism, like fighting ideological and religious extremism and the oppression they produce. This position contradicts both the master narrative of Feminism Past haunting much of the rhetoric of the post-backlash/anti-feminist age, as well as the prevailing misogyny in Abu Ghraib coverage. Ehrenreich further challenges a number of key tenets of media anti-feminism. For she exposes the notion of a monolithic Feminism Past as a mistake, and admits that she herself was guilty of at least partly misunderstanding who women have been. She also rejects the suggestion that the women's movement wants to turn women into men; the women's movement wants to make women even better, she says, if better means more compassionate, less inclined to war. Finally, she sees the work left for feminism. Not only isn't the work of feminism finished; it hasn't really gotten started, she says.

Enter Peggy Noonan to set the record straight. She opens a *Wall Street Journal* editorial entitled, "A Humiliation for America," with a categorical statement about coverage of the Abu Ghraib scandal. Reports of American abuse were no doubt "hyped and sensationalized." The problem actually is not as bad as we are being made to think, she suggests, but in the event it turns out to be the case that American soldiers did horrible things, blame feminism. For surely feminism's pernicious influence sits at the heart of this scandal. Without feminism, this aberration in American behavior could not have taken place, she explains, for feminism has created a certain kind of female monster. For example, Noonan claims that when she first saw pictures of Lynndie England abusing Iraqi prisoners, she thought about gender politics. The photo did not show "equality" among the sexes, but rather, "mutual degradation." Indeed, there is nothing resembling equality about the horrors of Abu Ghraib — nothing about feminism, either. Yet, in the context of Noonan's argument, "equality" serves as code for feminist insistence that women be allowed access to combat positions in the military. And, as she slips from that observation to the following question, we see what she thinks of "equality": "Can anyone," she asks, "imagine a WAC of 1945, or a WAVE of 1965, acting in this manner?" She answers her own question as follows: she can't. WACs and WAVEs, she explains, weren't just members of the armed forces, "*they were women*" (my emphasis). Further, these women felt no obligation to behave like men "or men at their worst." "But the young woman ... in the scandal photo," she notes, "looked, shall we say, confused about these issues." So, in the 40s and 60s military women felt more empowered than they do now to resist behaving like one of the boys. Yet in the wake of the women's movement that won them entry into the military and then moved them closer to combat, female soldiers serving in Iraq remain confused about feminist politics. The argument runs off-track and turns frivolous; surely, Noonan does not in fact believe that England was thinking about the history of women in the American military when she posed for the scandal photo. England's countenance was nothing to do with gender "issues"; she was torturing a prisoner over whom she momentarily enjoyed power and authority. Noonan stages a disingenuous salute to WACs and WAVEs as a cynical distraction from her implication of feminist politics and any women in the American military — the vast majority of whom do so with honor and at great peril — who might embrace those politics. These women, it seems, do not merit the title "women." Perhaps Noonan meant to write "*real* women," like the WACs and WAVEs of earlier wars she mentions, who were non-combatant members of the army and navy, and whose role was primarily to happily provide support for the men fighting abroad.

Here we see how terminology consistently haunts the feminist movement. Noonan claims the term "women" for herself, as if to redefine it as an honorific, and glibly attributes which females are (or are not) worthy the title. Indeed, the following characterization of WAC spirit by Eleanor Roosevelt seems in keeping with Noonan's notion of proper womanhood:

> They take everything in the spirit of soldiers, keeping their troubles to themselves. They suffer from homesickness, they experience the hardships of severe climates and the actual perils of war, yet they remain ever cheerful. Their smiles are wonderful medicine for the men they care for ["Women," *Reader's Digest*, 1944].

As paragons of womanly selflessness and care, WACs posed no threat to prevailing notions of proper gender behavior. When they took on masculine roles and took "everything in the spirit of soldiers," they retained their feminine cheerfulness and suffered no ill effects from masculine influence, or the horrors of war, à la the ever cheerful Girlies featured on the patriotic posters of the same period. They buttressed the good work of American men, quietly and without complaint. Significantly, Noonan seems to be confirming that American men in Abu Ghraib behaved quite badly; she longs in this piece for the old days when women didn't have to look to the "coarse and vulgar part of their nature ... to prove they were one of the guys." She does not deny that American men engage in barbarous, indefensible acts of cruelty in war; still, she gives those men a pass and singles out military women as all the more guilty for seeking to behave like men and failing to behave like proper "women." It appears that in Noonan's world, which tries to ignore the influence of feminism, most women could avoid the former (behaving like men) and embrace the latter (proper femininity). Still the argument cannot resist a feint in feminism's directions: Noonan could not imagine WACs and WAVEs engaging in such conduct because "they were *women*" — not *feminists*.

Noonan throws feminism out as the welcome distraction that it is for her hyper-conservative audience, a kind of lure drawing attention away from the actual causes of the Abu Ghraib disaster, like illegal or repugnant orders, the horror of war, or (gasp) the corruption of George W. Bush's administration. Moreover, Noonan presses her point that feminism and the changes it has wrought upon the armed forces explains the confusion of the woman in what she calls "the scandal photo."* In this *Wall Street Journal* piece, Noonan seriously undertakes to invite readers to see in Lynndie England's snarling cruelty a confusion about (and clear recognition of) the changed status of women in the world brought about by feminism. The "issues" of women debasing themselves to fit into the military world of men, insists Noonan, confounded Lynndie England: "she looked, shall we say, confused about these issues." Noonan asks us to believe that at the time the photo was snapped, England was perplexed about her gender identity and that she was actively reflecting upon her role as a woman in the American armed forces and, moreover, was considering the influence of feminist politics upon her career and behavioral choices. On the face of it, the argument is untenable, politically motivated, and just absurd. For example, Noonan argues earlier in the piece that "the dim might miss" her point; yet "the intelligent" will probably "get it."

Indeed, one would have to possess a very special kind of intellect to "get" that England's behavior stemmed from ideological confusion, which Noonan apparently spied out through close examination of that photo of England grinning maliciously and holding the leash. England's expression was "chilling," according to Noonan and, "[p]erhaps," she continues, "we should be worrying about that, too." The political cynicism here is award winning; no reasonable person would assume that England was snarling in ideological confusion, but rather that she was enmeshed in horrifying circumstances and the prevailing culture of abuse saturating Abu Ghraib. As one last bit of political deflection, the final line of the editorial asks readers to look away from the actions of the Bush administration and to concern ourselves instead with feminism's influence upon our culture; the "*that*" which should concern us refers to "chilling" moral degradation brought about by feminism itself and poor Lynndie's ideological confusion. In a perfectly seamless rhetorical move, Noonan ends with a cynical distraction and a cheap shot. She uses feminism to explain away the Bush administration's tolerance for torture, and she uses torture at Abu Ghraib to demonstrate the weaknesses and dangers of feminism.

Noonan laments, "This is not who we are," and she fears these events will diminish the standing of American troops worldwide. While "this" is not who "we" (read: Noonan's notion of America) are, it is apparently who feminists are. And while the "scandal photo" should not be used to tar-

---

The one showing Lynndie England pointing to a naked Iraqi prisoner.

nish the characters of the (male) troops, it shall be used by her to tarnish the character of women in the military and the movement that helped put them there. Within the anti-feminist media paradigm, when the post-backlash dream of women's return to conventionality fails to materialize, any difficulty for women, like sexual harassment, glass ceilings, balancing work and family, even domestic abuse and rape, becomes evidence of feminism's breakdown. Similarly, these events provide ample opportunity to argue in favor of a conservative notion of American femininity. In the case of America's War on Terror, the war itself calls attention to myriad feminist sins. For example, coverage of the war in Iraq repeatedly paints women as too weak to "carry a medium-sized backpack" and "too vicious" to be trusted; feminists are also accused of being either painfully naïve about women's capacity for violence or ignorant of women's feminization (softening) of the armed services. When not being blamed for women indulging their violent tendencies, feminism is blamed for forcing women to suppress those same tendencies when they join the armed forces. Either way, feminists exert a insidious influence upon the military. (See the Jessica Lynch story.) Finally, the media story goes, in most aspects of life feminism wrongly encourages women to engage in behavior more rightly reserved for men. Contradictory messages like these reveal a number of misogynous rhetorical threads running through American popular discourse, and one consistent truth: conservative media have grown very comfortable with blaming feminism for the ills of not just American culture but also American foreign policy. Anti-feminism has a singular, sweeping goal when addressing the war on terror: to demonstrate that "The Bush administration never makes a mistake," and to underwrite "the ideologically soothing notion that Abu Ghraib is the sad, but predictable, by-product of permitting women in the military" (Cottle).

> *But the idea that it's shocking that women could commit these acts is preposterous. We're all human beings, good and bad.*
> Robert Galley, Letter to the Editor, *Buffalo News*

Discussions of Abu Ghraib often suggest that because feminists argued for women's inclusion in the armed forces, feminists must bear the entirety of blame for any misdeeds done by women while serving. No such categorical declarations are made of men in the military, obviously. Only political movements contravening the status quo or threatening to expose misdeeds on the parts of those who hold power are credited with more influence than they could ever truly hold over their members; think, for example, of the movements for women's suffrage, abolition or Civil Rights, all of which at some point or another were professed to be precursors to the ends of all that our culture valued, held dear, or believed in. To make such uncompromising claims is to reveal the anxieties provoked by movements for social justice and to attempt to undermine or end them. Investing this kind of culture-destroying power in these movements escapes the boundaries of reason, but the rhetorical strategy makes good sense; for example, if we hold the feminists working on behalf of women in combat responsible for all women's conduct, then the movement cannot help but weaken under the weight of the first misdeeds or mistakes to come to light.

In her opinion piece, "Here's the Real Issue in Abuse Photos," Bernadette Malone barely suppresses a gleeful misogyny underwriting her argument. First, she contends that if "female personnel" had not been present, then abuses at Abu Ghraib would have been interpreted quite differently. Had men forced other men to strip, masturbate and simulate sexual acts without a female presence, she writes, the activities "would not be sexual, per se." Ideology is a powerful motivator, and fueled by anti-feminism and a none too thinly veiled misogyny, Malone presses her point to argue that these events would surely not contravened "military and international laws" had women absented themselves from them. What is the "Real Issue" of her title, then? Women in the military, of course, for they put military men at risk. And not by failing to shoot straight or follow orders, but by casting bad behavior in an even worse light. Can reports that include stripping Iraqi men, piling them in humiliating poses, and forcing them to masturbate or simulate masturbation in the presence of others be cast in a worse light? Can penetrating prisoners with light sticks and photographing these humiliations along with the bodies of the dead be made more horrific? For whom could a photo of a naked female prisoner sodomized by one U.S. soldier as another pulls her hair savagely, forcing her head back and exposing her agonized grimace for the camera, be made worse or to seem more awful? But no matter who was in that prison, no matter their political bent or gender, American soldiers tortured, humiliated and raped Iraqi prisoners. And photographed the whole thing. Apropos of Malone's argument, regardless of who was in the room, this was rape. Apropos of my own, when a woman transgresses in precisely the same manner as a man, the guilt somehow sticks to her more than to him, particularly if the transgression is sexual in nature. This is an all too familiar story.

Masquerading as a nostalgia for a simpler, more innocent era, antifeminist rhetoric takes on a sepia-toned hyperbole, blaming feminism for putting at risk not only the foundational truths of our society, but also our moral compasses, our children and our relationships with the world. (Not to mention prevailing myths about America's role in all wars up to this point.) Only through a rejection of progressive politics, a return to a past when conventional gender codes prevailed, can we be saved. Otherwise, Malone asks, "What kind of lesson about 'gender equality'" are American forces modeling for the benighted Iraqis? Aren't we, she asks, "supposedly educating, civilizing and democratizing" the Iraqis? A willful naïvete is quite common within defenses of the official U.S. responses to 09/11/01, particularly our invasions of Afghanistan and Iraq and of course Abu Ghraib. These are the politics of diversion, waving patriotism and misogyny in one direction while prisoners are being gang-raped and tortured in another. If I wave "feminist tunnel-vision" with my right hand, perhaps no one will notice the Geneva convention violations and offenses against human decency I hold in my left. Like cats, we are encouraged to move away from harm and toward the shiny things of patriotism and misogyny.

Arguments like these rely for their cachet and effectiveness on a prevailing anti-feminist sentiment within the American press as well as the market niche reserved for not only this very sentiment, but also misogyny. For example, Malone fails to contain her sexist distain for the women in the infamous photos. She invites her reader to picture Iraqi soldiers "pointing and laughing at the exposed genitals of U.S. servicewomen." The point seems to be to suggest the peril we put American women in when we behave in sexually aggressive ways toward the enemy. Disturbingly, the fantasy continues and overwhelms the political argument: "Imagine," she tells the reader, "a naked U.S. servicewoman on a leash held by her male Iraqi captor." Behind these images, Malone performs a dismissive rhetorical sweep of her hand: "All's fair in love and war, isn't it?" In other words (glib words), all women would deserve whatever horrors they suffered for the crimes committed by women in Abu Ghraib. Unpacking the argument, we can conclude that Malone would likely blame any rapes of women in combat on other women in combat, and that those rape victims might be getting what they deserved. Or, to put it more mildly, those women might be reaping what other women have sown. Not men; no quid pro quo is suggested anywhere regarding men, no fantasy of sexual violence against them (neither in Malone's piece nor throughout media coverage generally). No expressed wish that they might one day be naked on the ends of leashes held by their captors.

Those of us with only passing familiarity with the history of war have always understood the significant role rape has played; the U.S. men and women in Abu Ghraib did not invent sexual abuse of prisoners of war. Nevertheless, Malone enacts the totalizing strategy that feminism must be blamed for every aspect of all American women's behavior in that prison. She argues that in the wake of Abu Ghraib we should expect the Iraqis to reject us and our otherwise civilizing influence for two reasons: first, the "un–American" aspects of the scandal — soldiers behaving badly; and second, the definitively "American" aspect — the feminization of our armed forces. Here she contends that Abu Ghraib is a distinctly American event due to women's presence there; it is also quite "un–American," she argues, due to women's presence. The rhetoric tangles around an untenable thesis: the scandal is both entirely American and entirely un–American and it's all (women and) feminism's fault. And adding insult to injury in this case, women may also be responsible for our enemies' perception that the American military culture has been poisoned by femininity, not in the form of feminine violence or feminist politics, but by an essential female weakness. Unlike our enemies, we have failed to keep the girls out. Americans may be sexist, Malone reminds us, we may be indifferent to the rules of war, but Americans will not be seen as sissies, as mere girls. Here Bernadette Malone echoes what seems for the anti-feminist press the cruelest cut of all: the possibility that women might diminish the myth of hypermasculine American power.

But if Abu Ghraib demonstrates a problem with women in the military, why does it fail to demonstrate the problem with men in the military? Because the goals of such arguments are not served by that notion; anti-feminist, indeed, American, conventionality endorses men in combat. Therefore, when the conservative media struggles to rationalize all aspects of "King George's War on Terror," it often turns to feminism for fodder. Why is Abu Ghraib an "outgrowth of a feminist culture which encourages female barbarians," rather than, say, an outgrowth of an imperialist culture which encourages all manner of barbaric violence? Because in the latter case, one risks the truth of American foreign aggression, for American military misdeeds, even savagery, would out, and then even the standard fall gal, feminism, would not suffice as a distraction.

Indulging this distraction on the pages of the *American Spectator*, George Neumayr insists that if only more mommies stayed home then girls and women could avoid becoming "equal opportunity abusers." For "bereft of maternal role models"—that is, living with the curse of working mothers—girls are "catching up to teenage boys in arrests for violence." If absent mothers make girls act like boys; then why isn't this a problem of male behavior? Why not sound the alarm that those who dominate our culture—males—are setting bad examples, and behaving themselves in unacceptable ways? Instead, mothers go to work and girls' behavior becomes nearly as bad as boys, and the argument remains that women are somehow perverting their own and young girls' proper roles. Absent fathers and violent teen boys totally escape examination here, like the male soldiers at Abu Ghraib, elided in the powerful misogyny of the argument. Who is better pleased by such violent developments in female behavior, by the increasingly masculine violence of women, than feminists? No one, the argument continues; feminists love this stuff. At this point in postbacklash history the motives and convictions of few groups are invented with more impunity than feminists.*

> This is Eleanor Smeal's vision come to life.
> George Neumayr,
> The American Spectator

Despite that in 2005 U.S. District court judge Alvin K. Hallerstein ordered all photos taken in Abu Ghraib be released to the public, very little coverage that contradicted the goals of the Bush administration's war in Iraq appeared in the mainstream. As rhe *Village Voice* and other more left-leaning publications observed at the time, "Practically ignored in the Abu Ghraib torture scandal are the Iraqi female prisoners who have told their attorneys they were raped by U.S. soldiers" (Ridgeway). Reports of U.S. servicemen raping Iraqi women did not surface at this time, no photos of Iraqi women prisoners being forced to expose their breasts for the camera managed to gain the popular press' attention. Only those photos which served pro-war or anti-feminist politics were widely circulated, those images that could be made to support the argument that the events at Abu Ghraib were an American exception, or an aberration created by the social disease that is the women's rights movement were especially welcome. Rape, then, was not an issue in this war.

---

*Save, perhaps, women on welfare, rap stars and young women appearing in Girls Gone Wild videos.

Actually, that's not entirely true. In the case of Jessica Lynch, the media toyed with the truth of rape in war for as long as the image of the lithe, spunky, blonde Lynch served to make the crime all the more appalling—and to further demonize the Iraqi enemy. Here is how Rick Bragg, who told Lynch's story in *I Am a Soldier, Too*, describes the crime:

> The records do not tell whether her captors assaulted her almost lifeless, broken body after she was lifted from the wreckage, or if they assaulted her and then broke her bones into splinters until she was almost dead.

And in case we missed it, Bragg invites his reader to "fill in the blanks of what Jessi lived through on the morning of March 23, 2003." Indeed, when the *New York Daily News*—where I culled the excerpt above—reported that Lynch's book confirmed she'd been raped, that report itself made headlines.

That is, the scrubbed, well-spoken, delicate Lynch served the cynical media as a metaphor for the enlightened American way of life threatened by the benighted forces of terror. So, yes, we could say Jessica Lynch had been raped. Sure, no problem. In fact, Amber Pawlik of MensNews Daily.com couldn't say it enough. In her piece on Jessica Lynch written for a men's zine, she says rape, or a version of the word, no fewer than eight times in a two-page article. A sample: "Something worse happened: she was *raped*. Mercilessly, by Iraqis who were professional *rapists*—known for *raping* women and children under Saddam's terrorist regime" (my emphasis). Like Pawlik, the mainstream press overstated the case, sifting available medical records and quizzing experts for weeks about the possibility that Lynch had been sodomized by her captors. These developments lead to statements like those of Pawlik and others who can "see no positive benefit to women joining the military," as she herself writes after Lynch's capture and "rescue" was announced. Unless, Pawlik adds ironically, you consider "the added benefit of letting our 19 year olds go off to be raped by Saddam loyalists." Due to the possibility of rape, then, "letting women join has ... decreased military effectiveness"; the relationship between rape and military effectiveness is not generally made clear in arguments like these. Keeping this ugly image active in the press served as a patriotic boon, and Lynch was a true hero. Blonde, pert, virginal—and violated by the enemy; this image buttressed alarmist conservative attacks on both those who objected to the war and feminism in general. Until, that is, Lynch began telling her own story, the one in which she does not recall being raped, never shot her weapon (or killed a single Iraqi), and praised her caregivers in the Iraqi hospital where she was treated. Then there was the controversy over medical records and whether Lynch had indeed been sexually assaulted. The value of her story — and what she suffered — seemed to hinge entirely on whether or not she'd been violated in this way. Looking back, the media's obsession with uncovering the truth of her sexual assault and broadcasting the litany of other possible abuses suffered at the hands of her captors strikes one as overdetermined; clearly, the media was looking only for the evidence it needed to serve a political argument (the nobility of the war in Iraq). Now, in light of Abu Ghraib, the media's enthusiasm for Lynch and her story seems almost ingenuous in its naïve hope that this young woman might serve to rationalize the costs of the Iraq war. Others were equally enthusiastic in using her to justify removing women from the military.

But what happened to Jessica Lynch and in the cells of Abu Ghraib does not prove that women should not be in combat; it exposes, rather, the horrors of war itself: terror, torture, degradation, violence. Men have shown themselves over thousands of years of history to be more than willing and able to create war without women. But in an era when Ronald Reagan feels entitled to invent a Welfare Queen as a rationale for cutting social programs, Do-Me feminists claim empowerment through the satisfaction of men's sexual appetites, a 21-year-old unpaid intern is held responsible for the dissipated behavior of a sitting president, and women build editorial careers by arguing that feminism overreacts to rape, are we surprised by the disregard for sense and reason driving the rush to blame the women's movement for the failures of George W. Bush's war in Iraq? Only 15 percent of all the military are female, yet the dominant image of Abu Ghraib manages to be female; where were the other 85 percent when the press was selecting images representing the latest failure of Bush's bogus war on terror?

Piling on at this time, conservatives in the media moved beyond issues of Abu Ghraib and argued that the events after 09/11/01 reveal how American feminists take their safety and privilege for granted and their indifference to the suffering of other women around the world. Indeed, according to American media and punditry, the terror of 09/11 revealed American feminists as spoiled and self-interested. The murders of 09/11 and the subsequent intense media focus on the story became one more opportunity to defend the American status quo and condemn feminism. At this time, however, the anti-feminist scheme was tied not to a war on terror but to pure patriotism. The American-feminists-are-just-spoiled argument went (for a time) something like this: Afghani women need to be rescued by our military, and the patriarchal capitalist regime that supports that military will ultimately rescue them. Therefore, if you seek to alter that regime in any way you are denying help to those who are much less free than you. According to these terms, then, any critique of American culture could easily be characterized as perverse, as an unenlightened lack of appreciation for the differences between American women under George W. Bush and Afghani women under the Taliban. In continuing to recognize their own political inequality, American feminists display a horrifying ignorance of what women under the Taliban have suffered and demonstrate how out of touch they have become with real suffering. Again the question presents itself: Why feminism at this time? Why single out this category of women (indeed, this category of American) in service to the larger media project of reifying the Right, using mainstream political conversations to promote a conservative political agenda? It has become de rigeur to do so because since the age of Reagan, and the strategy has proven tremendously successful in that it both underwrites and motivates conservative political action (that is, institutional misogyny.)

Behind this righteous smokescreen of care for Afghani women, reside motives regressive to all women, designed to discredit feminism and further the work of backlash advocacy. We are reminded over and over in the post-backlash age that if American women properly appreciated their freedoms, their elevated and privileged status compared to most other women in the world, they would turn their backs on feminism and embrace a return to conventionality. What would this "return" look like? Precisely what we've been hearing for 25 years: go home, be quiet, and reject all feminist ideas and progress. For example, in October of 2001, almost exactly a month after the 09/11 attacks, Peggy Noonan confessed in a *Wall Street Journal* OpEd entitled, "Welcome Back, Duke," that she was once a feminist, and only after manly men ran up the steps of the World Trade Center on that horrible Tuesday did she realize that feminist principals made her a "jackass" and had led directly to the end of American "manliness." Noonan recalls that dread day when feminism defeated chivalry so many years before: when a man offered to help her put a piece of luggage in an overhead compartment, she was impolite; "I can do it myself," she "snapped." Indeed, she's certain that her feminist "rant," as she calls it, shocked the man out of his mannerly ways. He probably never offered to help a "lady" again, she laments. Surely this single encounter with her feminist stunt double ruined his life: she bets that her curt tone transformed this gentleman into a sissy — that is, an "intellectual or a writer" — rather than "a good man ... who says, 'Let's roll.'"

The shift from "feminist" to "lady" provides the giveaway here; ladies accept help, swoon over firemen, and apologize years later for an ordinary, harried (albeit a bit cranky) moment in a crowded airplane aisle. A distinct class snobbery comes through, as well, a kind of self-congratulatory stance; she was once a feminist and has now graduated to the status of a "lady." A lady has no need of messy political movements, does not suffer under the weight of poverty, inadequate healthcare or diminished employment opportunities. Noonan also demonstrates absolutely no class alliance with the heroes she praises in the piece. As a highly paid, highly influential intellectual who moves in the upper reaches of American power — former speech writer for Ronald Reagan, best-selling author, highly recognizable member of the punditocracy — Noonan praises the working class heroes of 09/11 as "masculine men who push things and pull things," do the heavy lifting, race into burning buildings, and direct people to safety. These "masculine men" include welders, construction workers, police and firemen. We count on them to "put the fire out" and then to "build whatever takes its place." Noonan's bloated rhetoric, her elaborate gratitude toward a class to which her work otherwise rarely refers, belies the class prejudice behind her sentiments; indeed, in this piece she mimics Paglia's disingenuous admiration of stay-at-home moms: better them than me. Moreover, Noonan recounts how she and her friends once visited the site where men working 12-hours shifts at ground zero would pass in their trucks and, she boasts, "all we did was cheer." Leaving the safety of her home and the life in which — unlike the guys on the trucks she reminds us — she had routinely been "applauded," she and other "professionals" saw fit to applaud these men and then congratulate their own willingness to do so in the *Wall Street Journal.** She looked around with satisfaction that day at those standing in solidarity with the working class. Noonan fires off a representative list of her pals: "Investment bankers! Orthodontists! Magazine editors!" Like spectators at a parade, Noonan and her comrades watched the trucks pass and remained clean, untouched by the workers on board; they were also immune to the kinds of professional difficulties faced by these rescue workers, like harrowing recovery work, fatigue, horror, and the psychic and emotional costs to themselves and their families. Instead, Noonan ignores the women altogether and creates a mythology of the men which confines them within a category to which she'll never belong, with which she'll never spend working hours. She quotes herself. Turning to her friend, she says,

---

**Noonan was apparently totally unaware that women work for the city of New York.*

"I have seen the grunts of New York become kings and queens of the City." I wonder if these guys knew they were regarded as, even in the wake of 09/11, "grunts of the city."

Noonan further trivializes their sacrifice when she compares these workers to her teenage crush, John Wayne, a fictional construct who fought bravely on film and never in real life.* All swagger and curious inflection, the Duke pushed women around and appeared in films full of barely disguised prejudices against pretty much anyone not white and American. Such a comparison — between a fantasy of utter safety and artificial heroism and the devastating sacrifices made by rescue workers and their families in New York — would insult the most cynical sensibilities. But Noonan presses the point, summing up her fantasy New York Fire Department (NYFD) hero: "I think he [John Wayne] returned on Sept. 11" in the form of a superhero in an NYFD uniform. Having dashed up the stairs and tossed a kid over his shoulder "like a sack of potatoes," this death-defying fantasy began shoveling rubble with one arm tied behind his back. Indeed, the fantasy continues (embarrassingly), as Noonan imagines the Duke even now in Afghanistan facing the world's most notorious terrorist" and "with his slow swagger and simmering silence," threatening bin Laden thus: "Yer in a whole lotta trouble now, Osama-boy." The dating-service language notwithstanding, Noonan's rhetoric both misrepresents the very difficult and likely traumatizing work done by New York rescue workers and makes light of the invasions that followed. As with so many conservative defenses of Bush's spurious war, Noonan's rhetoric ignores that, unlike in the movies, people actually die in war. When Noonan's arguments collapse into cartoonish fantasy, reducing genuine tragedy, physical violence and terror to unconscionable silliness, the dark heart of the argument reveals itself: slavish fealty to the administration's lies, blind support for its mistakes, and total indifference to other's suffering.

> *I think after September 11th the American people are valuing life more and realizing that we need policies to value the dignity and worth of every life.*
> Karen Hughes, George W. Bush Adviser

As we move further along in this period of media-driven antifeminism and follow the shift in American politics toward the Right, rationalizing political misogyny gets trickier. I do not mean to say more

---

*Not unlike the president she similarly idolizes, Ronald Reagan.

difficult, but rather that to successfully tie anti-women sentiment to virtually every major media event requires some creativity, and the arguments become, well, trickier. For example, 09/11 was cynically exploited as a wake-up call to those women engaged in a feminist lifestyle, a warning that gender codes were at the heart of international relations. After 09/11 manly men and traditional definitions of heroism were routinely celebrated in the media. For example, the violence of that morning, surely frightened women back to their conventional senses, according to the *New York Times*. In a style piece dated September 30, 2001, the *New York Times* predicted "that single women would no longer be so picky in their choice of mates because, as a result of the terrorist attacks, they were now 'alone and scared in their bachelor pads'" (in Gewertz). Perhaps the 350,000 women currently serving in the armed services would find the concerns of the *Times* Style section heartening, and the one in seven soldiers fighting in Iraq who are female might find the matchmaking advice helpful.

The heroes of 09/11 were also touted as women's dream men, for now that we had experienced the collective horror of mass murder, shouldn't women seek men like these? And then go home and back to the kitchen? The lack of reason is unmistakable in this case; the cynicism depressing—and instructive. For such commentary reveals how powerfully conservative politics are motivated by gender bigotry and ideology and how felicitously such intolerance can be deployed to rationalize international politics. When one reads the mainstream press and interrogates politics strictly through this medium, it becomes clear how thoroughly Americans identify through gender — not just as individuals but as political and intellectual beings and as citizens of the world.

Consider this observation by Jan Nindy Pettman, Director of the Center for Women's Studies at the Australian National University, writing in the *Brown Journal of World Affairs*:

> The myth of protection foists upon men responsibilities of soldiering and on women the function of being those for whom men must fight, underlining men as agents and women as passive pawns in international politics, regardless of what individual men and women are doing [89].

American post–09/11 foreign policy under George Bush reflects this myth quite thoroughly and cynically. Women are "those for whom men must fight" only when that fight serves the larger goals of the administration, one of which is to undermine feminist progress of the past several decades; women are called to passivity when we are asked to renounce an active engagement in the world, to turn back to homemaking and spouse-hunting* and to leave the difficulties, indeed violence, of living to men. This is precisely what the women's movement refuses to do. Further, women who do stay home are doubly insulted by this attitude to their labor; not working outside the home is not the same as doing nothing, does not mean quiet leisure. Further, any cursory perusal of political commentary proves that one can be totally insulated from political realities inside or outside the home, with or without children.

Anti-feminist sentiment attaches to virtually every major media event erupting in the past two and a half decades, as I have been arguing, but the tenor of what comes after history-making calamity concerns me in this chapter. When the media deflect attention away from violations of the rules of war, from accusations of child rape and torture by U.S. soldiers, we have truly entered an age of frightening media collusion. Moreover, the anti-feminist tack strikes me as just lazy and therefore symptomatic of a pervasive lack of outrage regarding the appalling behavior of some members of the American military and our leaders' endorsement of that behavior. So, while anti-feminist discourse has become not only excessive but also irresponsible, it paradoxically demonstrates an intellectual and political listlessness in the media. Can we seriously be expected to see a viable connection between the murders of 09/11 and the women's movement? Between the abuse at Abu Ghraib and women's political progress? I am not referring here to the much-mocked comments by Pat Robertson blaming a feminist impulse toward witchcraft (along with a host of other liberal social developments) for the attacks on New York and the Pentagon, but the exploitation of tragic events sure to garner sustained media presence and attention for the purpose of not just discrediting feminism, but also proving feminism to be somehow a primary cause. No reasonable person would draw this connection. And yet, here it is, repeated, endorsed, confirmed at nearly every turn since the towers fell.

Tying these social prejudices and ambitions to world politics requires a certain rhetorical and ideological finesse, as I've said, and luckily for anti-feminists writers, the rhetorical groundwork has been laid. Indeed, as anti-feminism emerges as a popular genre, the arguments begin to rely for consistency upon established conventions. They become, therefore, easier and easier to make. It's almost a matter of merely cutting and pasting from document to document: feminism turns women unmarriageable and violent, makes them abandon their homes and their children, violates their

---

*See the recent rebirth of the Mommy Wars.

non-violent tendencies, and either created or exacerbated circumstances leading to: *the latest tragic event*. Anyone can write an anti-feminist piece. Take for example the following comment appearing in 2006 on the Prague Post, a website featuring news and commentary from readers all over the North America and Europe. Apropos of a discussion of social developments in Europe, one George Rolph from London posts the following Reader's Comment:

> All over the globe men are suffering appalling sexism, and real deprivation, as well as serious ill health as a result of feminist policies being adopted by government. It has reached the point that men in every western country are threatening revolt. Families are being destroyed and children are suffering in ways not seen except in the old Soviet Union in the 1920s [10/28/2005].

We might be tempted to overlook such declarations as incidental, mere hyperbole or intransigent misogyny from a bitter man; however, as I've said, women claiming the feminist moniker make similarly reactionary statements about the powers of feminism and its pernicious influence on American culture. Remember Camille Paglia's claim in a 1995 *Playboy* interview that "the price of women's liberation is being paid by the children"? She elaborates her claim in the interview, making the case that all women's suffering can be attributed to the lack of choices offered them by the feminist movement:

> The problem is the alternative handed to them by feminism. I look at my friends who are on the fast track. They are desperate, frenzied and frazzled, the most unhappy women who have ever existed. They work nights and weekends and have no lives. Some of them have children who are raised by nannies.

And absolutely without irony, she later adds: "What I'm doing is pointing out the bind the women's movement has created not only for women *but for the culture as well*" (my emphasis). To her credit, Paglia resists comparing the feminist West with the Stalinist Soviet Union; still, her claim that her fast track friends are "the most unhappy women who have ever existed" certainly presses the boundaries of reason and credibility. But as the arguments that appear a decade after this interview indicate, to speculate wildly and attach dubious motives to feminist choices has become standard practice. And the tacit suggestion that to hire a nanny is to abandon one's children does that very same thing. Paglia shares with many other writers publishing at the time the tendency to see feminism as responsible for problems that more rightly are attributed to the culture at large —

and to completely ignore the challenges facing ordinary women. For example, many of us struggling to manage our careers and raise our children would welcome the consistency and security provided by a nanny. The truth is that most women under these circumstances (that is, living and working outside the class privilege with which Paglia so breezily identifies) manage to meet their responsibilities only by juggling work hours with favors from friends, family, and the clever use of sick days and vacation time; most working mothers have to make the best of the daycare they can afford and too often must shave hours off their work days here and there, fighting to squeeze more work into fewer hours, hoping not to be penalized by co-workers and supervisors. The anti-feminist position, however, cannot be troubled with realities like these; instead, it relies upon half-baked notions of women's motives and circumstances, mere guesses, and a willful ignorance regarding how most women live. Anti-feminism is, as I have said, a rhetorical position, one that earns book contracts, OpEd space and notoriety; the position retains currency, then, not through a realistic examination of women's lives, but by propping up the status quo embraced by the hyper-conservative American media machine. And how better to do this than to blame feminism for the failures of the war on terror and to grant political and rhetorical consideration to women who oppose women-centered politics.

> *My patriotism is tied to possibilities. The possibilities to get past racism and misogyny.*
> Angela Davis

The invasion of Afghanistan and failed attempts to capture Osama bin Laden gave the American press ample opportunity to build a case against American feminism (sometimes called in this case Western Feminism). Images of women in burkas and an increased awareness of the sometimes horrific conditions imposed upon Afghani women by the Taliban led (naturally, many would argue) to an ideological attack on the American Women's Movement. For example, 09/11 demonstrated how wrongheaded American feminism had become, according to Cathy Young of *Reason Magazine*. In "Feminism's Slide Since September 11," she argues that within a year of the attacks "the feminist movement," which she argues, was "already at low ebb," has now moved "into irrelevancy."

Feminists haven't been the only women singled out in the post–09/11 age. As Pettman points out, "gendered civic identities also legitimize the military solution as a humanitarian, indeed progressive intervention" and rhetoric about Afghani women plays out this strategy (89). So at this time the American war machine exploits the very women with whom the feminism they malign have always concern itself—victims of violence, state-sponsored repression, systemic rape, and so on—as symbols of what America isn't, and of our Western goodness. Images of these women are also used to rationalize the violent spread of American values. What is the relationship between terrorist attacks on America and feminist politics? One answer: the suffering of women under the Taliban, who, according to Young ought to not only make American feminists "realize what real oppression look[s] like," but also recognize the absurdity of many of their concerns — concerns which she dissolves into the shorthand: "policing sex jokes at work." Finally, swallowing whole the post–09/11 Bush administration rationale for our military response to that day, Young castigates "feminist luminaries," like Gloria Steinem, Alice Walker and Eve Ensler for ignoring that the war "loosed on the world by the Bush administration'" would, as she put it, actually improve the lives of Afghan women. One wonders if Young followed the political fortunes of Afghani women in the years before 09/11, or if she merely relied upon Bush administration reports. Did she realize that the U.S. supported the Taliban during times when it was politically expedient to do so (read: oil)? Did she remember that America had been ignoring the Taliban-led violence against Afghani women for years? Can Young identify specifically how a U.S. invasion would enhance the lives of Afghani women?

If she can, she isn't writing much about it and neither are her ideological compatriots. Freeing Afghani women was not the reason for the U.S. invasion of that country; if women were our concern, obviously, the U.S. would have invaded years before. Women's issues are of virtually no interest to Bush, Rice, Rumsfeld, et al., not now, not in the days following September 11. Only when it became politically useful to seem to care did the administration even mention the horrors visited upon women under the Taliban. None of us can truly be naïve enough to believe any differently; care for Afghani (or any other) women became strictly a rhetorical posture. Cathy Young knows this, as does every other pundit or editorialist chastising American feminists for their ingratitude to America and their failure to endorse the war in Iraq.

While Young contends that American feminists are generally ungrateful and holds that feminism itself is irrelevant, she recognizes feminism's substantial power and political significance. Historically, women's equality hasn't been seen "as a natural right," she explains; rather, we must see women's rights as the *"achievement of a complex, advanced civilization"* (my emphasis). Young makes the observation to trump all objections to her assertion that feminism has slid into irrelevancy; yet the assertion argues that feminism stands as a defining characteristic of the most advanced societies. True to the totalizing rhetoric of anti-feminism, Young still manages to find fault with feminists in the face of their achievement. Feminists "perhaps more than anyone else," she argues, ought to recognize that "the West is worth defending." Young accuses all feminists of throwing out the baby of Western civilization with the bathwater of an illegal war. If feminists can recognize the injustices around them and the work yet to be done on behalf of women, the argument suggests, then they must have no appreciation for their own society or their own good fortune. The sort of windshield wiper defense of Bush administration militarism is typical. The smallest burp against George W. Bush and the conservative media simply wipes away feminism and all feminists as irrelevant. We're right (swish); you're wrong (swish). But for any power play to redound flatteringly to oneself, one's opponent must be formidable, so before dismissing feminism as irrelevant, it must be elevated in status (civilizing influence upon society). It's the equivalent of the propagandistic claims coming out of the Bush White House post–09/11, claims that if Americans don't back the administration unquestioningly (or go shopping), "the terrorists win." Feminists who do not endorse Bush's foreign policy — which could quite reasonably be credited with creating the enemies angry enough to attack New York City — must see the West itself as not "worth defending."

Earlier I described such rhetoric as tricky because at times it is downright convoluted. Take, for example, Phyllis Chesler's description of her turn to the Right: earlier in her career, she says, she "did not think that conservative libertarians were a philosophical option ... since political and religious conservatives strongly opposed feminist ideas. (This has changed to some extent today)" (in Glazov). She further adds that despite that she didn't know much about them, she had assumed that "colonialism, imperialism, or capitalism" were "antithetical to freedom, especially to women's freedom." So what's the problem? Political and religious conservatives *do* oppose feminist ideas — quite strongly, in fact. Colonialism, imperialism, capitalism *are* "antithetical to freedom." Why does Chesler make these remarks in the past tense, as if to suggest those days are over? What has she seen or experienced since the publication of her first book, *Women and Madness* (1997), that has moved her ideology to the Right and urged her rethink the value of conservatism and imperialism? Feminism's collapse, of course, she tells her interviewer, Jamie Glazov, in FrontPageMagazine.com, and violence in the Middle East — the blame for which Chesler also manages to attach subtly to feminism. Feminists have failed, she argues, to reach broadly enough around the globe, failed to show adequate concern for women outside their own small sphere of interest. The blame lies with feminists, who, she argues, should follow their own beliefs and "support the victims rising everywhere," not just at home. In fact, American feminists have responded to the difficulties of women around the world, and Chesler agrees: "To be fair," she says, feminists have raised awareness about atrocities around the world, like genital mutilation and honor killings, for example. American women even spoke out about horrors perpetrated under the Taliban. Still, she persists in her claims against feminism: "they did not manage to forge a feminist foreign policy." The complaint strikes me as excessive. Under what circumstances can one imagine successfully building a woman-centered foreign policy in the United States? Chesler claims such a foreign policy has not come about because feminists "refused to work with a Republican administration." On the contrary, feminists have failed to achieve a feminist foreign policy under many administrations, Democrat and Republican. Like Paglia, Chesler condemns feminism for the failings of a society she seeks to defend. Seems to me that the proper complaint would be against a U.S. government which fails to create a foreign policy which undertakes to serve the needs of both men and women worldwide.

The anti-feminist logic with which this study concerns itself is especially apparent here because it is especially brittle; it takes very little reasoned resistance to break the stated connection between feminism bashing and pro-war rhetoric. Chesler wishes for a feminist political intervention that would establish "feminist foreign policies," for example, and would tie treaties and aid programs to women's rights. Her wishes reflect what any of us calling ourselves liberal, feminist, or concerned citizen would heartily endorse. Unfortunately, Chesler's argument strays from pro-women politics and wanders into an endorsement of American military aggression — via an attack on feminism. Feminists must retract their critique of American foreign policy, she insists, because it directly contradicts their beliefs. We would call for help if a man were "beating his wife to death" or if a rape were taking place, therefore, it is "contradictory for feminists to resist" a military response when women around the world are being "stoned to death, hung, jailed and tortured — repeatedly gang-raped." "Terrorists," she explains, "jihadists, torturers, and tyrants are not open to reasonable 'dialogue.'" Anti-feminist discourse is itself anything but "reasonable." As I've said, it tends toward the patently cynical, carelessly using women and the violence perpetrated against them around the world (see Chesler's list above) to promote a war, foster further prejudice, or solidify class distinctions. The post–09/11 American media tends to repeat an argument that renders women who suffer in the U.S. or around the world invisible, until they become important to a larger political agenda. In that case, women become pawns in a game played by politicians and a media largely sympathetic to their wishes; while the women tend to remain in harm's way, these players risk very little, garnishing great wealth and even greater power along the way.

Abu Ghraib offered too easy evidence for some that women do not belong in the military, are a disruption of military order, as if torture and mistreatment were invented by the American women in that Iraqi prison. But if this event demonstrates a problem with women in the military, why does it fail to demonstrate the problem with men in the military? Because the goals of such arguments are not served by that notion, post-backlash conventionality endorses men in combat. I would argue, however, that if Abu Ghraib revealed that women can be, like nearly all human beings, debased, cruel, and susceptible to the horrors of group-think, then women are merely and entirely human, fallible, and entitled to participate in the world in all its violence, horror, wonder and beauty as fully as men do.

6

"MacKinnon Was Wrong": A Little Rape Never Hurt Anyone

If I was really standing in the middle of an "epidemic," a "crisis"—if 25 percent of my women friends were really being raped—wouldn't I know it?

Katie Roiphe, 1993

All those backlash babes who think they'll get to be in the boys' club if they trash other women enough? They're telling sexist lies about women so they can get ahead in a man's world.

ginmar, "Alas, a blog," 11/25/05

Of all the anti-feminist statements emerging from the post-backlash era, those regarding date rape are arguably the most irresponsible and without doubt the most transparent in their regressive misogyny. That is to say that if the goal were to undermine feminist apologists working on behalf of rape victims and to redefine rape virtually out of existence in the mainstream, then the anti-feminist movement has succeeded. As I have argued, since the early 1990s anti-feminism has fundamentally altered the terms of feminist discourse and the manner in which we discuss many of its primary concerns, like rape. Beginning in the 1970s the women's movement enjoyed about twenty years of progress on rape with an increased awareness of its prevalence and positive legal changes, like making spousal rape a crime and giving voice to victims of acquaintance rape. When the 1990s arrived, women found the ground had shifted; indeed, in the years between *Against Our Will* and *The O'Reilly Factor*, the discussion of rape had deteriorated precipitously. The mainstream conversation turned against the interests of rape advocacy; now women found that we must argue not only that rape is a violent crime with genuine, devastating consequences, but also that the crime in fact takes place. Anti-feminist voices in the media embraced a blame-the-victim attitude; increasingly they portrayed crimes against women, like domestic violence, sexual harassment, stalking, and rape, in glib, dismissive terms, and called the behavior of victims of these crimes into question. Serving the interests of the hyper-conservative, male-identified media marketplace, and ensuring that they had yet another anti-feminist product to sell, conservative women (who often call themselves feminists) were largely responsible for this turn of events. Not only did they offer themselves up as public spokeswomen for this new attitude to rape and violence against women, but they in fact invented the attitude themselves.

> *if you get raped, if you get beat up in a dark alley in a street, it's okay. That was part of the risk of freedom.... Go with it.*
> Camille Paglia, in *SPIN*

If these women had played an organized sport, Katie Roiphe would surely have been voted team captain. I recognize how often Roiphe has been quoted on this issue and how frequently in the past decade some writers* have attempted to disabuse readers of her poor research and bogus conclusions, but for the purposes of my argument a thorough examination of her claims remains in order. For in her work we can identify the seeds of the date rape debate as well as a number of the red threads running through mainstream anti-feminist discourse: the cursory examination of statistical/documentary evidence; the manipulative and highly selective use of that evidence; and the tendency to mine the Western literary canon† for support of anti-feminist claims. Objections to the first two are fairly obvious. The third may not be. Positioning Western literature as evidence of women's lives, behavior and desires should concern us because the canon of Western literature tends to be dominated by masculine authors and exceedingly conservative in its treatment of women.§ In

---

Most notably Katha Pollitt's work in The Nation *and Paula Kamen's article for Fairness and Accuracy in Reporting, "Erasing Rape," available at FAIR.org.*

†*The canon goes by many names, such as "The Great Works" or "Books by Dead White Men." Either way, men like Chaucer, Shakespeare, Milton, Hawthorne, Melville, Hemingway, and Joyce form the spine of this list which represents the most conventional approach to literary studies and appreciation.*

§*For a fastidious representation of the traditional Western canon, see Harold Bloom's book,* The Western Canon. *The table of contents, which covers works from the fourteenth through the twentieth centuries, mentions just four women writers.*

1991, Roiphe began her anti-feminist career with an appearance in the *New York Times* and an attack on the very notion of date rape. Roiphe argued that date rape was a feminist myth, one invented to describe nights (and sex) with men that some women would just as soon forget. The idea stuck, and I will treat Roiphe's argument extensively below. Roiphe maintains that in order to deal with the disappointment of regrettable sexual encounters, on campuses all over America and at the urging of the feminist movement, women were crying wolf (that is, rape) the morning after.

In 1991 Roiphe wrote a *New York Times* Op-Ed, entitled "Date Rape Hysteria," while finishing a doctorate in English Literature at Princeton, and this background shows when she critiques feminist responses to rape on campus. The "metaphor" of rape, she insists, eventually seems "paranoid." Her evidence? That in literature classes much of the overwrought romantic overtures of Henry James characters are misnamed rape. Overuse drains the "specificity and meaning" from the term and threatens to align our gender ideology with the "18th-century patriarch" Henry Fielding, who Roiphe reminds us dismisses "ladies'" cries of terror in the face of violence like rape, as mere "vehicles of sound and without any fixed ideas." When Roiphe says we must avoid Fielding's "vision" she seems poised to treat date rape more seriously than Fielding does his female characters' fears and even on the verge of a critical treatment of this patriarch's sexism. Alas, dear reader, this is not the case. While Roiphe does use Fielding's language to lay the groundwork for her own view of women's issues, she does so not as we might have hoped, but rather as we might have feared.

Roiphe suggests a relationship between studies of rape imagery in scholarly works of literary criticism, where rape is often (safely) metaphorical, and the actual events happening on campus around her, where it is not. Like most literature, eighteenth-century novels reveal many cultural predilections of their period, but (also like most works of literature) they should not be consulted to discover, for example, empirical rates of violent crime, poverty or sexual violence. Works of fiction are neither sociological studies nor documentary representations of actual events happening to actual people. Still, we often look to them for clues about human behavior. For instance, since rape is not an uncommon occurrence in eighteenth-century novels, and female characters are being ravished right and left in those works to the bemused empowerment of the male characters, that period's treatment of women might rightly be characterized as misogynist, scandalous and cruel. So, a study of rape imagery serves our understanding of the treatment of gender and power by certain authors and within certain periods. However, such examinations of literary works do not provide clinical evidence and, more to my point, can not seriously undermine studies of date rape two centuries later. To use Henry Fielding's eighteenth-century novels as a basis for the critique of twentieth-century sociological issues like rape trivializes the crime and moves attention away from the central and very serious concern (violence against women) through distractions. Roiphe herself engages "vehicles of sound and without any fixed idea" in her alarmist warnings against taking date rape seriously. Indeed, she takes violence against women no more seriously than Henry Fielding does "ladies'" cries for help. Roiphe's affinity for Fielding provides the political giveaway, here, for the sexism of such novelists is well established. In fact, those of us who enjoy literature like Fielding's often must overlook glaring offenses to our ideological sensibilities in order to indulge our aesthetic ones. Fielding is a towering novelist, a great humorist, but not a celebrated advocate for women's rights.

Moreover, using literature to discuss cultural events occurring outside of literary studies generally fails to serve in the way writers and critics sometimes hope. Literature exposes us to diverse ways of thinking, understanding, and seeing and in so doing makes us more humane, more reasonable creatures. Literature does not reflect the "real world," however, as it is reported in the *Post*, *Times* or by Fox News or CNBC.* That is, it is the nature of great literature to lead us back to ourselves, to our most deeply held beliefs, and not into the political stew of the OpEd world. As literature "means" to us and we document those meanings, we tend to reveal ourselves in that we expose our own belief systems in our writing whether we intend to or not. So, for example, Roiphe's use of Fielding's language suggests a rather literal and undertheorized treatment of his works, and understanding this approach to literary studies helps make sense of her larger body of OpEd and anti-feminist writing. For, when one relies for one's understanding of the world upon the works of "patriarchs" like Fielding and reads their language as a transparent indicators of the truth of human existence, one will invariably find oneself (1) acting in fealty to the powerful and (2) standing in no position to identify either the nuances of language or the differences between a single man's fantasy and the lived experiences of nearly everyone else. Like her approach to the eighteenth century novel, Roiphe's approach to the date rape controversy

---

*I remember in graduate school once asking a professor why the characters in D.H. Lawrence's Women in Love *didn't talk like "real people." She replied, "It's not real life. It's Modernism!"*

exposes her conservatism and her veneration of the patriarchal powers that be.

In our age, Roiphe continues, "the cry across campuses is 'date rape.'" Of course, the idea that women "cry" date rape retains the eighteenth-century preciousness she reflects earlier: that women perpetually and noisily overreact to the slightest "fright" and that female noise invariably amounts to nothing (retains no "fixed idea[s]"). Certainly, the suggestion that women would call a disappointing night of regrettable sex "date rape," reflects this powerful, centuries-old sexism. Further reflecting the petty misogyny of Fielding's remark are Roiphe's assumptions about women and dating. She claims later in the OpEd to be rejecting "our grandmother's" assumption that "men want sex, women don't," but her own rhetoric suggests this is precisely how she herself sees the situation between the sexes. For example, the piece mocks the advice offered to college women in a book entitled, *Avoiding Rape On and Off Campus*, which warns them to exercise caution when they consider going to a man's room in order to avoid "any unnecessary risk." Roiphe asks, "When did the possibility of sex become an unnecessary risk?" Well, that isn't the risk to which the above advice refers, obviously; the advice is about rape, not sex. But Roiphe makes no distinction here between rape and sex, and further assumes that going to a man's apartment or dorm always implies an offer of sex on the part of the woman — an offer made by the woman in service to the man's desire and not necessarily her own. Also, Roiphe apparently doesn't leave room for the possibility of such visits being platonic social events. When she puts forward an ostensibly rhetorical question — "Should we really subject our male friends to scrutiny?"— the answer is not self-evident. The complexity of the issues behind her inquiry belies the limits of Roiphe's analysis. She maintains that no scrutiny of men or gender dynamics is necessary, for a woman's visit to a man's apartment or dorm always contains the promise of sex. Period. The fault lines in Roiphe's position reveal its genuine sexism; men can expect sex from women who come to their rooms, and therefore nothing that happens in those rooms should ever be called rape.

Why is it that some women are always trying to persuade other women that their troubles are grossly exaggerated?
Katha Pollitt, in *The Nation*

The voice of Roiphe's piece on rape is, stunningly, sexually naïve and, less surprisingly, politically defensive. For example, she insists that many feminists misunderstand their own political points of view when it comes to date rape rhetoric. By framing date rape as a "liberal concern," she says, these feminists overlook what is "fundamentally sexist" about their position and expose a conservative bias lurking beneath. I'm not sure what is conservative about the notion of date rape, the notion that too frequently men use bullying, the threat of physical force, drugs or alcohol to coerce women with whom they are acquainted into nonconsensual (and sometimes violent) sexual encounters. I can't identify a conservative bent inherent in caring about the physical or psychological damage women report and suffer after such encounters. But then Roiphe provides a clue when she concludes the above statement with a breathtakingly cheeky move: "More than just a polemic against rape," she argues, "it [objecting to date rape] reveals a desire for dates." This totalizing gesture collects all victims of date rape and the feminists who care about them into a single category: women who want dates and can't generally get them.* How could a desire for dates inspire women to accuse innocent men of rape, or to invent the notion of date rape?

When in her OpEd Roiphe unpacks her claims regarding the conservatism of feminists and their disquieting desire for dates, she adds a page to the media rule book for the treatment of women who claim to suffer sexual abuse at the hands of famous men.† She also provides a handy rationale for such abuse—feminism is confusing everyone, especially men. In creating an atmosphere of "sexual suspicion" and then overreacting with demands for increasingly "rigid courtship structure[s]," feminists reveal, according to Roiphe, a nostalgia for the time when "Johnny pick[ed] Susie up for a movie and a Coke." That is, to say, conservative fantasies of sexual innocence and conventional gender roles. To begin, feminism is not about courtship, as Jessica at Feministing.com reminds us, "[T]he last time I checked, feminism wasn't a fucking dating service!" Feminists talk about rape because they want men to stop raping women. Further, feminism does not cling to a nostalgia for the 1950s—that's the false Master Narrative of the anti-feminist media—nor is a desire to call attention to date rape seriously indicative of the Johnny-Susie nonsense above. (Like many characters in eighteenth-century fiction, Johnny and Susie merely corroborate a prevailing and soothing belief about sexual relations between men and

---

*Remember Pat Califia's assessment of feminist sensibility: "Preaching these antimale, antisex sermons is a way for them [feminists] to compensate for various heartaches—they're just mad at the beautiful girls" (in Friend, 55).
†More on this in a moment.

women.) Feminism insists that if a woman enters a man's room and does not want to have sex with him, he is not entitled to force her. Feminism insists that even famous and powerful men sometimes abuse women. Feminism does not insist the world look like the Disney-fied Soda Shop scenario Roiphe describes and does not work to secure its adherents better social lives. Feminism seeks only to ensure that women be allowed to move more safely in the world. The only way to make sense of casting date rape as a desire for the past is for you yourself to miss the past, to miss the old days when stories of date rape were not taken seriously. Further, in Roiphe's squeaky-clean fantasy of the 1950s, apparently, rape was an impossibility. In other words, Roiphe's position actually harkens to a fictional idea of "the good old days" which never existed but are so often "remembered" (or conjured) in the conservative media. Conservative arguments against feminism often encourage women to embrace this fantasy as real, to time-travel back to a time when women never mistook men's intentions, rarely found themselves in harm's way, and Johnny, in dominating the relationship with Susie, treated her with chivalry and utter care. Ignoring the real world and the reports of actual events happening to actual women, this fantasy is populated conveniently by girls who don't bother thinkers like Roiphe with contradictory evidence of the true behavior of some Johnnies toward some Susies.

On the other hand, Camille Paglia argues, in "Rape and the Modern Sex War," that nothing can save women from sexual violence. Feminism is wrong to try to protect women; in truth, she says, the movement increases women's risk of rape. Feminism "keeps telling women they can do anything, go anywhere, say anything, wear anything," she complains. "No they can't," she says, because women "will always be in sexual danger" (50). She adjusts her argument at this point in her essay, for while she acknowledges that rape has been "a horrible problem for women for all of recorded history," she continues to lay blame squarely upon feminism. Before feminism, she says, men protected women from rape, or at least avenged the act:

> Once fathers and brothers protected women from rape. Once the penalty for rape was death. I come from a fierce Italian tradition where, not so long ago in the motherland, a rapist would end up knifed, castrated, and hung out to dry [50].

Either rape has been a problem for women throughout history or a political movement specific to the last 150 years is the problem. These are mutually exclusive claims; both cannot be true. But, as we've seen, folks claiming the feminist moniker and arguing against women's empowerment find themselves at home in contradiction. Interrupting this tortuous history of male-dominated rape culture, of course, was feminism, luring women and girls into thinking they were entitled to move safely in the world, that their bodies were not to blame for masculine violence against them and that to remain tethered to fathers and brothers for protection was not true independence. Rejecting the rule of men constitutes mere foolishness, according to the scholars quoted here. According to Paglia, women must look to their own behaviors as the source of rape, then seek further masculine violence (vengeance) for solace. Another scholar, Wendy Shalit, also argues for feminism's culpability in perpetuating rape culture, only her ideas are the inverse of Paglia and Roiphe's. She argues that in not seeking a return to the old days feminism has led women into sexual danger. If feminists had simply left well enough alone between the genders, patriarchal culture would be a safe place for women. Feminists "want men to be gentlemen without having to be ladies," she argues, because feminism has lost sight of the power of "female modesty," which "gave men a frame of reference for a woman's 'no.'" Exhibiting a familiar nostalgia for the days before progressive politics, Shalit reminisces thus: "Before, it was a woman's prerogative to say no — she didn't have to join some political rally to enjoy this right — while now it is a man's prerogative to expect sex" (43). I think Shalit's been talking to Roiphe's grandmother, for at no point in her life could she herself have witnessed this kind of interaction between the sexes. Her argument forces us to conclude that any woman who fails to display proper modesty when visiting a man's dorm room should expect to be battered, and that's feminism for you. In order to understand the post-backlash rhetoric of rape, one must embrace mutually contradictory notions and believe that both point to feminism's failing. It's what my grandmother used to call "talking out of both sides of your mouth."

Again, others have made similar observations over the years about the so-called date rape debate, others have found Roiphe's claims objectionable distasteful and have thoroughly disassembled her argument, yet *The Morning After: Sex, Fear, and Feminism on Campus* (1993) enjoys considerable credibility and cachet in the popular reporting of women's issues. Folks continue to take Roiphe as a kind of expert in date rape. I hear the highlights of her argument regurgitated in my classrooms and throughout the media. In fact, eight years after its first appearance, Carol Iannone, writing for *Commentary*, has this to say about Roiphe's book: "remarkable — the first intelligent cry of protest from Roiphe's generation against what feminism hath wrought" (51). As her work is continuing its pernicious influence, a continuing examination of the terms of the date rape debate is essential. If woman-defined feminism is to continue to exist and if the movement is to turn popular attention back to issues of female safety and genuine empowerment, we must vigilantly identify and contest the roots of mainstream misogyny.

This misogyny includes the public abuse of the woman who accused Kobe Bryant of date rape. This media event perfectly reflects Roiphe's position on date rape. For months the alleged victim was accused in the media of being foolish for (1) having visited Bryant's hotel room and then (2) objecting to what allegedly happened there. Like the refrain of a bad song, we heard the same question repeated over and over again: "What did she think was going to happen?"—as if her mere presence in a man's hotel room meant rape was inevitable and excused anything Bryant may have done to harm her. The pervasive misogyny of mainstream media and the welcome reception sexist accusations against women receive there strike me as particularly cynical and mean-spirited in cases like these; when it comes to discussing what happens to the female body, too many members of the American punditry are not their better selves. Through careful staging of "clerical errors," leaked information, and just plain spite toward the accuser, popular media enacted the thesis offered above by Roiphe and the attitude toward women it reveals: preserve the patriarchal status quo at all costs, even if it means sacrificing a few women along the way.

Remember Kobe Bryant's public confession of date rape?:

> After months of reviewing discovery, listening to her attorney, and even her testimony in person, I now understand how she feels that she did not consent to this encounter [in Lithwick].

Most probably don't remember the specifics of this statement, since it was part of a much longer speech and released in the media to mark the end of the ugly scandal. The rest of the statement also took pains to paint Bryant as a good guy, chagrinned and made new by the pain he'd caused his wife and the trouble he'd put everyone through. But in the statement above he admits that the event between himself and his accuser was date rape: "she feels she did not consent," he says. This is textbook date rape; she didn't want to have sex, he being bigger and stronger, easily overpowered her and had sex with her anyway. Previous to the dismissal of the case, his accuser had been subjected to the lurid tabloid-level journalism reserved for women in these cases, particularly those accusing rich, powerful and beloved men. The system had been turned against her from the start; due to a "clerical error" her name was released to the media and a frenzy of harassment and public ridicule began. She was labeled a slut, a gold digger, and even subject to death threats. Finally, it became obvious that the rape shield law designed to protect alleged victims from further invasive trauma and unnecessary violations of their privacy would not be enforced by the presiding judge. Big surprise, Bryant's accuser refused to testify and the charges were dismissed.

> *I care about how men in public life treat women.*
> Andrea Dworkin

Take for another example the treatment of Andrea Mackris, the woman who accused Bill O'Reilly of sexual harassment. As a woman accusing a powerful public man she was crushed, caricatured as "a crazy broad" driven by hysteria and greed. According to legal documents widely available on the internet (I used TheSmokingGun.com), O'Reilly made the following comment to Mackris when she suggested that other women he'd harassed at FOX might report his behavior:

> If any woman ever breathed a word, I'll make her pay so dearly that she'll wish she'd never been born. I'll rake her through the mud, bring up things in her life and make her so miserable that she'll be destroyed. And besides, she wouldn't be able to afford the lawyers I can or endure it financially as long as I can.
> And nobody would believe her, it'd be her word against mine and who are they going to believe? Me or some unstable woman making outrageous accusations? They'd see her as some psycho, someone unstable.

O'Reilly reflects what we have sadly come to expect in this country. Conservative media welcome all manner of public abuse of women, and O'Reilly merely corroborates above his gleeful participation in public misogyny and the security it affords him. Those who control the flow of news and information in this country enjoy carte blanche regarding their treatment of women.* He and his accuser settled and she finally simply dropped off the media radar.

So, the time of "sexual suspicion" is indeed upon us, as evidenced in our everyday lives and the media. To deny this fact would require one to ignore the actual abuse suffered by real women everyday and the offensive depiction of such abuse on television, in movies and in the news. Two years

---

*I would add that such egregious disregard for honorable reportage and fair play also applies to Iraqis, the poor and women seeking abortions.

after her inaugural OpEd, Roiphe will do just that, ignoring documentary evidence about women and rape in a well-known piece entitled "Date Rape's Other Victim" (1993). In this essay, she bases her argument about rape on campus upon a review of a study she apparently didn't bother to read. The study, which reported that one out of every four female college students will experience rape or attempted rape, was conducted by a psychologist, Dr. Mary Koss, and was not an imaginative work of literature, but a survey through which Dr. Koss undertook to discover rates of sexual assault on college campuses. The results of the survey were published in the *Journal of Consulting and Clinical Psychology* in 1987. This OpEd, the book from which it was excerpted, the myriad responses from *New York Times* readers, feminists, and Koss herself have been well examined in the intervening decade. As have Roiphe's misunderstanding of the methodology of the study and her glaring disregard for its facts. My concern here is in the seeds of later discussions of rape and feminism planted by Roiphe's work.

The training Ms. Roiphe received in the English Department of Princeton University would certainly have included a healthy dose of literary criticism, theory and rhetorical analysis; unfortunately, Ms. Roiphe seems to have been absent the day the last one was taught. Had Ms. Roiphe submitted the *New York Times* magazine piece as a graduate-level essay in rhetorical analysis, she would surely have received an unsatisfactory grade and been encouraged to review the conventions of argumentation and the proper uses of textual evidence. As a Ph.D. in literature myself and a professor of English, I recognize both Ms. Roiphe's training and her weaknesses as a student of rhetoric. My own study might be described as an ideologically inflected rhetorical analysis of media treatments of feminism and its concerns. For the purposes of my study, then, Roiphe's weaknesses must be examined because her work on date rape helped to initiate the notion of "date rape hysteria," to establish the market niche for antifeminist skepticism toward rape in general, and to standardize the conventions of the particularly specious method of rhetorical analysis specific to post-backlash attacks on this issue. This brand of analysis borrows certain academic techniques to retain just enough high-flown style to appear to be the result of a higher education; it has evolved into a writing style meant to both mock the academic voice and exploit its apparent authority. So when Roiphe mentions Henry Fielding, for example, or Camille Paglia drops in a mention of Alain Robbe-Grillet as if they were talking about buying groceries, they enact the very class snobbery both accuse feminism of promoting and both claim to reject. For these are not authors with whom most of us are familiar, not because Fielding and Robbe-Grillet are beyond most folks' understanding, but because they tend to appeal to very particular tastes and disciplines. Large numbers of OpEd readers do not have degrees in literature, much less Ph.D.'s in that field.

The carefully blasé attitude to literature and literary terms belies a snobbery on the part of the writer, an assumption that she enjoys a higher level of education than her readers, and therefore greater cultural capital. The gesture strikes me as similar to sitting at a dinner party when someone mentions with studied casualness, "Oh, *darling*, you remember, the *last time* we were in Prague..." (Camille Paglia does a similar thing, as does Naomi Wolf, Cathy Young, Rene Denfeld and Christina Hoff Sommers, to name only a few.) The style is learned, an acquired idiom with an evolving jargon of its own, and appears to be taken quite seriously in the mainstream. Whereas, generally within academic English departments we use the tools of literary studies for the purposes of discovering the meaning, import and implications of various texts on their own terms, the anti-feminist uses of academic analysis tend to apply those tools only selectively and in service to a larger political agenda.

Nonetheless, scholars like Roiphe routinely conflate fiction with fact: "While real women get battered, while real mothers need day care," she complains in the *New York Times*, "certain feminists are busy turning rape into fiction." Her proof?—"Every time one Henry James character seizes the hand of another Henry James character, someone is calling it rape." Roiphe turns from "real women" and "feminists" to fictional "characters" and "someone," making the point hopelessly oblique. So, I am suggesting here that we all agree that the Henries — Fielding and James — have nothing whatever to do with rates of rape on twentieth-century and twenty-first-century campuses; that we all agree that critical objections to Fielding's sexism and James' heavy breathing are in no way relevant to feminist responses to violence against women on campus. I would like to suggest further that the metaphor of Victorianism and the use of fiction to promote regressive politics be abandoned; the move diminishes the serious study of literature and distracts us from looking directly at the non-fiction of women's lived experiences. Of course, mine is wishful thinking. Rene Denfeld titled her book *The New Victorians* in 1996, and Roiphe, Paglia and Shalit, for example, routinely take portrayals of female characters in literature as accurate demonstrations of female desire and behavior.

For example, she tells *Playboy* (yes, *Playboy*) that "[m]ost women want to be seduced or lured," she argues, and she urges her interviewer to "[l]isten to *Don Giovanni*. Read the *Faerie Queene*" (*Sex, Art and American Culture* 59). The argument is misleading in the extreme. *Don Giovanni*, an opera by Mozart which was first performed in 1787, and the *Faerie Queene*, written by Edmund Spenser a hundred years later in England and which features a number of rapes, were both authored by men and written from a male point of view. Using these works as examples indicate only that Mozart and Spenser imagined that women "wanted to be seduced and lured," not what actual women of those (or any other) times actually wanted. The character Don Giovanni commits murder and (depending on each performance's director) commits any number of rapes or seductions; either way, he uses and dupes women throughout the libretto to his own violent ends. The story itself portrays women as single-mindedly indeed, stupidly, suppliant to this narcissistic libertine; they fairly cling to him, drunk with lust, weepy and wretched throughout. (If this is not a standard male fantasy of female sexual availability, I'll eat my hat.) The women in the opera find themselves seduced and victimized by Don, and their characterizations are studies in libertine excess and sexual carelessness. These women do not reflect a sensibility of their own or of their gender; instead, they mirror the fantasy life of Don Giovanni who fancies himself wildly seductive and clever.

While Paglia insists that rock groupies enact a similar sexuality and calls this sexuality typical of all women, I would argue the opposite, for like the authors of much great literature, Paglia the cultural critic conceives of the entirety of female sexuality through the very narrow lens of masculine prerogative and excess. She and Mozart both corroborate the views of their times, as well as reflect (perhaps) the content of their own imaginations.* Like Roiphe, Paglia sticks with major works of the eighteenth and nineteenth centuries — periods during which, in proportion to works by men, little literature by women surfaced. And much of the language of violence against women didn't yet exist. A woman living during these centuries could not have given what happened to her names, like "domestic abuse," "stalking," "harassment," "date rape," or "marital rape," for example.†

Of course, we have not safely transcended these views of women and sexuality, as many women besides Roiphe and Paglia show us. Consider the following defense of Don Giovanni *written by a female reviewer: "Come on! This is Don Juan, the famously charming and fabulously successful seducer of women. The Don of the libretto does use force, but only when seduction or escape fails him."*

†*Notice these critics don't call on the works of Zora Neal Hurston, Virginia Woolf, Margret Atwood, or Isabel Allende, for example, to further their arguments. For, these are all* (continued)

A rape scene from the television series *Rescue Me* that aired in 2006 could have been written a century earlier. Two characters engaged in an ugly divorce argue over the disposition of property (in this case a chair), and the man, Tommy, becomes enraged by the woman's, Janet's, resistance to his wishes. He hits her, tears off her clothes and rapes her. The show's creator and the author of this scene, Peter Tolan, explains the filming of the scene and rationalizes the violence against Janet:

> I never wrote the words "don't" or "no" at any point in the scene ... I pretty much told [the actress playing Janet] she had to stand up to Tommy — that he had taken so much away from her over the years, that she had to stare him down from a position of strength *while he was forcing himself on her* [Gould; my emphasis].

Tolan's comments could have been written by any number of women who resist the very notion of date rape. Tolan believes that at the conclusion of the event he describes above — Tommy "forcing himself on" Janet — the female character could feel empowered, imagine herself in a "position of strength." Just as Camille Paglia thinks rape must be accepted as a consequence of feminism and Faye Weldon argues that "rape is not the worst thing that can happen" to a woman, Tolan totally overlooks the violence of the act. This rape clearly isn't "the worst thing" that ever happened to the character, Janet, because the teleplay requires her to grin ambiguously at the end of the scene and accept Tommy's apology for ripping her blouse. But we must not draw conclusions about real rape from fantasies depicted by men in positions to film, stage, publish or otherwise publicly transmit their own fantasies. Tolan could have written the end of this scene any way he chose. Monkeys could have suddenly filled the room with whipped cream, aliens could have landed, Janet could have stabbed Tommy in the back. But those things weren't in the script. The scene ended as Tolan chose to write it: with the woman accepting a smirking man's apology for ripping her blouse during a rape. Tolan seems even less cognizant of what he's saying than Kobe Bryant. If you recognize that the woman with whom you have had sex did not feel the experience was consensual, you have confessed to date rape. If you write a scene featuring a man "forcing himself upon" a woman, you have written a rape scene.

female authors of the twentieth century who confront issues of race, class, female sexuality and the myriad abuses visited upon those who are vulnerable to the culture around them. Their works include straightforward depictions of rape and other kinds of violence, and tell the stories of women who do and do not always survive the challenges of being a woman in patriarchy. Of this list, only Virginia Woolf appears in Bloom's book on the Western canon, by the way.

6. "MacKinnon Was Wrong"

> *Rape is not actually the worst thing that can happen if you're safe, alive and unmarked after the event....*
> Faye Weldon

The greater the media's willingness to indulge rape fantasies and to portray rape as not so bad, the greater the likelihood that the crime will be misperceived by those who have never experienced it. The same thing happens when critics rely upon fiction about rape to discuss the reality of the crime. So, when studies and statistics demonstrating the prevalence of rape on campus and other sex crimes against women become available, the mainstream media bends toward soothing fictions of feminist overkill rather than seriously treating the scientific literature. I do not say that Roiphe produced the conventions of anti-feminist rhetoric entirely on her own or even knowingly; her weakness as a writer and literary critic may account more for the birth of this trend than any political axe she might have had to grind. As Koss and her research partner Fitzgerald observe of Roiphe's *Magazine* piece, "having formed her opinion, she did not wish to be confused by the data." Moreover, the foundational texts of anti-feminist attacks on rape and rape victims all indulge a convenient disregard for inconvenient facts — that is, evidence — and create arguments driven very often by ideology alone.* For example, Roiphe appears to seriously undertake an interrogation of the language of Koss' study when she looks at a key question of the study and potential responses. The question, "Have you had sexual intercourse when you didn't want to because a man gave you alcohol or drugs," introduces, she argues, "the issue of agency." For, she continues, "If we assume that women are not all helpless and naive, then they should be responsible for their choice to drink or take drugs." Even if a woman's judgment is compromised, sex under those circumstances, she says, "isn't always the man's fault," and therefore not rightly considered rape. Here Roiphe uses a familiar academic term, "agency," but seems not to understand its meaning. Perhaps confusion lay in the fact that she is using the language we use to discuss literary figures — that is, fictional characters —

**Those texts, of which Roiphe's* The Morning After: Sex, Fear and Feminism on Campus *is surely the best known, also include Paglia's* Sex, Art and American Culture, *Denfeld's* The New Victorians, *Hoff Sommers'* Who Stole Feminism? *and hundreds of articles by Pat Califia, Cathy Young, Phyllis Schlafly, Susie Bright and Mary Gaitskill, among others. This list disappoints and misleads, however, in the narrowness of its scope because at the height of the date rape debate myriad books were also being published sympathetic to victims and taking the suffering of victims quite seriously. These titles greatly outnumbered the anti-feminist titles, but did not catapult their authors into the mainstream world of anti-feminism.*

to interrogate a study of what happens to actual women. Agency refers to the source of an action taken by a character, or the place from which cultural power and authority is generated. For example, when we discuss power, we often ask about agency: Where does the power originate? Who can use this power — or, who is its agent? Which characters or institutions does the use of this power benefit? So when characters enjoy agency, we might say they enjoy cultural authority and therefore move safely and autonomously in the world in which they find themselves. For example, we might rightly say that Lady Macbeth embodies agency; Ophelia does not. Elizabeth Bennett in *Pride and Prejudice* possesses considerable agency of her own; her sister, Jane, virtually none. Moreover, we do use "agency" to describe the lived experiences of individuals in courses on Cultural Theory, for example, but when we use the term, we recognize that the notion to which it refers originates in our study of fictive characters and metaphorical language. As a result agency serves us only as a helpful descriptor of actual experience; the terminology moves our analysis forward, but cannot substitute for studies like Mary Koss.'

In order to properly examine agency or any theme within a text, one must focus consistently upon that theme; Roiphe does not do this. In an effort to claim that women of our age are fully empowered, her example slips from what women do, like choosing to "drink or take drugs," to what men do. We can all agree that grown women are generally responsible for their own intake of drugs and alcohol. The point here: the survey under consideration above isn't interested in events in which women come to no harm. The study asks if rape — something harmful — has ever happened to individual women. Perhaps Roiphe would object to a survey of mugging victims which did not ask about all the times they walked home safely. If women had sex they didn't want to have as a result of being given drugs or alcohol, we can assume that the intake of inebriating substances was somehow nonconsensual or somehow rendered it impossible for a sexual encounter to be. At any rate, Roiphe claims that if women choose to risk being impaired, choose to drink or take drugs and then choose to have sex, "it isn't always the man's fault." Indeed, *sex* is no one's fault; only if sex were inherently shameful for women would it make sense to lay "fault" at the feet of all men. Further, no reasonable person would claim that all sex under the influence is date rape; nor is that a claim of the study Roiphe critiques. So the argument drifts uncritically, demonstrating a cursory reading of the text Roiphe herself calls into question, and shifting the terms of Koss' work. According to Roiphe's argument, if women become inebriated they simply must accept that they may be subject to unwanted sexual advances by men, accept that they may have to pay for their intoxication with a sexual attack. And if an attack happens, it's their own fault — making women the agents of their own victimization. Roiphe, then, endorses the notion that an impaired woman is fair game, and attempts to conceal this misogynist position behind not only misrepresentations of Koss' work, but also great leaps of illogic. Following the sense of her argument, anyone who leaves her car unlocked deserves to have it stolen; anyone taking a short cut through the wrong side of town deserves to be mugged (or worse). Apparently, Roiphe is not willing to hold responsible those who commit crimes of opportunity, especially sex crimes. She insistently camouflages rape as sex, disguises impaired sex as consensual, and labels anyone who can identify date rape as "always" unreasonable.

But Roiphe misreads Koss' survey question: "Have you had sexual intercourse when you didn't want to *because* a man gave you alcohol or drugs." The question doesn't ask if a woman chose to have sex while under the influence of alcohol or drugs; it asks if she had "intercourse" when she "*didn't want to.*" And further asks if this happened "because a man gave [her] alcohol or drugs." When Roiphe suggests then that the question "raises the issue of agency," she is simply wrong. There is no question of the woman's agency here; the survey asks if women had nonconsensual sex due to being deliberately impaired by a man, addressing issues of power and consent but not agency. An empowered woman accepts a drink through her own agency we might say; if that drink is spiked, drugged or otherwise not what she expected, we move out of the realm of academic descriptions of subjectivity and toward the commission of a crime. The survey does not define date rape as drunken sex college women later regret; Koss' work actually classifies the act of date rape quite clearly and unambiguously.

Nonetheless, Roiphe persists; this time misreading the implications of the numbers reported in Koss' report:

> The one-in-four statistic ... is measuring something elusive. It is measuring her word against his in a realm where words barely exist. There is a gray area in which one person's rape may be another's bad night ["Date Rape's Other Victim"].

As Dr. David Curtis, a clinical and school psychologist, observes in a report on acquaintance rape: "Some of these authors [like Roiphe] are women (a few identify themselves as feminists) who ... justify their ideas by drawing conclusions based on their own personal experiences and anecdotal evidence," and not upon "wide-scale, systematic research." The he said/ she said watering down of rape, like Roiphe's romanticizing notion of a "realm where words barely exist," demonstrates a total misunderstanding of the differences between regrettable sex and rape. Indulging a rather unsophisticated metaphor, think of it this way: it's the difference between loaning one's car to a careless friend and being carjacked. Perhaps, "words barely exist" for Roiphe in her sexual connection with her lovers, but the same might also be said for the connection between rape victims and their suffering. Words often fail to convey the depth of depression, trauma and anguish experienced by victims of that crime. No one who had ever spoken to a rape victim (date or stranger) about her experience would say that being raped is the same thing as having a "bad night." The glib insensitivity to other women's suffering demonstrated by Roiphe takes one's breath. Would anyone say such a thing of other crimes? One person's beating is another's bad night? One person's mugging is another's bad night? Regarding the limits of Roiphe's treatment of the issue, Dr. Koss and Louise Fitzgerald make a helpful observation:

> We submit that Ms. Roiphe, however gifted she may be at English literature, is neither qualified nor apparently motivated to provide a competent critique of the scientific literature [on rape].

Indeed. For example, Roiphe expresses the following sentiment regarding a woman she met on campus who took the one-in-four statistic seriously: "What is amazing is that this student actually believes that 50 percent of women are raped." What is truly amazing is the clumsy use of evidence: one in four is 25 percent (not 50 percent), and Koss' study explains clearly that this number does not refer only to completed rapes, but to rape or attempted rape. Nowhere does Koss claim that one in four women will be raped on campus.

According to a study conducted by the National Institute of Justice and Bureau of Justice Statistics in 2000, Koss' numbers are entirely correct:

> Over the course of a college career—which now lasts an average of 5 years—the percentage of completed or attempted rape victimization among women in higher educational institutions might climb to between one-fifth and one-quarter.

So, while in any given year an individual woman's risk of sexual assault may be quite low, over the entirety of her college experience, that risk will be significant. This study, by Fisher, Cullen and Turner, covering the years

1992–2000 and entitled, "The Sexual Victimization of College Women," plainly corroborates Koss' findings and Roiphe's classmate's alarm. Further, according to the FBI, a rape is reported every five minutes; the FBI also calls rape the most under-reported violent crime in the United States (*FBI Uniform Crime Report*, 1997). According to the Justice Department, 1 in 6 women have experienced rape or attempted rape, and 67 percent of perpetrators were known to their victims. About one-third of all rapes are committed by strangers. The number of unreported rapes continues to outstrip those reported; only about 40 percent of rapes are reported, according to the Department of Justice. Koss' work also provides concrete numbers, hard data and specifics. For example, in a letter to the editor responding to Roiphe's "Date Rape's Other Victim," Koss and her collaborator, Louise Fitzgerald, state that no fewer than "15 published studies on college students, 7 studies of representative samples of community-based women, and a ... report based on a national sample of 4,000 women" have corroborated their findings; indeed, "not a single study of rape rates among college students, whether in this country or abroad, has failed to replicate" their findings.

---

the term acquaintance rape [has been] defined as being subjected to unwanted sexual intercourse, oral sex, anal sex, or other sexual contact through the use of force or threat of force.
David G. Curtis, Ph.D., Clinical Psychologist

Roiphe's objection to a date rape guide published by the American College of Health Association (ACHA) demonstrates that she is perhaps no more qualified to provide a competent critique of date rape statistics than she is a critique of the Victorian era. For example, she complains that "date rape pamphlets begin to sound like Victorian guides to conduct" because in them women are advised to "communicate your limits clearly." Further, the pamphlet goes so far as to recommend: "If someone starts to offend you, tell them firmly and early." I cannot help but wonder what she finds objectionable about this advice. She mockingly calls the intended audience of the ACHA "delicate readers," as if to plainly state one's preferences to a man were somehow ridiculous because it is so unnecessary. What is disempowering to women about such advice? And for what reason would encouragement toward direct communication be called "Victorian"? Roiphe's assumptions strike me as, well, nonsensical; but more to the point, they define all men as innocent and all women as suspicious, which repeats the totalizing move Roiphe accuses rape activists of making, only in reverse — and totally in service to masculine prerogative, as, significantly, Victorian codes of conduct for women tend to be. While Victorian codes did insist that women retain at least the appearance of virtue, the advice they received was much less direct regarding their own safety, favoring instead the maintenance of social conformity and the preservation of masculine prerogative. So when Roiphe quotes the following line from an 1853 conduct book — "Do not suffer your hand to be held or squeezed without showing that it displease you" — she mistakes a description of a compulsory social performance for sincere concern for female safety. That is, women of the Victorian period were to appear displeased with physical contact above all else and to perform this displeasure to great effect; conduct books were in no way truly invested in female sexual safety, merely its appearance and the performed assurance that prevailing social codes did not permit sexual vice. Conduct books and legislation document attitudes to women and social pressures brought to bear upon them in concrete ways. Scholars must approach these documents quite differently than we approach works of the imagination. The Victorian comparison does hold, however, in Roiphe's conservative preference for female sexual availability and domesticity; for, like the conservative anti-feminists under consideration here, the Victorian world took great pains to herd women into the home, from publishing conduct books like the one quoted above, to passing legislation.*

Roiphe mocks the notion that a date-rape epidemic has been discovered in all her work from this period. She argues that the event now called "date rape" didn't hurt or traumatize before certain feminists gave it a name. In the past not speaking the truth of this kind of sexual abuse rendered it impossible to experience, she argues. "If you don't tell the victim that she's a victim," Roiphe contends in *The Morning After*,

> She may sail through the experience without fully grasping the gravity of her humiliation. She may get through without all that trauma and counseling. Buried within this description of helping students overcome the problem of "recognizing their experience of victimization" is the nagging concern that the problem may pass unnoticed, may dissolve without political scrutiny.

Having raised two toddlers, I recognize this way of thinking; problems can be made to disappear through strenuous wishing or simple denial.

---

*See, for example, the Contagious Diseases Acts of the 1860s.

Roiphe argues above that if we simply ignore date rape, it will go away. And yet, she does acknowledge that grave "humiliation" takes place as a result of date rape and she further recognizes the possibility of "trauma" and the potential need for "counseling." She then insists that we not offer this to women. If we do not tell a woman she's been raped, she won't feel victimized.

No one needs to tell women they've been raped. Studies show that even among women who did not call the event "date rape," 30 percent contemplated suicide afterward; 82 percent reported that they were "permanently changed" by the event (Curtis). That's trauma, that's humiliation; counseling may help. Some women may dislike the term "victim," maybe prefer "survivor," or no term at all. That's fine. We are all entitled to name what happens to us as we see fit, but no one is entitled to deny another's lived experience. Indeed, Roiphe herself coined a term in an effort to write something into existence: "Date Rape Hysteria." Thanks to this language, many women working to combat date rape on American campuses have been labeled hysterical and categorized as politically wrong-headed. Semantics do not excuse any violence perpetrated against others, or excuse the rest of us from working to ease their pain and prevent further violence. Roiphe's argument is rhetorical in that she seeks to discredit the language used to name the lived events of other women, to write something out of existence. (Events which contravene her own sense of the world around her.) Since her ideology cannot accommodate this naming, Roiphe's argument tangles around an oxymoronic rhetorical stance: date rape is a feminist fantasy but if a woman does experience date rape, it's her own fault.

The naming that offends post-backlash thinkers like Roiphe et al., forces into the open the suffering and challenges endured by women in patriarchy and, further, compels us to consider more than rhetorical responses to these things. Giving voice (that is, language) to women's lives has, happily, produced positive political and material consequences for actual women. For example, without terms like "domestic violence" and "homelessness" we might never have seen a single much needed shelter, have never seen legislative and cultural changes designed to ease the suffering of real people in real pain.

The data clearly suggest that on average men are stronger than women and have access to more social power.
Mary Koss

Contrary to Roiphe's claims, one can not talk sex crimes into existence any more than one can talk into existence a plague of hysteria over them. Sex crimes simply exist; facing that reality by speaking it does not produce "hysteria." Consider Judith Lewis' piece, "What Part of No Do You Still Not Understand? Date Rape in the Time of Kobe, Roofies and *Girls Gone Wild*," *LA Weekly*, Thursday, November 20, 2003:

> By bringing date rape into the public parlance, Koss and Warshaw didn't so much turn women into victims as identify the already victimized — there's no reason to believe that having one's vagina forcibly penetrated by an acquaintance's penis was any less horrifying before the two women gave the practice a name.

Her claims against the Victorians might be read as claims against Roiphe's own time or culture; in protesting sexual repression of Victorian women (or other characters in fiction), perhaps Roiphe displaces a complaint against her own repression. Regarding my accusations of sexual naiveté, I should say that like so much anti-feminist or post-backlash discourse of this period, Roiphe's strikes me as wishful in its defense of masculine prerogative. As I argue in an earlier chapter, this position seems very much like an attempt to pretend violence doesn't really happen to women, and so couldn't happen to the author. Such a motive is totally unrecognized, or unconscious, on the part of the author; overdetermined arguments like Roiphe's expose anxieties produced by the reality of violence against women and showcase the myriad protective responses women have to that threat, including book-length studies in denial. One will find no stronger indication of this denial than in Roiphe's definition of real rape: events occurring in Bosnia. Or, she concedes, suburban girls beaten on their way home from the mall. Bosnia is on another continent, and attacks by strangers constitute the smallest percentage of violent crime, including rape. So, given the limited parameters within which she conceives of real rape, is it any wonder her thesis regarding rape boils down to: no problem *here*.

The question becomes, then, what motivates analysis that renders date rape a non-event? Why make date rape murky, ill-defined, almost impossible to identify? To misuse an often misused literary phrase, the author protests too much. Accusations of Victorianism seem more concerned with the author's own sexual availability than anyone else's. A self-referentiality pervades this period in anti-feminism, as I argue earlier, and here that certainly seems the case; many women arguing that there is no such thing as date rape seem simply to want their own sexual activities and identities to go unexamined. For example, colluding in the "You go, girl," Botox-and-breast-implants pop feminism, women like Roiphe rationalize their ideological position and personal choices with the myth of institutional feminist power. Hoff Sommers informs *Penthouse* magazine that had she "gone along with the sisterhood" of feminists on date rape, the advantages "would have been enormous" (in Stein, 70). One wonders how she has suffered in her reportage against feminism, how she could have sold more books or become more celebrated had she gone "along with feminist dogma" (70). At the time of the interview she was a best-selling author being interviewed by a major magazine, in the same issue that included an interview with celebrities like Tony Bennett. Her concerns for her career strike me as slightly overstated, if not entirely disingenuous, as do her claims about the world in which she lives. For example, she tells a story about her introduction to academic feminist theory. She explains to *Penthouse*, that when she first became aware of feminist philosophy, titles like *Women and Domination and Oppression* threw her for a loop, and she could see no value or relevance in what they had to say.* In fact, she drew the following conclusion: "These women are paranoid. This just doesn't have any relation to American society *as I know it*" (emphasis mine). And isn't that the point for most oppressed categories of individuals — those in the upper strata, the safe zones, simply have not experienced much of what the oppressed have. Further, isn't this just like anti-feminism to dismiss the claims of others based on nothing else but individual (very often privileged) experience? And to say, "Well, this has never happened to me, so it must not really happen at all?"

Even more troubling, Hoff Sommers lacked intellectual curiosity about women and oppression and turned instead to dismissing the claim before entirely exploring it. As a philosopher, she tells her *Penthouse* interviewer, she looks for the "truth," but she doesn't interrogate the truth of many of the claims she rejects. For example, she warns that women in college are told:

> One in four of you will be victims of rape or attempted rape. You will earn 59 cents on the dollar. You will be depressed. You will lose your self-esteem. Two-thirds of you will be battered by your husbands or boyfriends [70].

"Well, of course," she quite reasonably observes, "sensitive young women who believe this will be stunned by the injustice of it all" (70). Isn't this

---

The delightful significance of Hoff Sommers' complaints against a book on female domination and oppression appearing in Penthouse *magazine should not be lost on the reader.*

the response we would hope for from young women — a shocked recognition of the injustice around us? Education shouldn't only involve the transference of pleasurable information which enhances our sense of entitlement and safety. Nothing listed in the example provided by Hoff Sommers above can be disproven; the numbers are present in study after study — the 59 cents was reported by the U.S. government (the General Accounting Office). So Hoff Sommers' objection reminds me of "Outlaw Feminist"* Laura Miller's insistence that "it's a real accomplishment for women to learn how to approach pornography the way men do" or Roiphe's proposition that to honestly face the statistical realities of American women's lives carries us "somewhere we *just don't want to be*" (*Morning*, 89; my emphasis). She's half-right. We don't want to be battered, raped, poorly paid or depressed. I am baffled by these simple-minded denials; how does telling women about social inequality constitute a problem? Because frank talk — that is, education — is the only way to provide assistance to women. To frankly address women's lives might lead to change, might result in shifts in how we see and define gender and, more importantly, class. If anti-feminism is about anything, it's about maintaining class and gender structures that enrich — professionally and ideologically — the few at the expense of the many.

Take for an especially egregious example of the dehumanizing influence of this point of view an OpEd which appeared in the *Wall Street Journal* in 2006. In "Ladies, You Should Know Better: How Feminism Wages War on Common Sense," Naomi Schaefer Riley describes a rape victim as "moronic" and fails to mention the guilt of the perpetrator. The victim allowed herself to become so drunk, Riley explains, that "she didn't know that she had had sex with a Naval Academy midshipman," she says, "until he told a friend of hers the next day." Ventriloquizing every anti-feminist before her, Riley blames feminism: since many feminists believe that "social constraints, ... that require them to behave differently from men" are both tacitly and explicitly unfair, "feminism may be partly to blame" for the violation of this and other women. Why would a woman publicly defend the violation of an incapacitated woman, and argue that women are essentially fair game and, therefore, ought to "behave differently from men"? Conservative notions of gender relations have always protected women from sexual violence, according to Camille Paglia, and both Paglia's and

---

*"*Outlaw Feminism*" is* Penthouse*'s answer to* Esquire*'s Do-Me feminism. In the February 1995 issue of* Penthouse *Lisa Katzman interviews Laura Miller, Lisa Palac, Danielle Willis, Susie Bright and others whose feminist platform begins and ends with, "MacKinnon is wrong."*

Riley's arguments privilege masculine access to the female body over reasonable and humane codes of social interaction. That is, both suggest that women get what they ask for when they risk stepping out of the protective shadow of men or breach the boundaries of so-called lady-like behavior.

Of a woman brutally murdered by a bouncer in New York City, Riley again blames feminism and the victim; this time, arguing that not just alcohol but independence earned this woman what she got. The good news? Other women can learn from her appalling murder. The violence done to the victim, Riley argues, ought to serve as a reminder that we could all use a healthier dose of "common sense" when we dare move through the world alone. One wonders why this event doesn't serve to remind men not to brutalize and kill women. Understand, Riley explains, that grown women "*should know better*" than to be out in the world doing what many people do every night — staying up late, drinking in bars (my emphasis). Without saying it, she says it, the young woman was asking for trouble. And in a finally flurry of conservative nonsense, Riley borrows advice from that paragon of political empowerment and insight, Ms. Manners: "People who need to be told to use their common sense probably didn't have much to begin with." I wonder if she recognizes the brutality of her position, or that she just dismissed the innocent victim of a vicious crime as simply lacking the common sense to avoid her own murder. Despite antifeminist protestations to the contrary, the only analysis truly being blocked in the mainstream publishing and media outlets is the truthful examination of rates of rape and violence against women.

> *Educating myself about the prevalence of [sexual] violence and the cultural myths perpetuating it made me notice more and more things — all of which I didn't want to see.*
> Paula Kamen, *Feminist Fatale*

So while I may be flummoxed by the distasteful claims made above and the myth of special protections afforded rape victims, others are not and have made arguments virtually identical to Roiphe and Riley. For example, *In Who Stole Feminism?* Christina Hoff Sommers invented the twin myths that (1) Women's Studies courses were replacing the canon on universities around the United States and (2) women's issues (like rape prevention) were getting all the funding there these days. So, she naturally disapproves of feminist misinformation, since "[n]o matter how you look at it women on campus do not face anywhere near the same risk of rape as women elsewhere" (221). Indeed, where she lives, apparently, rape is not a problem. Hoff Sommers locates "elsewhere" on the map of women's history in "poor urban communities." She is quite concerned for poor *urban* women — that cynical and ever recognizable code for *non-white* women — so much so that every time a privileged women who can afford to go to college dares to complain about rates of sexual assault, well, Hoff Sommers is compelled to speak up. But her rhetorical strategy indulges the ugliest hypocrisy: exploiting a reference to an oppressed group for which her work otherwise shows no genuine concern, Hoff Sommers seeks to paint those who oppose her views on rape as racist. She avoids the term racism, of course, and simply implies the offense as she tacitly piles on evidence of feminism's unconscionable concern for the notoriously "self-preoccupied" and misguided "campus feminists" (221).

Nonetheless, the yawning gap in logic here results from Hoff Sommers' total fabrication of rape statistics and university funding trends. First, studies show that, in fact, women on campus are at greater risk of sexual assault than women who are the same age but do not attend college.* Second, there is no evidence supporting her alarmist claim that

> College women continue to get a disproportionate and ever-growing share of the very scarce public resources allocated for rape prevention and for aid to rape victims [221].

She made this up. The Directors of Women's Centers on campuses all over the country, who compete for grant money and then have to scrape for university matching funds, would be quite surprised to hear this. Mary Koss provides helpful calm and insight here:

> The denigration of the term "victim" and the backlash against a "victim mentality" by women can be seen as a defense against the powerlessness and second class status they would feel if they reality of rape were acknowledged ["Acquaintance Rape"].

And the "reality of rape" points to the truth of women's continued oppression even in an "advanced civilization" like ours. If rape is "the natural trump card for feminism" as Katie Roiphe has said, it's not because being raped or helping victims of rape empower feminist women over any other group; it's because rape is indeed the strongest demonstration of the potential power men hold over women, irrespective of who we are or where we

---

*See the Department of Justice report prepared by Bonnie S. Fisher, Francis T. Cullen, and Michael G. Turner, entitled, "The Sexual Victimization of College Women" (2000).

live. And if women who deny feminism are also seeking to deny a disempowered status, then denying rape makes perfect sense. As Koss observes above and the vigorous denials of the date-rape-hysteria crowd demonstrate, facing the truth of rape is no small task — for any woman.

7

Conclusion: A Signifier of One's Own

> *I do not believe that anyone who promotes the subjugation of women for men's pleasure (anyone's pleasure, really) is a feminist, whether he or she claims to be or not. The word must have some meaning.*
>
> Juliette Cutler Page, *Feminista!*

A struggle for definitional control has dominated discussions of popular feminism for two decades, and one result has been a proliferation of prefix feminisms, like Do-Me, post-, girlie, pro-life, sex-positive, third wave, power-, gender-, equity-, individualist-, goddess-, lipstick- and anti-feminist, to name a few. Clearly, women have felt underserved by the movement, for these definitions indicate various needs that the women's movement has not addressed to many women's satisfaction. These thinly sliced prefix feminisms reveal not only fissures within the movement, but also its perceived failures, those issues and concerns many women today believe the movement has overlooked or even abandoned. Moreover, prefixes act as descriptors which define and track shifting beliefs held by women about feminism's role in politics and culture. While laying claim to the feminist title, prefix feminists also tend generally to treat feminism as a feeble remnant of a once-strong political movement and to take as an a priori assumption that feminism has lost relevance for most women's lives. As a result, in the mainstream the term has become discursive fair game, acting as a kind of floating cultural marker, still capable of drawing attention and pissing people off, but largely signifying nothing. "Feminism," then, occupies a unique position in American nomenclature which has rendered it dangerous to women: it's a term drained of specifically political meaning, perpetually susceptible to redefinition, which nonetheless exerts a powerful influence upon women's political lives.

Prefix feminists constitute a most conspicuous symptom of what ails the women's movement; in their ostensible efforts to adapt the movement to the evolving needs of women, they, in fact, render the movement narrow and brittle — as concerning exclusively the single issue, activity, or life choice which they feel has been overlooked, like sex or marriage, fashion or Botox, kitten heel pumps or pornography. This semantic (as well as ideological) debate threatens, I argue, to refine the movement out of existence with a particulate approach which substitutes highly individuated political tastes and personal choices for the collective of social politics. This approach drains the politics from the term, and divides a social movement into ever more granular statements of personal preference and lifestyle choices. Perhaps inadvertently, yet undeniably, these thinly sliced "feminisms" serve the backlash against women, as the mainstream media eat them up, happily slicing and dicing the movement into increasingly restrictive varieties and espousing illiberal politics. Indeed, the trend in prefix selections tells the story, since most focus very tightly upon choices or beliefs that do not serve large populations of women or the needs of the many over the needs of the few. "Do-Me" feminism, for instance, has little to offer a woman being beaten; "lipstick-feminism" cannot enhance the lives of women needing abortions; "sex-positive" feminism ignores the wage gap entirely. It's helpful to note the prefixes which have *not* been attached to the term "feminism" over the years: we have not seen "equal pay"-feminism, for example, nor have we heard much about, "sexual harassment"–; "domestic violence"–; "health insurance for children"–; "funding for shelters"–; or "raise-the-minimum-wage"-feminisms, in the press or on university campuses.

Having come thus far in my discussion of mainstream misrepresentations and regressive redefinitions of the women's movement, the question presents itself again: Why all the definitional uproar? Women must be vigilant regarding the terms of feminist discourse because this trend in labeling and parsing co-opts the terms of the movement in order to undermine those terms and the movement's goals; such vigilance becomes especially pressing in light of the ground lost for women and minorities since the Age of Reagan. Also, we must consider the pernicious implications of the face of the prefix revolution: academic, popular and largely female. When women scholars and writers promote points of view detrimental to women's political status, critiques of those points of view become all the trickier, fraught, and even defensive. One might be disinclined to challenge, for example, the convictions of women calling themselves feminists, or women claiming to care about other women, for fear of being (1) seen as turning one's back on women, or (2) criticized as avuncular, even perverse. Folks might ask further, if women themselves endorse prefix feminisms, what's the problem with creating a variety of them? The answer to this question constitutes the larger argument of this book: prefix feminisms are markers of *private*, not *social*, ambitions. Further, most prefix feminisms cannot be said to enhance women's political status at all, or create greater understanding of women's political needs and situations; indeed, certain of their ostensible arguments for empowerment are questionable at best, seriously damaging to women's political status at worst. Have you met a "make-over" feminist yet, who argues that conceding to cultural demands upon the female body through plastic surgery makes one feel empowered? Have you indulged in stripper chic (which traces its lineage directly to "Do-Me" feminism) which has grown women learning to strip for their partners or spending girls' nights out at strip clubs? Have you considered purchasing thongs or animal print miniskirts for a girl under the age of ten recently? If so, thank post-backlash feminism, which under the aegis of any number of prefixes, like "sex-positive," "Do-Me," or "girlie," seeks to attach to these trends the hue of social action, the scent political conviction.

Are American women so hopeless about their political status that they have sought refuge and bylines in the hackneyed divide-and-conquer tools of their oppressors? One might draw that conclusion were one to peruse (even briefly) American media. Choosing sides and divvying up ideological commitments like allowance handed out at the end of each week, many public women, most often members of the commentariat, lay claim to the label feminist in order to buttress pronouncements about what is right for other women and what is wrong with feminism. Therefore, I fear that feminism will one day fail to be a political movement, and, stripped of its goals for social justice, dissolve into a fashion statement, a cultural attitude or a code of social conduct. My own embrace of "anti-feminism" is intended to tag the political positions under consideration in this book as not reasonably labeled feminist at all and as lacking a satisfactory — alternative — signifier of their own. My use of a prefix is not meant to add to the list above; plainly, I have not argued that the Do-Me movement, for example, is a viable political movement, advantageous to women, or even reasonably labeled feminist.

The confusing thing about prefix feminisms is that they seem genuine, even heartfelt, and their apologists vehemently defend their seriousness in popular and academic venues; yet, the arguments don't themselves seem terribly serious and their calls to action, well, not terribly active. Women have earned the right, they argue, to embrace their femininity and to dispense with all the disappointments of the past. And who can blame them? Feminine things can be lots of fun and disappointment just plain fatiguing. Too often, however, these responses to women's status are not feminist (that is, political) at all, but are in fact consumer trends, politics of shopping or flirting or fashion. But politics outside the mall is terribly serious business and creating social change nearly impossible without years of struggle and enormous commitment by significant numbers. So when women calling themselves feminists trivialize their own ideological identities, reduce their political involvement to a slogan on a t-shirt or a call to cosmetic surgery, they undervalue women's politics in general. And make it all the more difficult for women to be taken seriously as political beings. Any reasonable interrogation of popular, media-driven "feminist" trends must lead one to assume that some women have simply given up. Forget divide-and-conquer, welcome to sleeping with the enemy.

And so, women live in a state of cognitive dissonance, for the cultural messages are mixed. Women write that feminism is passé, while other women label themselves feminist, and argue against feminism's most familiar views. Moreover, when we look around, women seem to have arrived; they're everywhere. Women host news shows, report on the most important events of the past decades, like Chechnya, Darfur, 09/11, Afghanistan, Iraq, and Abu Ghraib; women are among the wealthiest individuals in the world; women write and sell book after book; women (sometimes) appear on the most prestigious Op-Ed pages in the country. In fact, the editorial page of my local newspaper often features more women's bylines than men's. It's no surprise, then, that my students often wonder why I still insist on talking about feminism. Because, as I tell them, while women may enjoy an increased presence in the media as anchors, reporters, and commentators (have you seen ESPN lately?), air time and column inches devoted to women's issues have been shrinking.

While we may be disappointed that women have participated in the parsing of feminism into near meaninglessness, we must remember that the gender of the messenger is less indicative of cultural trends than the message itself. We must not assume that all women embrace the term "feminism" for the betterment of women's political status; too often, the term is deployed as a lure, a distraction away from a regressive message harmful to women's politics. Too often, a conservative, even misogynist, endorsement of the status quo is marketed as a new and improved feminism. All women are not feminists; gender and ideology are not equivalent. So, we may see plenty of female faces on television and read plenty of female bylines in print, but increased numbers of women reporters does not mean increased reporting on issues of concern to women. Female editorialists, for instance, do not necessarily articulate positions of benefit to women — although that is not what media conservatives and anti-feminists would have us believe. We saw this same logic applied when the number of women in college outstripped the number of men (about 57 percent to 43 percent). Surely, the conservative media argued, since women have overrun American campuses, college curricula must be equally skewed. And we heard the now-familiar refrain: feminists can stop worrying; women should back off and let the men back into the fold. The fact is, enrollment statistics have little to do with university curricular decision making. American universities have not introduced radical shifts away from male-dominated scholarship, and they have not overturned centuries of patriarchal dominance over the production of knowledge and higher education. What's happening is simply that now more women than men are studying the same male-defined content. Despite the successes of the women's movement, American popular culture (like American universities) consistently bends toward misogyny.

And, I would argue, it bends toward cynicism. For prefix feminisms cynically invokes "choice" to explain personal and private inclinations and to depict the more socially conscious variations of feminism as outdated, irrelevant or unhip. This heavy-handed rhetorical move draws on the feminist issue of choice and suggests that feminism has freed women to make decisions, like whether to learn to pole dance, or use Botox, wear low-rise jeans or belly shirts. Of course, these kinds of choices do not represent feminist "choice" at all. Feminist choice always refers to reproductive rights, not ordinary decisions made in the course of everyday lives. Reducing women's very serious — and sometimes very dangerous — pursuit of political and private control over their own bodies in this way ignores much of the history of the women's movement and belies a fundamental indifference (perhaps hostility) to its goals. Further, these invocations of choice inherently demean the feminist commitment to social justice, which includes empowering women to control their own bodies in safety, challenging systemic sexism and improving the lives of the poor, underinsured, abused, and needy. Prefix feminisms further belittle feminist goals in their divide-and-conquer approach to women's politics; for a red thread running through them all is the assumption that no matter what women choose the old feminism will disapprove. As Katha Pollitt so nicely puts it in *The Nation*, within American popular culture, "Whatever women are doing wrong is feminism's fault." Take, for example, a recent development, the very unserious media-generated scandals dubbed "the Mommy Wars," which in fact are mere reruns of the arguments characterizing the backlash of the 1980s: conservative career women, well-paid and thoroughly nannied-up, who don't clean their own homes or pack school lunches, making a killing writing that women (*other* women) ought to stay at home for the good of the children and the family. This recent media scam aims to make women feel guilty for any other choice they might make regarding family, work, and children and then blames feminism for this guilt.

The media version of feminist politics lays all things lost or gained for women at the feet of feminism. The seamless logic (illogic?) of anti-feminism renders feminism responsible for the smallest mistakes women make, and any misfortune that might befall them; it also argues that feminists are hyper-critical of any successes women enjoy, or fun they might have. Feminism freed women to strip, and it is feminism's fault if they are criticized for doing so; feminism freed women to choose to stay home, and feminism consistently makes women feel bad for doing just that; feminism made women free to remain single, and now its feminism's fault that the (traditional) family is in decline. It is a sealed system, an argument wherein women circle inevitably back toward disempowered status via the old fashioned feminism. "[N]o success" for women, as Gaby Wood writes in the *Guardian*, "without its shadow of failure." And, therefore, she continues, "no impression of choice without an accompanying sense of sacrifice." Women today live with the sad truth that conservative notions of gender have always characterized our culture, and when challenges to these notions begin to gain political ground new strategies will emerge to quash them.

And still, feminism sells. Just check out the titles available at your local bookstore, published by university presses or online. Search titles with the word "feminism" on Amazon.com, for instance, and you'll get 39,572 hits; narrow the search to titles since the year 2000 and Amazon.com will still return 793 hits. Plainly, someone is interested in publishing and reading about feminism, its goals, definition and continued survival. Yet, I would like to argue that even in the face of an apparent proliferation of books, articles, essays, and commentary on feminism, the parameters of what is acceptable for publication have been changing, shifting away from radical notions of the movement and commentary which is too explicitly angry, dissatisfied, or even political. Some might explain away this publishing trend as evidence that our society no longer discriminates against women, so the rhetoric can mellow. I would argue that a publishing boom occurred around the battle for definitional control over the terms of feminism and that that battle itself grows out of the backlash of the past 25 years and media domination by the extreme Right. Since anti-feminist titles dominate this publishing niche, the explosion of book titles provides further evidence of the pervasive anti-feminism in American culture and the challenges facing any attempt to reinvigorate the feminist movement.

For example, in seeking a publisher for this book, I approached an editor working at a major university press. Our correspondence went swimmingly for a time, and he seemed genuinely supportive of my work, congratulating my argument, complimenting my writing style, asking for more chapters. But that all changed once the editor read my argument about Monica Lewinsky. While my aggressive readings of Third Wave and my critiques of Do-Me feminism as disastrous to women's politics were embraced and encouraged, I was not free to write in support of Ms. Lewinsky. Nor was I welcome to contravene the most conventional view of Lewinsky's identity. His final email rejection stands as an example of the very attitude to the scandal I critique, as well as my larger argument regarding the mainstream media and feminism:

> I agree that Lewinsky, like perhaps Donna Rice, Fawn Hall, et al., was not treated as well as one might have hoped, but Lewinsky was also extremely culpable in that affair. Yes, Clinton was the older, supposedly responsible figure and shouldn't have done what he did. But Lewinsky clearly pursued him, clearly wanted a relationship with him, evidently pestered him, and then wanted to brag about it.

The emphasis on culpability deserves some comment, for it seems that any attempt to defend Lewinsky ideologically, or to call the behavior of those around her into question, must be rejected as a defense of her role in the affair. (We see this in anti-feminist writings on the affair all the time.) My argument concerns cultural definitions of gender, sexist and selective defenses of (or attacks on) women in popular culture by women claiming to be feminists — not who started the affair or who "pestered" whom.

This editor further reflects a potential misreading of my argument about Do-Me feminism: "I agree," he argues, "that this [female sexuality] is still a reasonable target for feminist critique, but are all visual expressions of female sexuality culpable?" My hope is that my point will not be misunderstood in this way, for I do not say that female sexual display offends feminist sensibilities. Many women (and men) enjoy display; create identities tied quite closely to their appearance. One might argue it's nearly impossible not to do so in this culture. Indeed, my point has never been that women shouldn't dress however they like, shouldn't enjoy the variety of fashion choices at their disposal and present themselves in ways that make them feel comfortable, happy, sexy, empowered or whatever they are personally seeking from their own appearance. My point remains simply that no amount of female display can replace a political movement; if we want to credit the women's movement with creating greater choices for women in this part of their lives, that's appropriate, totally accurate. But to suggest that we replace doing the larger political work of the movement with wearing belly shirts or high heels, Birkenstocks or lipstick, is to return to identifying women exclusively through their appearance, to caring too much about how women look and not enough about what they do, and toying dangerously with defining female identity strictly through fashion codes and body types. Have we circled round to the point where women who chose *not* to wear thongs, *not* to learn to pole dance or buy low-rise jeans will be seen as submitting to convention, as slaves to patriarchal demands on female appearance? In this world, women in comfortable shoes would risk being defined as slaves to fashion, emphatically disempowered. The problem with such terms, of course, is they imply that if we do not sanction and engage in stereotypically feminine and highly sexualized display then we deny ourselves as political women. If we happen to spy out the dangers of sexual capitulation, or to understand that some choices aren't truly made free of social or ideological duress, where does that leave us?

The editor's rejection suggests an answer: "Are we left with an Islamic fundamentalist view of how women should present themselves? In hijab, veils, covered totally? Naked female arms freak out more than one culture. Is this feminism?" Obviously this is not feminism. But if writing this book has taught me anything, it is that to discuss the female body and the politics of public discourse on the subject — with men or women, feminist or not — is to invite all manner of personal reactions, and to nudge up against all manner of investments that extend beyond political ideologies. For the sake of full disclosure I confessed earlier to a love of short skirts and Nine West pumps, as well as to anxieties about my own appearance and a sometimes harrowing obsession with the state of my mid-40s', post-childbirth abs. I do not say in this work that female beauty, cultural standards and fashion do not exist, or do not influence women's lives in very real ways (hence the on-going feminist critique of these things), or that covering female skin is somehow inherently more righteous than exposing it. I do say that embracing a particular mode of display is not the same as embracing an identifiably political ideology and practicing it. Think of it this way, to simply pin a pro-choice button on our backpacks is not the equivalent of canvassing neighborhoods, writing OpEds, passing out leaflets, working at the polls, making phone calls, or escorting women seeking abortions through throngs of angry protestors. Further, if the mode of fashion or physical appearance required for entrée into the prefix feminist fold requires women to be of a certain size (small-ish) and of a certain class (upper-ish), then we are no longer in the world of liberal social movements, but rather in the world of prejudice and exclusion.

So, while my project professes openly to read against widely held, and to my mind, mis-named, "feminist" positions, there remained a boundary the book editor could not cross, and crossing this boundary seems precisely feminist to me, perhaps the strongest, most radical, political position offered by this work: that Ms. Lewinsky deserved better than she got, that it was undeniably a feminist gesture to stand with her, and that public feminism largely failed her and women in its refusal to do so. Reactions like the editor's described above suggest to me that at the heart of any discomfort with this position is a discomfort with certain revelations about female sexuality and sexual behavior provided by her scandal. For example, Ms. Lewinsky did not refuse an adulterous affair, never really seemed sorry for her behavior, and failed to perform proper modesty once she was exposed. Indeed, her reaction to Clinton's final rejection — reported as a kind of "hissy fit" at the gates of the White House — became further evidence of not only her silliness, but her insignificance as a woman. (Rather, than, as I would argue, emblematic of her undersized status before the behemoth of patriarchal and presidential authority.) If my own rhetoric in this case seems aggressive, my own examinations of shifts in feminist discourse feel unforgiving, it is because my goal is to arrest the retrograde anti-feminist movement and to help correct misrepresentations of women-centered politics; one cannot accomplish such things, I believe, by continuing to allow openly misogynist attitudes to collect around the term feminism. Nor will this happen if we go quietly. My goal is not to prescribe my own definition of feminism, but rather to highlight those notions that cannot reasonably be called feminist — and expose the celebration of such notions as too often ideologically disingenuous performances serving an overwhelming media appetite for anti-feminism. I further hope to reset public discussions of feminist issues by exposing the co-optation of the "feminist" label, demonstrating the need for a purposeful response to this co-optation and modeling reclamation of the terms of feminist discourse. If these are my goals, then an unapologetic look at feminist reactions to Bill Clinton and Monica Lewinsky seems to me a reasonable (although, clearly treacherous) place to begin.

The manner in which feminists describe ourselves, as well as how we allow ourselves to be described, matters. Language produces material consequences, arguments create political realities; think of the War on Terror and the thousands who have died, or the invasion of Iraq, and the lies — the language — harnessed in service to making that war happen. Whether people live or die, have access to power or not, are allowed to marry or not, live in safe neighborhoods or not is very much determined by the language used for or against them, the manner in which they have been defined. There are no shelters for women without the term "domestic violence," for example; no equity training without the phrase "sexual harassment." So, feminists must reclaim the language of the movement and renounce its uses against women; we can no longer allow "feminism" to mean "man-hating reactionary" anymore than we can allow it to mean "girls who like porn and cosmetic surgery." While we remain committed to protecting the rights of all women, we must insist upon a signifier of our own.

Bibliography

Alfonso, Rita, and Jo Trigilio. "Surfing the Third Wave: A Dialogue Between Two Third Wave Feminists." *Hypatia* 12:3 (Summer 1997): 7–16.
Austin, Elizabeth. "Lipstick Feminists." *The Washington Monthly Online,* 30:11 (November 1998). (accessed 21 April 2006)
Baumgardner, Jennifer, and Amy Richards. *Manifesta: Young Women, Feminism, and the Future.* New York: Farrar, Straus, and Giroux, 2000.
Beck, Joan. "Feminists Shed Principles to Back Clinton." *The Online Service of the Arizona Daily Star.* www.azstarnet.com (accessed 29 March 1998).
Beggan, James K., and Scott T. Allison. "Tough Women in the Unlikeliest of Places: The Unexpected Toughness of the *Playboy* Playmate." *The Journal of Popular Culture* 38:5 (2005).
Chavez, Linda. "Girls Have Gone Wild." Catholic Exchange.com, 18 February 2002. www.catholicexchange.com (accessed 26 November 2005).
Cohen, Adam. "The Burden of Proof." *Time,* 2 February 1998.
Cottle, Michelle. "G.I. Jane." *The New Republic,* 230:19 (May 24, 2004).
Curtis, David G. "Perspectives on Acquaintance Rape." Publication of the American Academy of Experts in Traumatic Stress, 1997.
Dean, John W. "A Letter to Monica." *New York Times,* Editorial Desk, 9 August 1998.
Denfeld, Rene. "Cry Rape: The Feminist Crime Against Women." *Hustler,* December 1992.
Dowd, Maureen. "The Slander Strategy." *New York Times,* Editorial Desk, 28 January 1998.
Dreifus, Claudia. "Ms. Behavin' Again." *Modern Maturity,* May/June 1999. www.aarp.org/mmaturity/mayjun99 (accessed 14 February 2003).
Ehrenreich, Barbara. Barnard Commencement Speech, 2004.
_____. *Nickel and Dimed.* New York: Henry Holt and Company, 2001.
_____. "The Week Feminists Got Laryngitis." *Time,* 9 February 1998.
Epstein, Kate. "Femme Feminist." *Moxie,* 2000. http://www.moxiemag.com/moxie/articles/style/femme.html.
Faludi, Susan. "All the President's Flings: Let's Separate the Women from the Girls." *L.A. Weekly,* 20–26 February 1998.
_____. *Backlash: The Undeclared War Against American Women.* New York: Bantam Doubleday, 1991.
_____. "Where's the Feminist Conspiracy?" *The Nation,* April 1996.
Ferguson, Andrew. "It's the Sex, Stupid." *Time,* 2 February 1998.
Flanders, Laura. "The Pundit Spectrum: How Many Women — And Which Ones?" *Fairness and Accuracy in Reporting,* 21 November 2005. http://www.fair.org/index.php?page=1336 (accessed 16 February 2006).

Freedman, Estelle B. *No Turning Back: A History of Feminism and the Future of Women.* New York: Ballantine Books, 2002.
Friend, Tad. "Yes." *Esquire,* February 1994, pp. 48–56.
Gewertz, Ken. "Faludi Fears Feminism Trivialized: Author Speaks at Radcliffe on 'Gender Shock.'" *Harvard University Gazette,* 28 April 2005. www.hno.harvard.edu/gazette/2005/04.28/13-faludi.html (accessed 31 January 2006).
Glazov, Jamie. "The Death of Feminism," 4 January 2006. www.frontpagemag.com (accessed 31 January 2006).
Goldberg, Michelle. "Feminism for Sale," 8 January 2001. www.alternet.org (accessed 1 February 2003).
_____. "Ask Buffy: Is the War Between the Sexes Over?" *Ace Weekly,* 7 February 2002. www.aceweekly.com/backissues (accessed 7 January 2005).
Gould, Sara K. "Why Are Men Still Joking About Rape?" AlterNet.com (accessed 30 June 2006).
Gray, Kevin. "Slave Drivers." *Details,* January/February 2003.
Haywood, Leslie, and Jennifer Drake, eds. *Third Wave Agenda: Being Feminist, Doing Feminism.* Minneapolis: Minnesota University Press, 1997.
Henry, Shannon. "Male-Female Salary Gap Growing, Study." *Washington Post,* 4 January 2002.
Herbert, Bob. "In America: The Feminist Dilemma." *New York Times,* Editorial Desk, 29 January 1998.
Hoff Sommers, Christina. *Who Stole Feminism? How Women Have Betrayed Women.* New York: Simon & Schuster, 1994.
Horn, Miriam. "Feminists Don't Know What to Think." *U.S. News & World Report,* 28 September 1998.
Iannone, Carol. "Sex and the Feminists." *Commentary,* September 1993.
Iley, Chrissy. "Shopping Is the New Feminism." *The Daily Mail.* 6 December 2004. (online.) 10 January 2005.
Jeffords, Susan. *Hard Bodies: Hollywood Masculinity in the Reagan Era.* Brunswick, NJ: Rutgers University Press, 1994.
Jervis, Lisa. "The End of Feminism's Third Wave: The Cofounder of *Bitch* Magazine Says Goodbye to the Generational Divide." *Ms.,* Winter 2004.
Jong, Erica. "Ally McBeal and *Time* Magazine Can't Keep the Good Women Down." *New York Observer,* 13 July 1998.
Kanner, Bernice. *Pocket Power: How to Reach the Hearts and Minds of Today's Most Coveted Consumer — Women.* New York: McGraw-Hill, 2004.
Karp, Marcelle, and Debbie Stoller. *The Bust Guide to the New Girl Order.* New York: Penguin, 1999.
King, Florence. "Italics in Amber (How One Female Writer Could No Longer Write the Articles *Cosmopolitan Magazine* and Editor Helen Gurley Brown Wanted)." *The National Review Online,* 24 May 1993. www.nationalreview.com (accessed 20 November 2005).
Kinser, Amber. "Negotiation Spaces for/through Third-Wave Feminism." *National Women's Studies Association Journal* 16.3 (2004): 124–153.
Koss, Mary P. "Acquaintance Rape: A Critical Update on Recent Findings with Application to Advocacy." University of Arizona. http://vip.msu.edu/theCAT/CAT_Author/MPK/colorado.html.
_____, and Louise F. Fitzgerald. Letter. *New York Times,* 14 June 1993.
Levy, Ariel. "Dispatches from *Girls Gone Wild.*" *Slate*.com, 22 March 2004.
Lewis, Judith. "What Part of No Do You Still Not Understand? Date Rape in the Time of Kobe, Roofies and *Girls Gone Wild,*" *LA Weekly,* 20 November 2003. http://

www.laweekly.com/general/features/what-part-of-no-do-you-still-not-understand/2204/.
Lithwick, Dahlia. "Hall of Blame." Slate.com, 2 September 2004.
Lukas, Carrie. "Sex (Ms.)education: What Young Women Need to Know (But Won't Hear in Women's Studies) about Sex, Love, and Marriage." Special Report, Independent Women's Forum, 2004.
Maciulis, Tony. "Teen Magazines." Transcript from WNYC radio show *On the Media* ... 2000. www.onthemedia.org/maciulis092800 (accessed 21 November 2005).
Malone, Bernadette. "Here's the Real Issue in Abuse Photos." Editorial. *The Union Leader,* May 9, 2004.
McElroy, Wendy. "In Defense of Beauty Pageants." www.lewrockwell.com (accessed 19 November 2004).
Meek, James Gordon, and Dave Goldiner, "JFK had an Intern, Too: Historian Says Teen Traveled for Trysts." *New York Daily News,* 12 May 2003.
Meyerowitz, Joanne. "Women, Cheesecake, and Borderline Material: Responses to Girlie Pictures in the Mid-Twentieth Century U.S." *Journal of Women's History,* 8:3 (Fall 2006): 9–35.
Moseley, Caroline. "Feminism: The Next Generation?" *Princeton Weekly Bulletin,* 90: 26. www.princeton.edu/pr/pwb/01/0430/6a.shtml (accessed 30 April 2001).
Neal, Terry M. "In Punditland, a Little Imagination Could Yield Needed Diversity." Washingtonpost.com, 4 April 2005 (accessed 17 February 2006).
Neumayr, George. "Thelma and Louise in Iraq." *The American Spectator,* 5 May 2004.
Noonan, Peggy. "A Humiliation for America: Why the Abuse of Iraqi Prisoners Is So Disheartening." OpinionJournal, *Wall Street Journal* Editorial Page (accessed 5 June 2004).
_____. "Welcome Back, Duke." OpinionJournal, *Wall Street Journal* Editorial Page (accessed 12 October 2001).
Orr, Catherine M. "Charting the Currents of the Third Wave." *Hypatia,* 12:3 (Summer 1997): 29–45.
Page, Juliette Cutler. "Why Do Feminists Support Clinton?" *feminista!* 2:11. www.feminista!.com. (accessed 29 March 2003).
Paglia, Camille. *Sex, Art and American Culture.* New York: Random House, 1992.
Pawlik, Amber. "Jessica Lynch: Proof That Woman Should Not Be in the Military." MensNewsDaily.com, 11 November 2003.
Peri, Camille, Fiona Morgan, and Dawn MacKeen. "We Believe You, Juanita (We Think)." Salon.com, March 1999. http://www.salon.com/mwt/feature/1999/03 (accessed 27 March 2003).
"The *Playboy* Interview: Camille Paglia." *Playboy,* May 1995.
Pollitt, Katha. "Did Someone Say 'Hypocrites'?" *The Nation,* 13 April 1998.
_____. "Feminism's Unfinished Business." *The Atlantic Monthly,* November 1997. www.theatlantic.com/issues/97nov/pollitt.htm (accessed 26 October 2003).
_____. "The World According to Dowd." *The Nation,* 28 November 2005.
Ratnesar, Romesh. "The Trouble with Monica." *Time,* 9 February 1998.
Richards, Amelia, and Jennifer Baumgardner, "In Defense of Monica." *The Nation,* 21 December 1998.
Ridgeway, James. "Rape at Abu Ghraib." *The Village Voice,* 25 May 2004.
Riley, Naomi Schaefer. "Ladies, You Should Know Better: How Feminism Wages War on Common Sense." *Wall Street Journal,* Editorial Desk, 14 April 2006.
Roiphe, Katie. "Date Rape Hysteria." *New York Times,* Editorial Desk, 20 November 1991.
_____. "Date Rape's Other Victim." *New York Times* magazine, 14 April 1993.

———. "Monica Lewinsky, Career Woman." *New York Times,* Editorial Desk, 15 September 1998.

———. *The Morning After: Sex, Fear and Feminism on Campus.* Boston: Little, Brown & Co., 1993.

Rosenthal, Phil. "Give the Lady a Cigar." *Chicago Sun-Times,* 20 March 2003.

Sandoval, Chela. *Methodology of the Oppressed.* Minneapolis: University of Minnesota Press, 2000.

Scott, Linda M. *Fresh Lipstick: Redressing Fashion and Feminism.* New York, NY: Palgrave Macmillan, 2006.

Sere, Adriene. "What If the Women Mattered?" *Eat the State: Politics with Bite,* 23 September 1998. eatthestate.org (accessed 27 March 2003).

"Sex, Lies, and TV News: Network News Coverage of the Monica Lewinsky Scandal." *Media Monitor* online, September–October 1998. www.cmpa.com/Mediamon/mm0910.htm (accessed 19 April 1999).

Shalit, Ruth. "Canny and Lacy: Ally, Dharma, Ronnie, and the Betrayal of Postfeminism." *The New Republic,* 6 April 1998.

Shalit, Wendy. *A Return to Modesty.* New York: Free Press, 1999.

Sidler, Michelle. "Living in McJobdom: Third Wave Feminism and Class Inequity." In Leslie Heywood and Jennifer Drake, eds., *Third Wave Agenda.* Minneapolis: University of Minnesota Press, 1997.

Stein, Harry. "Christina Hoff Sommers," Interview. *Penthouse,* January 1995.

Steinem, Gloria. "Feminists and the Clinton Question." *New York Times,* Editorial Desk, 22 March 1998.

Straus, Tamara. "Girl, You'll Be a Woman Soon." *Northern California Bohemian,* 9–15 November 2000. www.metroactive.com/papers/sonoma (accessed 20 November 2005).

"Study Finds a Growing Gap Between Managerial Salaries for Men and Women." *New York Times,* 24 January 2002.

Thibault, David. "Abu Ghraib Abuse Is a Feminist's Dream, Says Military Expert." CNSNews.com, May 10, 2004.

Walker, Rebecca, ed. *To Be Real: Telling the Truth and Changing the Face of Feminism.* New York: Anchor Books, 1995.

Wolf, Naomi. *The Beauty Myth: How Images of Beauty Are Used Against Women.* NewYork: Anchor/Doubleday, 1991.

———. *Fire with Fire: The New Female Power and How It Will Change the Twenty-First Century.* London: Random House UK, 1993.

Young, Cathy. "Feminism's Slide Since September 11." *Boston Globe,* 16 September 2002. Also published on Reasonline, 17 September 2002. http://www.resononline.com (accessed 22 May 2006).

Index

Abortion politics 5, 9, 92
Abu Ghraib 48, 122, 124, 125, 126, 127, 128, 129, 130, 131, 132, 133, 134, 135, 137, 142, 148, 179, 189, 190
Alfonso, Rita 74, 84
Allison, Scott T. 186
American Enterprise Institute (AEI) 7
Anderson, Pamela 121
Anti-feminism 11, 123, 131, 142, 144, 148, 150
Are Men Necessary? 101
Ask Amy 85
Austin, Elizabeth 21, 45

Backlash: The Undeclared War Against American Women 15, 20, 54, 123, 186; see Faludi, Susan
Ball busting women 95
Baumgardner, Elizabeth 76, 81, 93, 189
Beauty Culture (Miss America) 107
Beck, Joan 51
Berry, Halle 88
bin Laden, Osama 144
Bobbitt, Lorena 27
Brewer, John 79
Bright, Susie 1, 26, 31, 163, 172
Brown, Janelle 104
Brownmiller, Susan 3, 46, 51, 60, 68, 83
Bryant, Kobe 157, 162; see also Date rape
Bush, George H.W. 19, 23
Bush, George W. 5, 125, 129, 137, 138, 140, 146
Bushnell, Candace 107, 108
Bust 75, 96, 97, 101, 103, 106, 115, 187
The Bust Guide to the New Girl Order 103, 187
Butler, Judith 71, 72

Center for Military Readiness 125
Charen, Mona 79
Chavez, Linda 65, 79, 118
Cheever, Susan 18
Cher 88

Chesler, Phyllis 146
Consumer culture 97, 99, 101, 102, 103, 106, 110, 113, 114, 115, 116, 117, 164, 180, 183, 186, 187
Convention on the Elimination of All Forms of Discrimination Against Women (CEDAW) 5, 36, 72
Cosmopolitan (magazine) 187
Cottle, Michelle 126
Curtis, David G. 165, 167
Cutler Page, Juliette 63, 176

Date rape 161, 162, 173
Davis, Angela Y. 13, 71, 144
Dean, John 42
Denfeld, Rene 7, 21, 28, 31, 52, 65, 67, 160
Details 21, 28, 29, 187
Dirty Dancing 113
Disney 13, 14, 155
Do-Me feminism 1, 5, 7, 9–11, 13, 15, 17, 18, 20–23, 25–33, 35–39, 41, 45, 47, 50, 52, 56, 65–72, 75, 84, 89, 92, 93, 94, 96, 97, 99, 101, 102, 104, 107, 112, 119, 123, 127, 137, 143, 149, 150, 155, 159, 160, 162, 163, 172, 174, 176, 177, 178, 182, 189; see also Bright, Susie; Denfeld, Rene; *Esquire*; Paglia, Camille; Roiphe, Katie; Wolf, Naomi
Dowd, Maureen 40, 51, 52, 65, 72, 79, 112
Drake, Jennifer 86, 187, 189

Ehrenreich, Barbara 16, 51, 83, 123, 126
Epstein, Kate 104, 105, 108
Esquire 1, 6, 11, 15, 17, 21, 25, 27, 28, 30, 31, 32, 33, 34, 35, 37, 172, 187; see also Men's magazines

Fairness and Accuracy in Reporting 78, 150, 186
Faludi, Susan 7, 15, 20, 24, 47, 53, 54, 103, 123
Farrell, Colin 29
Feminism past 97, 98

191

Feminista! 176
Ferguson, Andrew 60
Fielding, Henry 151, 152, 159
Fire with Fire: The New Female Power and How It Will Change the Twenty-First Century 190
First Wave feminism 72
Fisher, Cullen and Turner 166
Fitzgerald, Louise F. 188
Flanders, Laura 78
Flowers, Gennifer 41, 43, 45, 57
France, Kim 103, 117; *see also* Consumer culture
Freedman, Estelle B. 65, 89
Fresh Lipstick: Redressing Fashion and Feminism 99
Friend, Tad 1, 17, 26, 27, 31, 39; *see also* Do-Me feminism

Girlie feminism 66, 68, 92, 93, 94, 95, 96, 97, 98, 99, 101, 102, 103, 104, 105, 106, 108, 109, 110, 111, 112, 113, 114, 115, 116, 117, 127, 188
"Girls Gone Wild" 107, 118, 119, 135, 170, 188
Glazov, Jamie 147
Goldberg, Michelle 32, 97, 103
Goldiner, Dave 188
Goldstein, Marianne 22
Goodman, Ellen 52
Gurley Brown, Helen 97, 187

Hall, Fawn 41, 182
"The Happy Feminist" 5
Haywood, Leslie 86
Hegemony 8, 11
Herbert, Bob 47
Hill, Anita 3, 41, 59
hooks, bell 71, 72
Horn, Miriam 63
Hypatia 74, 81, 186, 188

Iannone, Carol 156
Iley, Chrissy 98
Independent Women's Forum (IWF) 35, 36, 37, 52, 65, 78, 118, 188
Iraq war 9, 48, 125, 126, 127, 128, 131, 133, 134, 135, 136, 137, 141, 145, 158, 179, 185, 188

James, Henry 151, 160
Jane 97, 101, 102, 106, 113, 114, 115, 116, 117, 164, 186
Jensen, Michelle 65, 82, 90, 108
Jervis, Lisa 98
Jones, Paula 41, 43, 51, 55, 58, 59, 64
Jong, Erica 24, 31, 99
Jong-Fast, Molly 98, 99

Kinser, Amber 73

Lamm, Nomy 89
Levy, Ariel 96, 118
Lewinsky, Monica 3, 41, 42, 43, 44, 45, 46, 49, 50, 52, 53, 59, 61, 63, 64, 79, 80, 81, 85, 87, 119, 124, 182, 185, 189
Lewinsky-Clinton scandal 3, 19, 23, 41, 42, 44, 45, 47, 48, 49, 50, 51, 53, 54, 55, 56, 57, 58, 59, 61, 62, 63, 64, 80, 81, 82, 83, 87, 126, 185
Lewis, Judith 170
Love, Courtney 88
low-rise jeans 103, 110, 180, 183
Lucky 97, 101, 103, 106, 117
Lynch, Jessica 9, 131, 136, 137, 189

MacKeen, Dawn 189
Mackris, Andrea 158
Madonna 42, 88, 119
Malone, Bernadette 124, 132, 134
"The Man Show" 107
Marxist feminism 4, 99, 109
McElroy, Wendy 107
McLachlan, Sarah 88
Media 8, 14, 42, 188, 189
Men's magazines 1, 6, 11, 15, 17, 18, 21, 22, 23, 24, 25, 26, 27, 28, 29, 30, 31, 32, 33, 34, 35, 37, 41, 112, 119, 121, 143, 160, 171, 172, 186, 187, 189
Millett, Kate 68, 85
Morgan, Fiona 189
The Morning After: Sex, Fear, and Feminism on Campus 156
Ms. Magazine 27, 40, 41, 42, 43, 44, 46, 48, 49, 51, 53, 56, 57, 59, 60, 61, 62, 64, 66, 69, 75, 76, 98, 118, 159, 166, 173, 182, 184, 186, 187, 188

National Organization for Women 36, 48, 49, 50, 51, 52, 82
Neal, Terry M. 79
Neumayr, George 134, 135
New York Fire Department (NYFD) 140
Nickel and Dimed 16, 186; *see also* Ehrenreich, Barbara
Nindy Pettman, Jan 141
Noonan, Peggy 128, 138

"The O'Reilly Factor" 149

Paglia, Camille 1, 7, 9, 10, 13, 15, 18, 23, 25, 26, 27, 31, 36, 37, 56, 65, 67, 70, 71, 119, 143, 150, 155, 159, 160, 161, 162, 163, 172, 189
Pawlik, Amber 136
Penthouse 15, 17, 21, 22, 23, 112, 171, 172, 189
Playboy 15, 18, 21, 23, 24, 37, 41, 112, 119, 121, 143, 160, 186, 189
Pollitt, Katha 6, 57, 64, 83, 121, 150, 153, 181

Pornography debate 28, 30, 31, 40, 57, 63, 83, 102, 154, 158, 163, 172
Post-backlash 99; *see also* Prefix feminism
Post-feminism 15, 18, 19, 20, 22, 24, 26, 28, 30, 32, 34, 36, 38, 42, 44, 46, 48, 50, 52, 54, 56, 58, 60, 62, 64, 66, 68, 70, 72, 74, 76, 78, 80, 82, 84, 86, 88, 90, 92, 94, 96, 98, 99, 100, 102, 103, 104, 106, 108, 110, 112, 114, 116, 118, 120, 124, 126, 128, 130, 132, 134, 136, 138, 140, 142, 144, 146, 148, 150, 152, 154, 156, 158, 160, 162, 164, 166, 168, 170, 172, 174, 178, 180, 182, 184
Prefix feminism 4, 11, 15, 18, 19, 20, 22, 85, 87, 89, 91, 94, 95, 96, 103, 107, 142, 176, 186, 187, 188, 189

Radical feminism 4
Radicalesbians 15, 39
Rape 21, 22, 70, 135, 149, 150, 151, 153, 155, 159, 163, 165, 167, 169, 170, 174, 186, 187, 188, 189; *see also* date rape
Reagan, Ronald 8, 9, 10, 11, 15, 17, 18, 19, 23, 43, 47, 49, 54, 58, 64, 65, 67, 79, 87, 88, 92, 96, 98, 102, 110, 122, 123, 137, 138, 139, 140, 177, 187
A Return to Modesty 11, 97, 189
Rice, Donna 41, 182
Richards, Amelia 81; *see also* Richards, Amy
Richards, Amy 101, 102, 186
Riley, Naomi Schaefer 172
Riot grrrl 115
Robertson, Pat 18, 36, 142
Roiphe, Katie 1, 7, 10, 20, 25, 29, 32, 45, 47, 50, 65, 67, 69, 72, 75, 102, 119, 149, 150, 174
Roosevelt, Eleanor 129
Rosenthal, Phil 62

Sandoval, Chela 13, 71, 77
Schlafly, Phyllis 12, 35, 65, 163
Schroeder, Patricia 49
Scott, Linda M. 99, 101
Second Wave feminism 66, 72, 76, 77, 78, 80, 83, 84, 86, 90, 91, 94, 97, 99
Sere, Adriene 45
Shalit, Ruth 24, 39
Shalit, Wendy 11, 156
Sidler, Michelle 67
Stansell, Christine 86
Steinem, Gloria 25, 31, 47, 53, 58, 77, 90, 145
Stoller, Debbie 187
Straus, Tamara 106

Taliban 138, 144, 145, 147
Thibault, David 125
Third Wave 4, 66, 67, 68, 69, 71, 72, 73, 74, 75, 76, 78, 80, 81, 83, 84, 85, 86, 87, 89, 90, 91, 92, 94, 96, 97, 99, 101, 104, 117, 127, 182, 186, 187, 188, 189; *see also* Alfonso, Rita; Jervis, Lisa; Sidler, Michelle; Third Wave Agenda; Trigilio, Jo; Walker, Rebecca
Third Wave Agenda: Being Feminist, Doing Feminism 86, 187
To Be Real: Telling the Truth and Changing the Face of Feminism 190
Tolan, Peter 162; *see also* Date rape
Trigilio, Jo 72, 74, 186
Twain, Shania 88

U.S. Bureau of Economic Analysis 103

Vanity Fair 43
Violence Against Women Act (VAWA) 5

Walker, Rebecca 32, 35, 66, 69, 90, 95, 108
Wayne, John 140
Who Stole Feminism? How Women Have Betrayed Women 187
Wicke, Jennifer 62
Winfrey, Oprah 84, 88
Wolf, Naomi 1, 7, 15, 17, 20, 25, 33, 35, 36, 37, 67, 84, 112, 160
Women in Congress 2, 119
Women's movement 6, 7, 8, 15, 18, 19, 20, 22, 23, 24, 25, 26, 28, 30, 32, 34, 36, 38, 42, 44, 46, 48, 50, 52, 54, 56, 57, 58, 60, 62, 64, 65, 66, 68, 70, 72, 74, 76, 78, 80, 82, 84, 86, 88, 90, 92, 94, 96, 97, 98, 99, 100, 101, 102, 103, 104, 106, 108, 109, 110, 112, 114, 116, 118, 120, 122, 124, 125, 126, 127, 128, 130, 132, 134, 136, 138, 140, 142, 144, 146, 147, 148, 150, 152, 154, 155, 156, 158, 160, 162, 163, 164, 166, 168, 170, 172, 173, 174, 176, 178, 180, 181, 182, 184, 186, 187, 188, 189, 190
Wood, Gaby 181
Wurtzel, Elizabeth 85

Yes 25, 37, 187; *see also* Friend, Tad
Young, Cathy 7, 21, 35, 36, 48, 52, 65, 144, 145, 160, 163
youth market 103

Ziegfeld, Florenz 112

www.ingramcontent.com/pod-product-compliance
Ingram Content Group UK Ltd.
Pitfield, Milton Keynes, MK11 3LW, UK
UKHW042011140426
5217IPUK00015B/1116